Discoursal Construction of Academic Identity in Cyberspace

Discoursal Construction of Academic Identity in Cyberspace: The Example of an E-Seminar

By

Małgorzata Sokół

CAMBRIDGE
SCHOLARS
PUBLISHING

Discoursal Construction of Academic Identity in Cyberspace:
The Example of an E-Seminar,
by Małgorzata Sokół

This book first published 2012

Cambridge Scholars Publishing

12 Back Chapman Street, Newcastle upon Tyne, NE6 2XX, UK

British Library Cataloguing in Publication Data
A catalogue record for this book is available from the British Library

ISBN (10): 1-4438-3468-8, ISBN (13): 978-1-4438-3468-1

TABLE OF CONTENTS

LIST OF TABLES

ACKNOWLEDGEMENTS

I would like to express my gratitude to all those who gave me the possibility to complete this work. First of all, I am indebted to my supervisor and mentor Prof. Anna Duszak, for her constant guidance, stimulating suggestions, encouragement and appreciation of my work. I am obliged to the *Humanist*'s members who have agreed to take part in my research, and to the *Humanist*'s moderator, in particular, for insightful email exchanges. I am also grateful to my colleagues from the English Department, Szczecin University, for inspiring discussions and their friendship. I thank my family: my parents, Jakub, Natalia and Iga, for their confidence, support and patience. Special thanks go to Jakub for his programming expertise and assistance in "taming" the technology for me.

INTRODUCTION

The aim of this book is to specify and investigate the linguistic means of academic identity construction in electronic discourse, on the example of an Internet discussion group (also referred to as an electronic seminar or e-seminar). The development of the Internet and computer-mediated communication (henceforth CMC) has affected the world of academia, both globally and locally. First of all, these new network technologies have intensified the global academic exchange and internationalisation of scholarship. The deriving changes include the restructuring of contemporary academic institutions and networks of social relations, which in effect, increases their mobility and lack of stability. The progressing expansion of new technologies has also had consequences for language: new communicative situations have transformed the existing genre repertoires of an academic community and caused the emergence of novel electronic genres. All these changes have, in turn, generated new mechanisms of identity construction both for institutions and individuals, which is reflected in the discursive practices of an academic community.

In view of the above changes, contemporary linguistics has faced a challenge of investigating academic communication phenomena in cyberspace, and in particular, the mechanisms of identity construction in electronic discourse. An important research question is to compare how interpersonal meanings are realised in academic electronic discourse with how they are realised in "traditional" academic speech and writing. In this way, it will be possible to evaluate the relation between academic identity constructed by members of an academic community in cyberspace with identity constructed in real life.

What follows from the Hallidayan conceptual framework of language as social semiotic, there is a close relation between language use and the social context. More precisely, language is viewed as a product of the social processes and therefore should be interpreted within the broader socio-cultural context. The view of language as social semiotic also foregrounds the dual role of language. Language is not only to exchange information but also has a significant function of communicating identities and relationships. "By their everyday acts of meaning, people act out the social structure, affirming their own statuses and roles, and establishing and transmitting the shared system of value and knowledge" (Halliday 1978, 2; see also the dual role of communication in N. Thompson's discussion of language and communication, 2003, 10–12). This means that the social structure is implicated in Halliday's framework, which carries major implications for linguistic research of identity.

First of all, an individual's identity should be viewed as a social category, dynamically constructed in relation to social structures an individual is a member of and his/her social roles. However, it is also necessary to account more explicitly for an individual's active role in identity construction. As N. Thompson points out, "to a large extent, I choose who I am through my actions and interactions" (2003, 26). An individual's identity is socially constructed, but the effect of social forces is not deterministic. Rather individuals themselves reflexively draw on a number of socially available resources for the construction of identity, including institutional practices, values and beliefs (Giddens 2001, 4–6).

Secondly, linguistic theories of identity must address the increasing complexity of contemporary social life and its progressing diversification, the changes that affect individuals, communities and institutions. In the postmodern era, dominated by communications media, the issue of an individual's identity becomes more problematic and unsettled as societies become "displaced", structurally differentiated, fragmented and culturally pluralistic (Castells 1997; Giddens 2001). This has resulted in the advancement of more pessimistic accounts of identity. Some postmodern theories of identity are based on the premise that new communication technologies have caused a digital revolution and, as a result, undermined the stability and credibility of the self, requiring from an individual the formation of a new consciousness (e.g. Gergen 1996). In addition, as Mudyń (2002) points out, the ongoing digital revolution is responsible for the changes in the psychological condition of a contemporary human being, even if an individual avoids direct contact with the new technologies. On the other hand, researchers also argue (e.g. Barnes 2003; Turkle 1996) that although identity has become an unstable choice, the new era has brought the diversity and increased the possibilities of effective self-presentation.

The same ambivalence appears in the discussion of the changes in the formation and functioning of contemporary communities. For one thing, as a result of the digital revolution, the world has become a "global village", the term coined by Marshall McLuhan in the 1960s to express his conviction that electronic communication would unite the world. Information technologies, with computers, networks, satellites, multimedia and the Internet, have revolutionised communication, which, in turn, has led to an increased interaction on a global scale. Much of everyday interhuman interaction has shifted into cyberspace, leading to the proliferation of virtual communities. The term virtual communities is used to refer to dynamic collectivities of individuals constructed around various types of CMC, where individuals are bound by common interests rather than the shared geographical location (e.g. Rheingold 2000; Smith 1995). For one thing, virtual communities have the capacity to unite dispersed individuals in the fragmented world and bring revival of "true" community by strengthening social bonds globally and reversing the processes of social atomisation. For another, these new collectivities offer new opportunities for surveillance and control, which results from an uneven distribution of power in the Internet, not such an egalitarian medium as its enthusiasts initially thought (see also Kollock and Smith 1999).

The transformation of societies is also accompanied by the restructuring of contemporary institutions, which also carries major implications for identity construction by individuals. Contemporary institutions, including academic ones, are characterised by a new dynamics, in which social relations are "uprooted" from local contexts and moved into more global frameworks. This phenomenon intensifies the processes of reorganisation of time and space, necessitates the re-ordering of social relations on a global scale, and increases the mobility of contemporary institutions (Giddens 2001, 28–37). This, in turn, results in the lack of stability of contemporary institutions and threatens their identity and authority.

In view of the above changes it seems certain that there is a need for new identification of community and an institution, but more essentially of an individual, an analogue individual whose way of thinking and perception of the world and culture have been transformed as a result of "digitalisation". It appears compelling to investigate to what extent this new identification is present in electronic discourse and what are its linguistic exponents. In this book, my major focus is an academic virtual identity. My purposes will be to identify linguistic means of academic self-presentation in electronic discourse and to find out how members of academia give their identity constructed online institutional validity. The discussion will be empirically supported by the research of identity construction in a scholarly electronic seminar (e-seminar) *Humanist.* The communicative situation of this asynchronous type of CMC provides a challenging context in which to investigate the linguistic means of academic self-presentation as it combines private, public and institutional aspects of identity.

In my discussion I will emphasise the relevance of the conflicting characteristics of the electronic medium which intensify the complex interrelation between mass media, social structures and an individual (e.g. Goban-Klas 1999). I will argue that the construction of academic identity in electronic discourse is affected by such properties of the electronic medium as hybridity – related to the blurred boundaries between the public and the private, interactivity, flexibility, digitalisation and technological convergence.

The theoretical and methodological basis of my investigation is a discourse community approach to scholarly communication by Swales (1990) and the Hallidayan systemic-functional model of grammar. Swales' approach allows us to focus on shared communicative goals, norms and discursive practices as the factors that influence the negotiation of group and individual identity. Halliday's (1994) distinction between ideational, interpersonal and textual levels of language use is important because these three levels contribute towards discoursal construction of identity. My approach fits in within the current theorising of identity in linguistic research, where identity is viewed as a dynamic phenomenon, actively constructed in discourse (see overviews of discursive approaches to identity in e.g. Benwell and Stokoe 2006; Bucholtz and Hall 2005; De Fina et al 2006; Ivanič 1998).

As regards the terminology, despite the multiplicity of near-synonyms for *identity* and the imprecision of the term, in this book I will still adhere to its use. I will be using the term *identity* in the broad sense, recognising its multivariate and dynamic character. By *identity construction* I will be referring to identity work being accomplished in discourse. The term *construction* implies that identity work in discourse is a conscious activity on the part of an individual (see e.g. Joseph 2004a). Admitting that an individual's self-presentation in discourse is also largely subconscious, I have followed the use of this widely accepted term as it emphasises an individual's agency in identification processes.

The book is organised into four theoretical chapters (Chapters 1-4), in which I provide an overview of the most important issues that are relevant for identity research in general, and the analyses of identity construction in academic electronic discourse, in particular, and one empirical chapter (Chapter 5), which presents the analysis and findings based on the *Humanist* e-seminar. More specifically, the aim of Chapter 1, "Language, Community, Identity", is to provide a broad perspective on linguistic research of identity in general. I provide the arguments for the necessity of an interdisciplinary study of identity construction in linguistics. In relation to this, I discuss the contributions to identity research of such disciplines as social psychology, sociology, cultural anthropology and communication studies. Following a social view of identity, I survey the linguistic accounts of the communal aspects of identity construction and argue in favour of a discursive approach to identity. In Chapter 2, "Academic Identity in Speech and Writing", I focus on the studies of linguistic realisations of academic identity in the "traditional" media. My major aims are: to emphasise the interactional character of academic texts, and to provide an overview of frameworks that allow us to investigate interpersonal meanings in academic discourse. Chapter 3, "Electronic Discourse: Linguistic, Social and Technological Aspects", and Chapter 4, "Virtual Identities, Cyberspace and Academic Communication", introduce linguistic, social and technological aspects of CMC that are relevant for the research of identity construction in academic electronic discourse. In Chapter 3 I characterise electronic discourse as a new variety of language, distinct from speech and writing. I also present CMC as a new medium and discuss its defining properties. The aim of Chapter 4 is to discuss the concepts of *virtual identity* and *virtual community*: how they are theorised and empirically investigated. I will also talk about the changes that academic communication has undergone as a result of the development of CMC. Finally, Chapter 5 presents my research and analyses of the findings of identity construction in academic discourse on the basis of an Internet discussion group. Initial sections of Chapter 5 (5.1–5.4) present the research group, the *Humanist*, and the research material, i.e. the corpora of the postings contributed to the *Humanist* by its six active members. Then, in the subsequent sections of Chapter 5 I demonstrate how academic identity is constructed on three levels of discourse organisation: the features of lexico-grammar, textual macrostructures and genres.

Generally speaking, the results of my analysis reveal how important it is for scholars to maintain a legitimate identity in an e-seminar. Virtual academic identity as constructed in this context is as an extension of academic identity constructed in the real world. The new communicative medium seems to have extended the repertoire of effective means of self-promotion, and the presentation of academic achievements and expertise. These aspects have become important for academic interaction in today's world, which is characterised by such phenomena as the internationalisation and globalisation of scholarship, commodification of science and intensified competition.

The present book is based on my PhD dissertation, written under the supervision of Professor Anna Duszak, the University of Warsaw, and defended at the University of Szczecin, Poland, in March 2008.

CHAPTER ONE

LANGUAGE, COMMUNITY, IDENTITY

The aim of the present chapter is to look at how linguistics, taking an interdisciplinary perspective, has tackled the complexity of identity construction. Given a social view of language, in order to fully account for how identity is discoursally constructed, linguistics has to be informed by other disciplines that focus on the interrelation between the individual, a social structure and language. These are mainly social disciplines that emphasize the role of language as an identification and classification factor, used to mark affiliations and non-alignments, construct social bonds and the sense of group identity, convey solidarity, loyalty or detachment, etc. Thus, I will look at the findings of social psychology, sociology, cultural anthropology and communication studies, focusing on the concepts of social identity, social bond and group identity.

Then, I will proceed to an overview of linguistic frameworks that address the social context of language and explore discoursal construction of identities, frameworks that involve such notions as speech community, discourse community and discourse system, social network and small culture, community of practice and epistemic community, and face and face systems. What emerges from this overview is a domination of collective views of identity: an individual's identity is mainly theorised in relation to social structures and his/her social roles. My major focus will be on a discursive approach, the basis of which is the view of identity as a socially constructed phenomenon. I will speak in favour of the argument that identity is a discursive process, i.e. a public phenomenon which is dynamically and continuously negotiated in discourse. As my ultimate aim in this book is to investigate discoursal construction of identity in the Internet, which is considered to be a mass medium, I will also address a critical perspective for the analysis of identity construction in mass media discourse.

1.1. The social foundations of language and identity: an interdisciplinary perspective

The understanding we have of others and ourselves as persons is largely constructed through diverse linguistic practices we engage in. Languages have developed a range of resources (linguistic varieties, mechanisms and strategies) for handling social relationships and thus can be used to identify the social structure of a given collectivity (e.g. Crystal 1998; Foley 1997; Tabouret-Keller 1998). In other words, "there is an indexical correlation between the social context of a given linguistic interaction and the linguistic forms (…): the variables of social stratification are given concrete expression in the linguistic choices of actors" (Foley 1997, 313). This role of language as an identification and classification factor has also been addressed in other fields of study that take into focus the individual, society and culture, such as social psychology, sociology, anthropology and communication studies.

When discussing the conceptions of identity rooted in social relationships, it is necessary to point to the variability in conceptual meanings of the notions of *identity*, *self* and *person* in these fields of study. This variability has been numerously addressed in the literature of the subject (see e.g. Benwell and Stokoe 2006; Ivanič 1998; Joseph 2004a, 2004b; Kopytko 2002, 2003; Stryker and Burke 2000) and the disentangling of the complexity of the terminological problem is beyond the scope of my present discussion. However, in this section I would like to focus on those aspects of personhood and self-concept that I find directly relevant for the linguistic discussion of identity construction, especially in electronic discourse.

The near-synonyms for identity reveal some dualism in how identity has been conceptualised: identity understood as a cognitive or psychic phenomenon, and identity viewed as a public phenomenon interpreted by people in social interaction (Benwell and Stokoe 2006, 3–4; see also Ivanič 1998; De Fina et al 2006). For instance, in her overview of the terms synonymous with identity, Ivanič lists such alternative notions as *self* and *ethos* that emphasise the private, individual aspect of identity, whereas *person*, *persona* or *role* refer to the public, institutional aspect of identity (1998, 10). Ivanič also recounts the terms *subject*, *subject position* and *positioning* that may additionally indicate a deterministic effect of social practices upon peoples' identities.

In social psychology, a well-established concept related to the social presentation of an individual is that of social identity, fundamental to social interaction. In most theoretical conceptions of social identity, the main research interests lie in the forms of social identity that derive from individuals' real affiliations to social groups and categories. Thus, social identities emerge as the identities attributed to others in an attempt to situate them in social space (Snow 2001). They may be grounded in established social roles (e.g. teacher, mother), or in more inclusive social categories (e.g. gender, ethnicity, nationality) and thus are often referred to as "role identities" (Snow 2001 following Stryker 1980).

The construction of social identity is related to the formation of the sense of "We" that links an individual's self with others (even with the unknown others), despite the lack of direct experience (Grzelak and Jarymowicz 2000). The establishment of the mental construct "We" is ensued by the development of other forms of identification with others, such as the sense of social bond and community, or willingness to cooperate. Social identity may also be based on the symbolic affiliation to a social group: "We" may relate to a social group which we would like to belong to. Moreover, the formation of the so-called "abstract We" comes from the direct identification not with other individuals but their shared beliefs, values or goals. Consequently, social identity is shaped regardless of any real or symbolic membership in a social group.

In relation to the contribution of social psychology towards the explorations of identity in linguistics (a contribution which, according to Giles 1979, is, though, insufficient), two major approaches become available: Tajfel's theory of social identity and intergroup relations and Giles' accommodation theory (see e.g. Edwards 1985 for sociolinguistic explorations on ethnic identity, and Fasold 1984 for sociolinguistic studies of code-switching). Both theories attempt to examine the mechanisms responsible for group vitality.

Tajfel's Social Identity Theory (SIT), later adopted by Turner in his Self-categorisation Theory (SCT), is considered to be one of the most influential theories of social identity (see e.g. Grzelak and Jarymowicz 2000). According to Tajfel, social identity is part of an individual's self-concept that derives from his/her membership in a given social category, together with the value and emotional significance attached to that membership, shared with other members of this category. In Turner's SCT, social identity is defined as social categorization of the self based on the interpersonal similarities and differences stemming from group affiliation. In addition, Tajfel proposes a number of strategies that are available to members of groups in contact to enhance their positive identity (e.g. change of group, redefinition of negative qualities, creation of new evaluative dimensions). Similarly, speech accommodation, developed by Giles and others, focuses on identity adjustments that are made to increase group status and favourability (Edwards 1985, 150–154).

The interest of sociology in the processes of social identification and the question of how membership in particular social categories moulds the self has centred around the responsibility of social roles and identities for the definition, meaning and social perception of the self (see e.g. Ivanič 1998; Kopytko 2002, 2003; Sztompka 2002 for extensive overviews). Likewise, recognizing social behaviour as a necessary condition for the development of the self and its relevance for social categorisation, social psychologists have developed models of the interpersonally determined self, stressing the role of communication (symbolic interaction) in the relationship between the self and society (e.g. Mead 1975; Tanno and Gonzales 1998; Griffin 2002), the establishment (or breakdown) and maintenance of social relationships (e.g. Argyle and Kendon 1967; Argyle 2002), or the processes of group formation (e.g. Mika 1981; see also Kopytko 2002 for an overview).

As products of categorization processes, social identities attempt to reflect the increasing complexity of modern social life. Snow (2001) considers this a kind of sociological truism that the issue of identity in the postmodern era becomes more problematic and unsettled as societies become more structurally differentiated, fragmented and culturally pluralistic (a problem also recorded in e.g. Castells 1997; Giddens 2001; Graddol 1997). Still, the so-called phenomenon of simultaneous participation is a natural feature of a human society (Sztompka 2002, 190). Multiple membership in social groups, deriving from the multiplicity of roles performed, mirrors the plurality of everyday human activity. Each individual typically functions in multiple, often conflicting roles because of different social contexts and fields of interaction, and because of a variety of needs that need to be satisfied. What is important is that, nowadays, individuals have gained a bigger freedom of choices as regards their group affiliations. In addition, different conventions for interactions and expectations are ascribed to different social roles. Roles also vary in the extent to which they are rigid or negotiable, and in the overall effect they have on an individual's life. It might be argued that highly pervasive roles are likely to become central definitional aspects of a person's identity (Foley 1997). Another problem relevant for the conceptualisations of social divisions is posed by the complex and ambivalent nature of demarcation processes. "Identitarian ambivalence may result from contradictory socialization or adaptation to, and use of, multiple positions (e.g. code switching)" (Duszak 2002a, 3). Moreover, "it is generally assumed that group boundaries are fuzzy rather than discreet, that they form a continuum of ingroupness-outgroupness rather than a combination of disparate or partly overlapping constructs" (Duszak 2002 *op cit*). As a result, social identities emerge as complex, indeterminate and dynamic constructs, the elements of which become invoked or avowed depending on their situational relevance and their relative importance in relation to other identities (see also Snow 2001; Sztompka 2002; Tabouret-Keller 1998).

Other two terms that are relevant for the discussion of social identities are the *social bond* and *group* or *collective identity*. As it has been mentioned above, the way people construct and manage social identities is related to the processes of group building and bonding. In sociology and social psychology, a social bond is considered to be a basic determinant of social life: constructing and maintaining social bonds is one of the main aims of social behaviour (see e.g. Jacher 1987; Kerrick et al 2002; Kosiński 1987; Szczepański 1963; Sztompka 2002). Through bonding with others, people satisfy their basic social needs such as their sense of belonging, to open up a way to the realisation of other purposes: performing tasks, pursuing interests, or deriving material benefits. In addition, social bonds play a substantial role in helping to understand ourselves and others, winning and maintaining a position, keeping partners and allies, or boosting one's self-esteem (Kerrick et al 2002). As a central social category, a social bond is used to explain the existence, durability and functioning of social structures and processes: it is indexical of a social structure whose cohesion it ensures (Jacher 1987, 7).

A social bond is a multifold construct, the components of which attract varying research interests that attempt to grasp its nature. For example Kosiński (1987, 118–119) distinguishes 2 sets of components of a social bond: (1) spontaneous-subjective, related to the phenomena of the individual's identification with a social structure (of interest to social psychology); (2) formal-objective, including organizational aspects of a social bond (of interest to sociology). Kosiński also argues that a social bond is a dynamic phenomenon of varying intensity and duration that must include at least one of the following ten possible components (see also Szczepański 1963): (1) spatial contact, (2) psychic contact, (3) social contact, (4) interaction, (5) social activity, (6) social relations, (7) social dependencies, (8) social institutions, (9) social control and (10) social organization. The particular components of a social bond correspond to the subsequent stages of its development, pointing to the gradational nature of social bonds.

The gradation of a social bond, and, consequently, of human groupings, is also emphasized in Sztompka's typology of social bonds (Sztompka

2002, 182–192). Depending on the degree of its development, Sztompka differentiates the following types of a social bond: *objective, subjective, behavioural* and *co-operational*. The *objective bond* refers to the sense of community deriving from the similarity of a life situation, determined by such external factors as gender, age, race, citizenship, place of living, etc. (Sztompka 2002, 184). The next stage in the advancement of a social bond is the *subjective bond* marked by the emergence of collective identity: the basic sense of community becomes strengthened by members' identification with a grouping, revealed in a shared sense of "we-ness". Finally, the *behavioural bond* is identified by the sense of community expressed through common activity, whereas the co-operational bond relates to members' mutual indispensability in pursuing individual and collective goals.

The subsequent stages of bond building correspond to particular phases of group crystallization, resulting in the gradational nature of group divisions (see e.g. Kerrick et al 2002; Sztompka 2002). However, as Sztompka (2002, 194–196) notices, in reality there are frequent deviations from the complete schema of group formation. Not always is a social group characterized by the presence of objective and subjective bonds, the conscious realization of the sense of identity, and dense contacts or interactions. What is particularly pertinent to the discussion of virtual communities, the cohesion of a group may also grow from the imagined sense of community and identity, without any similarity of interests or sameness of any objective factors (see reference to *imagined communities* in Chapter 4, Section 4.3.1).

As it has been already mentioned, the processes of group building and bonding are related to the development of collective identity. Every group of interacting individuals is considered to possess symbols, slogans, values, objects, etc. that are necessary for group members to develop the sense of community and belonging to their group (e.g. Szczepański 1963). The emergence of the shared sense of "we-ness" is only a partial reflection of the growing social bond. According to Snow (2001), conceptually, the essence of collective identity dwells also in the so-called "collective agency", i.e. the action component of collective identity. More specifically, the collective agency indicates the possibility of collective action in pursuing shared interests, and even encouraging such action. Therefore, Snow emphasizes the multidimensional, dynamic and evolving nature of collective identity. Differentiating the concept of collective identity from personal and social identity, Snow argues that "collective identities tend to be more fluid, tentative, and transient than categorically based social identities" (2001). Also, collective identity is marked by the generation and maintenance of symbolic resources that strengthen group solidarity and function as boundary markers of distinguishing insiders from outsiders.

The social view of identity is also emphasised in anthropological research. To present the anthropological foundations of the dependency of the social presentation of the *person*[1] upon the establishment of social relationships and structures, Foley adduces Gergen's view of social functioning (Gergen 1990). According to Gergen, "the individual's well-being cannot be extricated from the web of relationships in which he/she is engaged", where "forms of relationships depend on the mutual coordination of actions" among interactants (quoted in Foley 1997, 262). Consequently, the person appears as "a lived history of structural couplings", bringing to each interaction the various patterns of relationships that they have been engaged in, as well as the social status that has been established in the previous encounters with others. A public social presentation of the person, in turn, will be contingent on their social status, their membership in social groups and the variety of social roles they perform.

Still, Foley (1997) also records some of the cross-cultural differences in the conceptualisation of personhood, revealed in a dichotomy of local beliefs between sociocentric and egocentric understanding of the person. Personhood defined in sociocentric terms, according to the social position a particular individual occupies, is common in cultures that do not single out the individual and his/her autonomy as the local understanding of a person. "The sociocentric conception of personhood regards the good of the social grouping as fundamental and subordinates individual wants and needs to the collective good" (Foley 1997, 266). In contrast, in the egocentric individualist ideology individuals themselves are more important than any constituent social grouping. Thus, a person is viewed as "an individual, an embodiment of absolute value in her own right, and not simply in terms of her position in any social pattern" (Foley 1997, 265).

Judgments about others as well as the classification of individuals into social categories are invariably based on sets of linguistic and non-linguistic criteria, which also vary cross-culturally. The non-linguistic parameters of social categorization include relatively permanent physical and psychological aspects of an individual's identity (e.g. gender, age, ethnicity), or relate to people's professional and economic status (e.g.

---

[1] The notion of *person* as understood in anthropology is "a social concept made of local notions of one's rights and obligations", which varies cross-culturally. The notion of *person* is contrasted with the notion of *self* referring to "a proposed universal human awareness of one's own individual embodiment" (see Foley 1997, 262–263).

educational qualifications, occupation, income, their style of living). The evaluations of a person's social position according to the latter group of non-linguistic parameters are frequently just subjective judgments. People's attitudes and practices related to the processes of social categorization are inculcated through the various processes of socialization (see e.g. Foley 1997).

Finally, taking the perspective of communication studies, the accent is placed on the multiple communicative and identifying roles of the linguistic code, in a wider perspective of the multifunctionality of the process of communication (see e.g. Goban-Klas 1999). The knowledge of the phenomena that influence interpersonal communication may contribute to a better understanding of the mechanisms that shape human social behaviour and, subsequently, will give a deeper insight into the processes of group building and bonding. In relation to the context of CMC, it is also relevant to mention the complex role of mass communication in bond building (Goban-Klas 1999). Admittedly, mass communication enriches the social landscape, but contributes to the mediation of social relations, which grow more distant, impersonal and weaker (Goban-Klas 1999, 114–116). Thus, on the one hand, mass communication conduces to the consolidation of dispersed individuals and generates the formation of new social structures. On the other hand, it leads to greater social mobility, atomisation of society and weakening of social ties and traditional communities.

1.2. Community-based approaches to identity

Modern linguistics, under the influence of related fields of social psychology, sociology, ethnography of speaking and cultural anthropology, has used a variety of approaches and methodologies to address the social context of language and explore the construction of social identities. In the 1960s, in his discussion of sociological linguistics, J. R. Firth recognized the significance of contextual analysis that makes allowance both for the situational and social context of language use (Firth 1964, 66). As people progressively become incorporated into the social organization, they accumulate a number of social roles that impose appropriate rules of linguistic behaviour under specific circumstances. Therefore, an efficient linguistic analysis must be concerned with the relation between the community's language and its social structure. A similar view appears in other works within the ethnography of speaking (e.g. Bauman and Sherzer 1974; Hymes 1964a, 1964b, 1968, 1974), and in Gumperz's works in cultural anthropology (e.g. 1971a, 1971c, 1974).

An important contribution of ethnographic research to the studies of language in its social context is the introduction of the notion of communicative competence. Hymes subordinates Chomsky's linguistic competence to communicative competence, arguing that effective communication in language involves not only the knowledge of language code, but also social and cultural knowledge of what to say and to whom, depending on a given situation, and speakers' ability to appropriately interpret linguistic forms.

Being concerned with how social information is encoded linguistically, Gumperz (1971a, 1971c, 1974) and Gumperz and Cook-Gumperz (1982) address some sociolinguistic problems of interpersonal and intergroup communication, focusing on face-to-face interaction. First of all, they recognize the complexity of the communicative environment, both at the level of everyday interpersonal interaction and intergroup communication across society. In modern, constantly changing societies, group membership, ethnic identity, communicative contexts and settings are rarely clearly definable (Gumperz 1974, 7). Moreover, since the study of sociolinguistic phenomena in relation to existing groups, institutions and settings cannot give a full account of everyday behaviour, Gumperz argues against the reliance on a priori social categories. Sociolinguistics needs analytical models that would consolidate the study of how individuals use their lexical, grammatical and sociolinguistic knowledge to interact appropriately in various social contexts. This argument is repeated in Gumperz and Cook-Gumperz (1982). In addition, Gumperz and Cook-Gumperz argue that the boundaries within which people's social identities are negotiated are dynamic, communicatively constructed parameters, such as those provided by gender, ethnicity and class. Given this, to fully appreciate the mechanisms of identity construction and maintenance, it is necessary to gain insight into the communicative processes by which social, political, and ethnic divisions arise (Gumperz and Cook-Gumperz1982, 1).

1.2.1. Speech communities

The essential concept for the link between language and social structure is that of a *speech community* (SpCom), whose origins are grounded in the general sources of sociolinguistics: historical linguistics, philosophy of language, dialectology, anthropology and early structuralism. This much defined and discussed unit of empirical linguistics has been used in the research of social groups and sub-groups of various kinds: urban and rural, large and small, specific and temporal, geographically-bounded and of groups that cut across geographic lines, or groups not defined in linguistic terms (for an extensive review see Patrick 2002). As the study of the numerous conceptualisations of a SpCom also reveals much divergence, Patrick notes "a general lack of analysis and synthesis concerning the SpCom" (Patrick 2002, 575). The disparities revolve around such aspects of a SpCom as group boundaries, group membership and group homogeneity vs. heterogeneity. Additionally, it is unclear whether a SpCom is a primarily social or linguistic object.

In Chomsky's (1965) conception of a completely homogenous SpCom, group membership (of ideal speakers-listeners) is contingent on a shared access to a code (linguistic competence). Shared linguistic knowledge becomes the only criterion of social inclusion and exclusion. However, Chomsky's idealization of a uniform community does not relate to what can be observed in actual communities, i.e. the prevailing bi- or multilingualism (Gumperz 1982, 19).

For Hymes, a SpCom is a unit of taxonomy of sociolinguistic situations: thus, a social rather than linguistic entity (Hymes 1964, 1974). He argues that the definition of a SpCom in terms of shared linguistic features is inadequate to the external and internal bounding of communities. Besides, a "primary focus on a single language or grammatical code tends to make variation seem peripheral or intrusive" (Hymes 1964, 386). This recognition of variation among speech habits reflects the increased concern of linguistic anthropology for the complexity of the social structure. Hymes extends the criteria of social membership in a SpCom: apart form sharing linguistic form, legitimate members of a SpCom must competently exploit the knowledge of the rules and norms governing their communicative practices (communicative competence). Thus, the leading themes in Hymes' conceptualisation of a SpCom are: (1) boundaries, (2) co-variation among linguistic and social features (Hymes 1964, 388), and (3) membership in a SpCom as different from mere participation (Hymes 1974, 51). Still, Hymes does not expand on the issue of group membership, arguing that its complexity requires the contribution of social science.

Initially, Gumperz defined speech communities in terms of linguistic communities which were purely social concepts. A linguistic community was a mono- or multilingual structure, whose members were united by their "frequency of social interaction patterns and set off from the surrounding areas by weaknesses in the lines of communication" (1971a, 101). As regards the size and range, linguistic communities could be small groups constructed on the basis of face-to-face contact, or they could spread across larger regions. Subsequently, in his more restricted definition of a SpCom, Gumperz stresses a shared linguistic knowledge as an essential criterion of a SpCom (1971b, 114). Moreover, he argues that regardless of the linguistic differences among them, speech varieties within a SpCom are systematic, as they reflect a shared set of social norms. Speech varieties serve as indices of social patterns of interaction in a SpCom, reflecting functionally related social roles (Gumperz 1971b, 116). Lastly, in his later conceptualisation of a SpCom, Gumperz questions speech communities being defined as functionally integrated systems with shared norms of evaluation, because this definition does not recognize social variability as an inherent property of linguistic systems (Gumperz 1982, 26). Therefore, a SpCom comes to be defined in functionalist terms as "a system of organized diversity held together by common norms and aspirations.... This variation shows systematic regularities at the statistical level of social facts (Gumperz 1982, 24).

The criticism of the models of a SpCom outlined above resulted in numerous elaborations and refinements of the notion (see e.g. Halliday 1978; Montgomery 1986; Patrick 2002; Romaine 2000/1994; Saville-Troike 1989). Halliday (1978) notices that a SpCom is a general label that might be applied to almost any aggregate of people. In its idealized sense (i.e. a linguistically homogenous group sharing reactions and attitudes to language, linked by some form of social organization), a SpCom is a construct to which human groups can only approximate (Halliday 1978, 154). The classical model of a SpCom proves to work reasonably well in rural contexts, whereas it begins to collapse when applied in urban situations of extensive linguistic diversity among and within individuals.

Montgomery (1986), in turn, observes that the conditions for an idealised SpCom are rarely simultaneously fulfilled. Secondly, part of the difficulty with the notion of a SpCom lies in the internal differentiation of human communities: material, cultural, political, by employment, occupation, gender, age, etc (Montgomery 1986, 134–135). As it is difficult to disentangle linguistic practices from the wider social processes in which they are embedded, the term SpCom should be concerned not only with the shared verbal practices, "but also with tension and conflict between them" (Montgomery 1986, 135).

In her discussion of a SpCom, Saville-Troike (1989) primarily addresses the distinction between participation and membership in a SpCom, arguing that membership cannot be based solely on sharing linguistic knowledge and skills. The focus in initially defining communities for study may also be placed on non-linguistic criteria, such as common geographical and political boundaries, culture traits or physical characteristics (Saville-Troike 1989, 17). Recognising the natural heterogeneity of human communities and the complexities of social settings, Saville-Troike speaks in favour of the concept of a SpCom that would make allowance for primary and secondary memberships, and for multiple and overlapping memberships in social structures. This conception, which makes possible the integration of complex patterns of membership, proves particularly relevant for the study of contemporary technologically mediated social relations and structures. Finally, with reference to the problem of boundary marking by means of language, Saville-Troike distinguishes between "hard-shelled" and "soft-shelled" speech communities (Saville-Troike 1989, 19). The "hard-shelled" communities have stronger boundaries that limit interaction between in-group and out-group members, and provide maximum maintenance of language and culture. In contrast, the "soft-shelled" communities allow a relatively easy two-way interaction across the community's boundaries.

The synthesis of Gumperz's and Hymes' approaches appears in Romaine's definition of a SpCom: "a speech community is not necessarily coextensive with a language community. A speech community is a group of people who do not necessarily share the same language, but share a set of norms and rules for the use of language. The boundaries between speech communities are essentially social rather than linguistic" (Romaine 2000/1994, 23). When focusing on membership in a SpCom, Romaine adduces the Prague School's distinction between *speech bond* and *language bond* (*Sprechbund* vs. *Sprachbund*). Shared ways of speaking frequently go beyond language boundaries; thus, membership in a community is determined in terms of interactional rather than language norms (i.e. through communicative competence).

To conclude, the multitude of conceptualisations and re-evaluations of a SpCom reveals much divergence and disagreement among researchers, which contributes to the concept's vagueness and deficiency. Admittedly, a SpCom was for long considered a basic defining factor of language (Duszak 2001) and a socially-grounded unit of linguistic analyses (Patrick 2002). However, some dilemmas still remain unsolved, such as the differentiation of linguistic competence of a SpCom, its internal heterogeneity of language, and an individual's participation in multiple speech communities (Duszak 2001, 8). The adequacy of the notion of a SpCom has been numerously challenged or rejected, giving way for alternative conceptualisations of the relationship between language use and social structures. These conceptualisations attempt to better account for the complexity and dynamics of the contemporary social reality of cross-cultural and cross-linguistic contacts, continuously enhanced by the ongoing development of communication media.

1.2.2. Discourse communities and discourse systems

One of the major concepts that developed as a reinterpretation of a SpCom and *interpretative community*[2] is a *discourse community*. Although much contested (e.g. Borg 2003; Duszak 1998a; Johns 1997), the concept of the discourse community has proved particularly useful in research on specialist discourse (for academic discourse analysis see e.g. Duszak 1997b; Valle 1994), the study of writing in academic contexts and writing for specific purposes (Bhatia 1993; Connor 1996; Duszak 1998b), organizational communication (Orlikowski and Yates 1994), genre (Bhatia 1993) and cybergenre theory (Berquist and Ljungberg 1999; Erickson 1997; 1999; Shepherd and Watters 1999; Sokół 2004; Yates and Sumner 1997).

An influential definition of a discourse community belongs to John Swales (1990), who grounded his conception on the analyses of English academic texts. Swales distinguishes six defining characteristics of a discourse community: (1) a set of common public goals, (2) mechanisms of intercommunication among its members, (3) the use of participatory mechanisms primarily to provide information and feedback, (4) shared genres, (5) shared lexis, and (6) a threshold level of members with a suitable degree of relevant content and discoursal expertise (1990, 24–27). Thus, the emphasis is placed on genres and lexis as elements that enable a discourse community's members to maintain their goals, regulate their membership, and communicate efficiently with one another. In Swales' original conception, a discourse community is united by written communication. After the reconsideration of this issue, Swales differentiates between discourse communities and "place discourse communities" which were united by both written and spoken communication (Swales 1998).

As regards the distinction between speech communities and discourse communities, the main advantage of a discourse community approach in Swales' view is its sociorhetorical perspective of analysis. Unlike a speech community, the term discourse community focuses on functional rather than social determinants of the linguistic behaviour of individuals. In terms of the structure of society, speech communities are centripetal, i.e. inclusive, while discourse communities are centrifugal: they tend to separate people into occupational or speciality-interest groups. A point raised in relation to the patterns of members' recruitment is that membership in a speech community is typically inherited by birth, accident or adoption, whereas in a discourse community – by persuasion,

[2] According to Stanley Fish (1980), an *interpretative community* is an open network of people who share ways of reading texts.

training or relevant qualification (Swales 1990, 24). Lastly, it is not easy to demarcate between sociolinguistic and sociorhetorical aspects of human communication skills, hence the border between speech and discourse communities runs on fuzzy grounds (Duszak 1998a, 254).

Another vital element of a discourse community approach is its recognition of gradable and multiple membership. Swales notes that discourse communities have changing memberships, and that the survival of the community depends on a reasonable ratio between novices and experts (Swales 1990, 27). The differentiation between experts and novices implies the gradational nature of members' specialist, textual and communicative competence. Full membership in a discourse community is marked by intensive communicative activity. Multiple membership in discourse communities, in turn, is a reflection of the multiplicity of social roles and identities that individuals adopt in their social life. Each role/identity involves the voluntary and conscious activation of a specific communicative, interactional and textual competence under particular situational, social and communicative circumstances. This suggests that people's social identities, as well as their memberships in discourse communities, are dynamic and undergo constant revisions and modifications.

Finally, the advantage of the concept of the discourse community is that it does not presuppose a reference to one language, just as speech communities do (Duszak 2001, 10). Since an index of membership in a discourse community is the competent use of established genres and compliance with the community's communicative norms, a member's initiation into other types of discourse competence remains of secondary importance. Discourse communities are constructed within and across speech communities, independently of the members' native language. Another important consequence of such global distribution of discourse communities is their freedom from territorial bounds. This element of the concept of the discourse community makes it an attractive tool for research into CMC-based social structures.

Still, despite its wide application, the concept of the discourse community is considered to be abstract (Johns 1997) and fuzzy (Duszak 1998a; Erickson 1997, 1999; Swales 1990), and some of its elements as imprecisely defined (Borg 2003). Johns, concerned with issues of academic literacies, expresses the necessity to specify the relationship between discourse communities and their genres and the mechanisms that make communities complex and varied. In addition, she inquires about the existence of levels of discourse communities: e.g. "can we hypothesize a general academic community or language?" (Johns 1997, 51). Given the complexity of the concept of the discourse community, Johns speaks in favour of a community of practice approach for the studies of academic discourse. In contrast, Borg (2003) argues that research is needed into the issues related to the size of a discourse community, the status of speech in maintaining a discourse community, and the stability of a discourse community and its genres.

The reinterpretation of a discourse community as a discourse system appears in the conception of Scollon and Scollon (1995), developed mainly for a wide range of cross-cultural studies of discourse: corporate, professional, generational and gender discourse. Scollon and Scollon discern four components of a discourse system: (1) ideology, (2) socialisation, (3) forms of discourse, and (4) face systems (1995, 98). Duszak argues that Scollon and Scollon's approach has the capacity to provide a more complete and integrated description of the phenomena that contribute to the formation of social structures in response to the specific interactional, communicative and practical (e.g. exchange of information) needs of individuals (1998a, 255). Additionally, as CMC-based communities are goal-oriented communities that exist across cultural and national boundaries, I find Scollon and Scollon's model particularly relevant for the cross-cultural studies of global interpersonal and group communication in cyberspace.

1.2.3. Social networks and small cultures

More recent approaches in linguistics that address the relationship between language, identity and social structure reveal a considerable deconstruction of the concept of community, resulting from the growing social diversification of language and culture, and multiplicity of social purposes (Duszak 2001; Gumperz and Levinson 1996). A powerful concept that developed as an alternative to a SpCom was the notion of a *social network*, which became a solid methodological tool for explorations into language variation. While social network analysis continues to develop (see modern social network analysis SNA; for an overview see e.g. Bergs 2006), (socio)linguistic research has offered a number of other network-oriented conceptualisations and frameworks for the studies of language variation from the perspective of a social structure, such as nested communities, cultural communities, small cultures, styling and crossing.

The acknowledgement and wide application of the concept of the social network came with Milroy's seminal study of Belfast English (1980). In Milroy's theory of social networks, the concept of a social network is primarily an analytic tool for exploring language variability in multiplex social relations. It offers better possibilities of capturing the dynamics underlying speakers' interactional behaviours and language change in general (Milroy 1980, 2002; Milroy and Gordon 2003). The concept of the social network is defined as "the aggregate of relationships contracted with others, a boundless web of ties which reaches out through social and geographical space linking many individuals, sometimes remotely" (Milroy and Gordon 2003, 117).

The theory's major premise is that the content and structure of individual network ties can be both directly observed and quantified. As a result, an individual's degree of integration into a community can be measured on the basis of a network's density, clusters and multiplexity (Milroy 1980, 49). Density and multiplexity, in turn, serve to discover a network's capacity to act as a norm enforcement mechanism: Milroy proves that "a relatively dense multiplex network structure has the capacity to impose specifically linguistic norms upon its members" (1980, 136).

In her overview of the previous research of social networks, Milroy notes that the main advantage of a social network approach lies in its focus on the characteristics of the linkages which connect individuals rather than on the social or personal attributes of the individuals in a social nexus (1980, 45). As the network concept refers to informal social relationships that individuals contract, it proves more universal, less ethnocentric and unlimited by intercultural differences. Moreover, a social network approach offers a set of procedures to examine individual behaviour and relationships without postulating group membership of any kind (Milroy 1980, 167). Finally, the advantage of Milroy's theory of social networks is its emphasis on the choice of communication channel that a community makes in a specific situation, i.e. the choice of a medium for transmission of language, which is relevant in any account of communicative norms.

The application of a social network approach for the study of face-to-face encounters in large populations appears also in the works of Gumperz (e.g. Blom and Gumperz 1972; Gumperz 1982). The studies of networks of social relationships which associate classes of individuals with interactive experience involves systematic tracing of the regularities in the communicative patterns of interpersonal contacts (Gumperz 1982, 41). Gumperz argues that looking at the sum of networks of a given set of individuals can give insight into such domains of social structure as kinship, friendship, religion and trade. In addition, an individual's status in a network can be discovered from his/her network position, i.e. the set of relationships that that person is involved in. Since a social network analysis examines both internal and external social ties, it is possible to measure the degree of a network's overlap and cohesion. "The greater the amount of overlap, the more cohesive and community-like the population and the sharper the boundaries that separate it from others. The smaller the overlap, the more difficult it becomes to draw social boundaries" (Gumperz 1982, 41).

Notably, a social network theory may seem an attractive approach for explorations into CMC-based social structures, although the focus on clear territorial boundaries in the studies of social networks cannot be directly transferred to the corresponding research in cyberspace (see e.g. S. Jones 1998; Rheingold 2000/1993; Bergs 2006).

Having presented an account of the concept of the social network, I will proceed to discuss other network-oriented concepts and approaches, beginning from nested communities, through cultural communities and small cultures to styling and crossing.

In modern social structures, binding factors extend over the boundaries of languages, to be replaced by local and specific social goals, shared systems of values, lifestyles, or practices. For Gumperz and Levinson, these social structures could be social networks or "sub-cultures", nested communities within communities, or regional or global specialist networks that crosscut linguistic and social boundaries of all sorts (1996, 12). Thus, the concept of a SpCom is redefined as a collectivity of social networks (Gumperz 1996). Gumperz (1996, 362) introduces the division of networks into the primary, multiplex networks of socialization, based on recruitment by kinship, and additional occupational, educational and other networks constructed as a result of further socialization processes. Moreover, extended interpersonal cooperation in network-specific pursuits is conducive to the institutionalisation of practices, and subsequently, the conventionalisation of communicative practices (Gumperz 1996; Hanks 1996). What is important, these network-specific practices not only facilitate communication within the group, but also play a boundary marking function, limiting access to participation in it by non-members.

Following the argument of the deconstruction of "large" culture being replaced by "small culture" that refers to local, frequently extemporary systems of values, experiences and worldviews, there are also "cultural communities" (Clark 1996) or "small cultures", (Holliday 1999). Clark defines cultural communities as cultural groups, systems, or networks whose members have communal common ground, i.e. shared facts, beliefs, assumptions, conventions, values, skills and expertise that are taken for granted (1996, 332–333). The extent of the communal common ground increases with the number of joint memberships in the communities established by interacting individuals. Clark argues that the shared knowledge reveals itself in a number of characteristics such as nationality, education, place of residence, occupation, sub-culture, etc. Each of these characteristics can be differentiated into a "nesting of communities" (1996, 334), each with distinct beliefs, practices, and assumptions that members can appeal to if necessary. In consequence, the social structure emerges as a large number of identifiable nested communities defined by cultural characteristics.

The small culture approach is pertinent to the studies of interaction in an increasingly multicultural world (Holliday 1999). A small culture can be any social grouping from a neighbourhood to a work group. Holliday argues that a small culture emerges from individuals' active interaction with an existing environment. Thus, the formation of a small culture proves to be a dynamic, ongoing group process, grounded in the activities taking place in a group. This is a process that "operates in changing circumstances to enable group members to make sense of and operate meaningfully within those circumstances" (Holliday 1999, 248). Any social grouping may be said to have a small culture when there is a discernible set of cohesive behaviours and understandings, i.e. social constructions such as conventions or routines, or products such as artefacts, art, literature values, discourse of and about culture (Holliday 1999, 248–249). Indeed, the suggested shift from a large culture to a small culture paradigm enables us to look at social groupings from a new perspective. First of all, "a small culture approach ... attempts to liberate culture from notions of ethnicity and nation and from the perceptual dangers they carry with them" (Holliday 1999, 237). Secondly, it may be an effective way to explore and illuminate the inter-cultural complexity of the contemporary social world.

Evidence for the progressing diversification of culture and social structures can be also found in those sociolinguistic approaches that view "styling the other" or "crossing" as ways to negotiate social identities in multilingual and multicultural contexts (Hill 1999; Rampton 1995, 1999). Language crossing involves the use of language varieties associated with social or ethnic groups that the speaker does not normally belong to (out-group language use; Rampton 1995, 14–15). Since such code-crossing entails a movement across social and ethnic boundaries, it raises the problem of determining the boundary of *self* and *other* (Hill 1999), and other important issues of social legitimacy that participants of an interaction need to negotiate (Rampton 1995). Still, as Rampton argues, language crossing gives the potential to investigate complex and often contradictory patterns of affiliation and non-alignment across a range of social categories, thus avoiding divisions of people into simple dichotomous groups (Rampton 1995, 8). Besides, language crossing gives a new perspective to study the development of an active sense of urban community and local group identity.

The multiple forms that language crossing can take are influenced by specific socio-historical factors, by local social relationships, and by specific interactional dynamics. Although language crossing is mainly about the local or situated construction of social identity, it is possible to shift the focus from micro-processes of talk to global macro-social phenomena (e.g. of political sensitivities; Rampton 1999; see also Hill 1999). In general, sociolinguistic analyses in terms of styling and crossing can provide insight into the complexity of identity negotiation in an increasingly multicultural, heterogeneous world, in which the grounds for inferences about meaning and identity are shifting and fluid (Hill 1999, 543).

1.2.4. Communities of practice and epistemic communities

Other two terms that incorporate the construction of social identities through language are: *community of practice* (CofP; Wenger 1998) and *epistemic community*. These two conceptualisations of social groups are related because of their practice-based approach, explicit focus on the social construction of individual identity, and their application for linguistic analyses of professional communication.

As regards the concept of community of practice (CofP), researchers have emphasized its affinity with speech communities and social networks (see e.g. Bergs 2006; Holmes and Meyerhoff 1999; Meyerhoff 2002; Milroy 2002), discourse communities (see e.g. Johns 1997), and teams or task forces in organizations (e.g. Nickols 2000). The concept has gained wide recognition in sociolinguistic research and recently become a potent theoretical and methodological basis for analyses of language variation and discourse in professional (see e.g. Nickols 2000; Orlikowski and Yates 1994 for the studies of organizational communication) and academic contexts (see e.g. Lave and Wenger 1991), or gender studies (see e.g. Bucholtz 1999; Eckert and McConnell-Ginet 1999; Holmes and Meyerhoff 1999).

According to a popular definition, CofP is "an aggregate of people who come together around mutual engagement in an endeavour" (Eckert and McConnel-Ginet 1992, quoted in Meyerhoff 2002, 527). There are three defining criteria of a CofP: (1) mutual engagement of the members, (2) sharing jointly negotiated enterprise, and (3) a shared repertoire of negotiable resources accumulated over time (see Meyerhoff 2002, 527–528). Mutual engagement signifies more or less intensive, but regular and mutually defining interaction among members. Joint enterprise refers to an ongoing process of negotiating and building members' contributions toward a shared goal. Finally, a shared repertoire includes a number of linguistic (e.g. specialized terminology, shortcuts to communication, styles displaying membership, common stories, "inside" jokes) and non-linguistic resources (e.g. normative practices, routines, gestures, objects). A significant part in the conceptualisation of CofP is the recognition of gradational membership (core and peripheral members), acquired through a social process of learning that involves e.g. the adoption of the shared repertoire, the assimilation of the shared goals or established patterns of engagement with other members.

With reference to the issue of language and identity, what is particularly advantageous in the CofP framework is its explicit consideration of the social construction of the self and emphasis on the members' agency. In the CofP framework, the members' social identity is actively negotiated in their joint pursuit of a common purpose. This involves understanding of the members' personal roles within the group, but also recognition of the individual's mobility and participation in multiple CofPs. Also, an interesting point is that the CofP framework accepts difference and conflict as natural aspects of membership in a CofP and maintenance of its boundaries. As research shows (e.g. Bucholtz 1999), identities are constructed through opposition to the identities of the members of other groups.

The concept of CofP, although in many ways similar to the notions of a SpCom and a social network, presents new perspectives for sociolinguistic and discourse studies. Holmes and Meyerhoff see in a CofP "an ideal framework exploring the process by which individuals acquire membership in a community whose goals they share; it provides a means of studying the acquisition of sociolinguistic competence … and language change" (Holmes and Meyerhoff 1999, 182). In addition, as it allows simultaneous observation of social diversity and meaningful patterns, the CofP concept may be an efficient tool of combining a micro- and macro-level analysis. Still, more work is required into specifying the extent of core and marginal membership. Lastly, the application of the concept of CofP may be extended to more global communities, and therefore may constitute an attractive framework for research into CMC-based communities, whose constitutive element are shared interests, values and regular practices.

The model of CofP was an inspiration for another theoretical framework in linguistics, developed with the aim of tackling the complex relationship between language and identity, with the emphasis being on the social group and its communicative practices. Riley (2002) introduces the concept of epistemic community and argues in favour of a theoretical framework for the study of domain-specific discourse from the point of view of social epistemology. More specifically, he postulates the necessity for "an approach in which the social knowledge system is seen as a set of structures and functions for the management of socio-cultural knowledge, and aims to show how that macrostructure is related to personal identity through discourse" (Riley 2002, 41).

Riley defines an epistemic community as a form of social configuration whose members are bound by their shared knowledge (Riley 2002, 44). This knowledge forms an individual's cultural or epistemic competence, which includes the information and skill necessary for his/her successful interaction in a community. The possession of the knowledge which delimits the boundaries of an epistemic community gives an individual the right to claim his/her membership to this community by using a domain-specific discourse. Such attempts to use a domain-specific discourse are identity claims, i.e. "utterances in which individuals affirm their membership of specific social figurations or sub-groups in order to foreground them with reference to the matter in hand and thereby orient their audience's behaviour and expectations" (Riley 2002, 57).

The appeal of the concept of epistemic community lies in its emphasis on knowledge as an essential constituent of identity, and thus it can be applied to study professional and academic discourse. Riley's approach foregrounds an important aspect of how individuals actively and consciously position themselves in their discursive choices relative to discipline-specific beliefs, norms and practices. An example of a study which investigates the extent to which the epistemic community determines discursive choices in professional communication is Rowley-Jolivet and Carter-Thomas' (2005) analysis of international scientific communication in English.

1.2.5. Face and face systems

Much of linguistic investigation into the social presentation of an individual has been conducted within Goffman's face framework and Brown and Levinson's theory of politeness, which is developed around the face concept. Goffman defines face "as the positive social value a person effectively claims for himself [herself] by the line others assume he [she] has taken during a particular contact. Face is an image of self delineated in terms of approved social attributes" (1972/1955, 319). Face is not embedded in an individual's body but is constructed, largely linguistically, in the flow of events in social encounters. Thus, maintaining face depends on such external factors as the rules of the group, the definition of the situation, other participants' judgments and an individual's social position. An important point about Goffman's theory of face is its applicability to both direct and mediated social encounters.

Goffman's face concept and the English folk term of face, constitute the basis of Brown and Levinson's theory of politeness (2000/1987). Brown and Levinson redefine face as the public self-image of an individual, consisting of two components: "negative face" (an individual's claim to freedom of action and freedom from imposition), and "positive face" (an individual's want to be appreciated and accepted). The vulnerability of face requires from the interactants their constant attention to it and co-operation in maintaining their face. In Brown and Levinson's terms, linguistic politeness is the redressing of the affronts to face posed by face-threatening acts to addressees. The twofold aspects of face result in the differentiation between positive and negative politeness strategies. "Positive politeness is redress directed to the addressees positive face, his [her] perennial desire that his [her] wants (or the actions/acquisitions/values resulting from them) should be thought of as desirable" (Brown and Levinson 2000/1987, 101). In contrast, "negative politeness is redressive action addressed to the addressee's negative face…; it is the heart of respect behaviour… [and] it performs the function of minimizing the particular imposition that the FTA [face-threatening act] unavoidably effects" (Brown and Levinson 2000/1987, 129).

While recognizing the culture-specific content of face and culture-specific distribution of politeness strategies, Brown and Levinson argue that the mutual knowledge of members' public self-image, and the social necessity to orient oneself to it in interaction are universal, thus warranting the pan-cultural interpretability of politeness phenomena. They emphasise the application of their theory of politeness to ethnographic explorations of the patterns of social interaction, and to the functionalist studies of the linguistic system.

The reassessments of Brown and Levinson's model of politeness (e.g. Brown and Levinson 2000/1987; Foley 1997; Kopytko 1993) and continued work on politeness phenomena resulted in elaborations of the original theory (e.g. Eelen 2001; Leech, 1983; Scollon and Scollon, 1995; Schiffrin, 1994).

When looking at the face concept from the perspective of linguistic pragmatics, Kopytko (1993) criticizes Brown and Levinson's reductionsist bias to politeness phenomena. Kopytko addresses Brown and Levinson's conceptualisation of face as self-image and face as wants. Firstly, this is because of the indeterminacy and unpredictability of a person's self-image in social interaction, face is a dynamic, changeable and multiple concept. Secondly, the reduction of face to basic wants calls for justification. In Kopytko's view, face is "more than just a want, if it is that at all. It is also (or perhaps primarily) a social value and a norm. Face is a value in itself" (1993, 97). Besides, being a product of socialization, politeness cannot be accounted for solely in terms of inherited wants.

Foley's (1997) main objection to Brown and Levinson's model of politeness is that it is presented as universal. In fact, Brown and Levinson's concept of face with its dual aspects is framed in individualistic terms. Foley adduces numerous comparative studies of politeness that reveal differences in the amount of significance accorded to the two aspects of face (see Foley 1997, 273–275 for a review). To give an example, Brown and Levinson's division into positive and negative face is unsustainable for East Asian cultures, with sociocentric conceptions of personhood, where the concept of negative face is marginal.

Still, in general, the concept of face and diverse linguistic practices used to minimize any threat to both types of face (politeness) prove useful in understanding human social interaction. Originally developed for studies of face-to-face interaction, the theory of politeness was elaborated to deal with interpersonal cross-cultural communication in spoken (e.g. Schiffrin 1994), written (e.g. Meyers 1989; Scollon and Scollon 1995), and recently in computer-mediated contexts (e.g. Bunz and Campbell 2002; Hongladarom and Hongladarom 1999; Morand and Ocker 2002).

An important elaboration of the theory of politeness appears within Leech's interpersonal rhetoric (1983). Leech views the Politeness Principle (the PP) as a necessary complement to Grice's Cooperative Principle (the CP): the instances of flouting the CP maxims involve, at a deeper level, the operation of the PP, redeeming the CP from difficulty. The PP has a highly regulative function in social interaction: it allows "to maintain social equilibrium and the friendly relations which enable us to assume that our interlocutors are being cooperative in the first place" (Leech 1983, 82). Leech develops a set of politeness maxims of varying importance, which roughly correlate with Searle's categories of illocution. In justifying these maxims, Leech draws on evidence of pragmatic asymmetries between a speaker and a hearer, of implicatures and of indirectness (see Leech 1983, 132–133 for details). While recognizing the culture- and situation-dependency of politeness, Leech argues that general pragmatics should restrict its attention to politeness in the absolute sense.

Schiffrin (1994) uses Goffman's concept of face (next to Gumperz's anthropological works) as the basis for interactional sociolinguistics, an approach to discourse that focuses on situated meaning. For Schiffrin, Goffman provides a sociological framework for exploring "the form and meaning of the social and interpersonal contexts that provide presuppositions for the interpretation of meaning" (1994, 133). Goffman's work demonstrates that all interactive activity is situated within such social contexts as the occasions, situations, encounters, contexts that provide structure and meaning to what is said and may themselves be organized by what is said. Thus, for Goffman, language is indexical to a social world: it provides an index to interactively constructed social identities and relationships. More specifically, Schiffrin analyses a "speaking for another" discourse strategy used as a contextualisation cue to signal speakers' identities and alignments. What is important, the perspective of interactional sociolinguistics allows us to view social identity as a dynamic, locally situated construct: "rather than an identity being maintained throughout an extended period of time (be it a speech activity, a situation, a span of life, or even a lifetime), different facets of identity may be highlighted or submerged during different periods of time; …identity is open to intentional manipulation by self, and to impersonal negotiation between self and other" (Schiffrin 1994, 374)[3].

In the study of cross-cultural, professional communication, Scollon and Scollon (1995) explore politeness phenomena within the framework of face or politeness systems. First of all, their conceptualisation of face systems is grounded on Goffman's concept of face and on the Asian concept of face that carries a range of meanings based on a core concept of "honour". Next, Scollon and Scollon argue that the construction of face as a public image involves both the negotiation of face and the assumptions about face made by participants of interaction. Thus, face relationships among participants consist of an unmarked set of initial assumptions and ongoing negotiations in which those unmarked assumptions are verified (1995, 41–42). Face or politeness systems, in turn, are defined as persistent regularities in face relationships, marked by the use of a fairly regular set of face strategies, and dependent on three factors: power, distance and the weight of imposition. Scollon and Scollon extend the

[3] The view of social identity from the perspective of interactional sociolinguistics is contrasted with the variationist view, in which social identities are social and cultural categories that are not easily susceptible to our own control or alterations by others (Schiffrin 1994, 374).

analysis of face relationships to the context of written communication. Given the limitations of face negotiation among participants in written communication, Scollon and Scollon argue that in some forms of written discourse (e.g. the press release and the essay), the considered face relationships will be those between the implied writer and the implied reader, rather than the real writer and the real reader (1995, 93).

A face model can also be a starting point in explorations of language choice in secondary multilingual settings (O'Driscoll 2001). O'Driscoll notes a current increase in communication in multi- or plurilingual contexts, i.e. non-traditional settings for intercultural contacts outside long-established communities, resulting from such activities as business, tourism, or student exchange (2001, 247). Such plurilingual settings are characterized by: (1) the relative permanence of community members and norms, (2) the varying levels of expertise in the language repertoire of community members, and (3) the lack of a neat ingroup-outgroup dichotomy in language and group divisions. For tackling identity in these settings, O'Driscoll develops a face model that could accommodate not only a priori identities that are inputs to interaction but also identities that emerge as outcomes of interaction. According to O'Driscoll, interaction in a plurilingual setting involves a configuration of three faces available to interactants: ethnolinguistic, cosmopolitan, and polite, relative to the language-ownership and language-status factors. Since the interaction in an electronic discussion may be considered a secondary plurilingual setting, O'Driscoll's face model could provide an interesting contribution towards developing a framework for managing identity construction in CMC-based groupings.

Finally, Eelen's (2001) noteworthy input to how politeness is theorised is an integration of linguistics, social theory and psychology. This approach allows us to better understand the relationship between language and social reality, but first of all, foregrounds the agency of the individual.

In Eelen's integrated view of social reality, politeness is considered as an active form of linguistic behaviour, whose main features are evaluativity, argumentativity, variability and discursiveness (Eelen 2001, 35). In other words, politeness and its norms are social practices that have social effects, purposes and motivations, and which are used to characterize people's conduct. What is important, while recognizing a dynamic interrelationship between the social and the individual, Eelen's approach to politeness brings into focus the individual's active role. Individual practices of politeness are shaped by both external, socio-cultural factors, "but also by the individual's perceived position within the social structure and the linguistic market, and his or her subsequent reaction of self-positioning" (Eelen 2001, 227). This acknowledgment of the individual and his/her psychological make-up gives way for the incorporation of creativity and change.

With reference to issues of language and identity, politeness, or more precisely, an interaction between politeness and social power, turns out to be an important social tool of identification and differentiation. As Eelen points out, "politeness is an active expression of the person's social positioning in relation to others and the social worldview in general", whereas power is viewed as social practice co-determined by individual action and thus can be "asserted, maintained, claimed and challenged" (Eelen 2001, 224, 226). Thus, social power is not a position in the social hierarchy that is reflected in polite behaviour, but as a form of behaviour itself, power is actively negotiated by the individual. I find the empowerment of the individual particularly relevant for the analysis of discoursal construction of identity in CMC, this being a dynamic and individuating medium of communication (see the characteristics of CMC in Chapter 3 Section 3.3).

1.2.6. A summary of community-based approaches to identity

An overview of the community-based approaches to identity reveals points of similarity and contrast between them, and demonstrates an evolution of linguistic conceptualisations of social structure. What combines the approaches is the view of language as a social phenomenon, and what comes with this, the view of identity as a socially constructed category. The reviewed approaches also share an assumption that identity is a matter of both collectivity and individuality; however, it is mainly the communal aspects of identity construction that are emphasised. Finally, all these approaches recognise the complexity and dynamism of identity construction.

As regards the divergences, the approaches differ with respect to the criteria of delimitation and membership for particular concepts of community, and the range of shared knowledge and competence. One of the problems concerns the demarcation of social structures in relation to linguistic phenomena. In addition, it is unsettled whether membership in a social structure should be based on external or internal criteria, and whether the necessary shared knowledge within a collectivity should be purely linguistic. There is also a dilemma: how to account for the evolving social reality, its complexity and heterogeneity?

Essentially, the evaluated approaches show an evolution of social structures, from larger, homogenous units, to smaller, dynamic and purpose-oriented ones, which follows from the deconstruction of the concepts of community and culture. Also, as a result of the researchers' concerns with the diversification of linguistic competence, its range has been extended. With the development of various notions of community, we additionally observe differing attitudes towards the extent of shared knowledge relevant for community construction and operation. In general, the focus changes from purely linguistic and grammatical conditions towards non-linguistic and pragmatic ones. Conceptions that developed as alternatives to the SpCom recognise the gradation of shared knowledge and enable us to concentrate on such aspects of social interaction within a collectivity as bond building, norms, beliefs and attitudes. Most importantly though, these various approaches contributed to the advancement of discursive approaches to identity, which allow us to give a comprehensive account of identity construction in discourse.

1.3. Discursive approaches to identity

A social-constructionist perspective that emerges from the cross-disciplinary approach to identity enables us to view identity as a discursive process (see overviews in Ivanič 1998; Bucholtz and Hall 2005; Benwell and Stokoe 2006; De Fina et al 2006). This means that identity work involves people's understandings of themselves and of each other in interaction, when they rhetorically perform social action. Thus, what a discursive approach corroborates is that identity is a social construction, i.e. a public phenomenon or action that is dynamically and continuously accomplished, managed and negotiated in discourse. This is the approach that I represent in this book, as it has a number of advantages directly relevant for my present purposes.

First of all, as Benwell and Stokoe (2006, 17) point out, a discursive approach to identity allows us to reconcile the divergent understandings of identity: identity as a private vs. public phenomenon, and what comes with this, identity as a fixed vs. a fluid construct (see Ivanič 1998). For one thing, although a constructionist view of identity has shifted the focus from the private, psychological domain, to the public domain of discourse, an "inner" self has not been altogether replaced by an "outer" one. As Benwell and Stokoe emphasise, it is rather "the very idea of an inner self and its *outward* expression that is constructed, metaphorically" when people accomplish social action (Benwell and Stokoe 2006, 4; the authors' emphasis). To others, discursive approaches "are able to explicate the processes by which people orient to consistency in their accounts of themselves and other people (underpinning the view of identity as "fixed"), whilst simultaneously showing that identity is contingent on the local conditions of the interactional context", and hence the view of identity as fluid and fragmentary (Benwell and Stokoe 2006, 17–18).

Another significant advantage of a discursive approach to identity is that it enables us to account for the role of the individual in identity construction (see especially Ivanič 1998; also Fairclough 2003). Since in discursive approaches to identity a collective view of identity predominates, researchers argue that the role of the individual is not sufficiently theorised (e.g. Ivanič 1998; Johnstone 1996). Although some approaches to identity point to the individual's agency in how identity is constituted in discourse (e.g. Eelen 2001; Foley 1997; Riley 2002; see Section 1.1 above), few accounts take the individual's perspective explicitly.

An interesting exception is Johnstone's work (1996), in which she carries out an inquiry into linguistic variation and the construction of social identity from the perspective of the individual rather than a social structure he/she belongs to. Following Le Page and Tabouret-Keller's view (1985) that speech acts are "acts of identity", Johnston notes that to some extent people's linguistic behaviour can be related to how they are externally defined in terms of demographic categories such as gender, social role, ethnicity, etc. However, she argues against deterministic ways of talking about language use, saying that "to correlate discourse choices directly with social categories is to abstract away from the real reason linguistic choices are made: in service of the expression and the creation of self" (Johnstone 1996, 89–90). Speakers make different choices about how to interact with others and how to persuade because they are expressing different selves.

In her account of discoursal construction of identity in writing, Ivanič (1998) also focuses on the individual's perspective and agency, and rejects the separation of the private self from the social context. She develops a framework that successfully integrates the private and public dimensions of identity and does not depreciate the role of the individual. I find Ivanič's approach valuable for my present purposes, as it stresses the individual's agency and shows that identity construction, also in institutional contexts, involves a constant interplay of the private and public facets of the self.

Ivanič argues that there are four interrelating aspects of the writer's identity: the *autobiographical self*, the *discoursal self*, the *self as author* and the "possibilities for self-hood" that are available in the writer's socio-cultural context (1998, 23–30). These "three selves are socially constructed and socially constructing in that they are shaped by and shape the more abstract 'possibilities for selfhood'" (Ivanič 1998, 24). The autobiographical self refers to the individual's social and discoursal history brought into the process of self-portrayal. This is an evolving self because the life-history of the individual constantly develops. The discoursal self is the self as presented through the characteristics of a text. In contrast, the self as author involves such aspects of the writer's voice as his/her stance, opinions and beliefs. Although it is essentially the discoursal self that can be reached through textual analysis, aspects of the autobiographical self and self as author also become apparent, as these three dimensions of the writer's identity are inseparable.

As I have mentioned above, an important perspective in Ivanič's approach is her emphasis on the individual's agency: the socio-cultural and institutional contexts of writing with its constraints is viewed as a source of the possibilities for self-hood rather than a deterministic factor. This is especially relevant for the investigation of academic texts, because it shows that the institutionally approved possibilities for self-hood are not inflexible. The author's creativity and reliance on the less privileged resources have the potential to redefine the available possibilities, and thus are likely to contribute to changes of conventions (Ivanič 1998, 28).

A similar approach is also represented in Fairclough's social view of discourse (1995a, 1995b, 2003). When accounting for the complexity and heterogeneity of identity construction in discourse, Fairclough argues for the dialectical interconnection between social identity and personal identity (personality), and, what comes with this, for an extension of the concept of agency (2003, 160–161). As he underlines, identity construction is not purely a textual process, but involves also self-consciousness as a precondition for the social processes of identification. Besides, people are also prepositioned within society according to their social roles, but as social agents they have the capacity to reconstruct their positionings thanks to their reflexivity and ability of collective change. "Achieving social identity in a full sense is a matter of being capable of assuming social roles but personifying them with one's own personality (or personal identity), enacting them in a distinctive way" (Fairclough 2003, 160–161).

In connection with the issue of agency, researchers also argue (Fairclough 2003; Ivanič 1998) that the use of the verb *to identify* and its nominalization *identification* better reflects the nature of the processes involved in the discoursal construction of identity. Using the nominalization rather than the noun *identity* emphasises an individual's agency, the processual aspect of an act of identifying, and shows that identity construction is a dynamic and fluid phenomenon.

Finally, an advantage of a discursive approach to identity is the possibility to combine the micro- and macro-level analyses of how identity is constituted in discourse (Benwell and Stokoe 2006, 116). In other words, particular language choices that convey an individual's representation in text and his/her alignments and non-alignments can be investigated in relation to the wider sociological and economic context. The assumption that language use reflects macro-social forces lies at the basis of a critical perspective for doing identity research (the perspective of critical discourse analysis), a perspective that proves useful for (mass) media studies.

1.3.1. Identity and Critical Discourse Analysis

With its focus on language use in relation to the institutional and socio-cultural context of media practices, critical discourse analysis (henceforth CDA) provides a framework for the multifunctional and intertextual investigation of the representation and constitution of relations and identities in media discourse (Benwell and Stokoe 2006; Fairclough 1995b). A CDA perspective enables us to show an interrelation between the individuals, society and its institutions with their embedded power relations.

One view of this interrelationship assumes a deterministic effect of the socio-cultural context upon language, where language becomes a site of ideological workings which shape people's experiences, identities and worldviews. This view is based on the Foucauldian framework of discourse analysis, in which identities are seen as products of dominant discourses and are dependent upon social practices and orders (see Aycock 1995; Benwell and Stokoe 2006; Thoms and Thelwall 2005 for overviews and critique). Consequently, this leads to social inequalities and disempowers an individual: he/she is presented as a powerless subject rather than a generator of action. However, Foucault's later conception of "technologies of the self" (Foucault 1988) does not seem to neglect an individual's agency totally. By "technologies of the self" Foucault refers to the different mechanisms of self-construction offered by available ideologies and systems of power, which both constrain and enrich the possibilities for self-hood. One such technology is the Internet, which has, on the one hand, challenged the credibility and agency of the self (see Gergen 1996; Thoms and Thelwall 2005), and on the other, opened up new ways of identity construction not only for individuals, but also for communities and institutions (see e.g. Turkle 1995; Benwell and Stokoe 2006; for the discussion see Chapter 4).

Another, less pessimistic framework for critical analysis of media discourse is advanced by Fairclough (1995a, 1995b). Essentially, Fairclough emphasises a dialectical relationship between language use and social practices, i.e. language use is both "socially shaped and socially constitutive" (Fairclough 1995b, 55). Thus, language use functions to reproduce and sustain identities and relations, but at the same time individuals have the capacity to creatively transform them. Drawing on the Hallidayan view of the multifunctionality of language, Fairclough stresses an interdependency of ideational, interpersonal and textual meanings in texts, and additionally subdivides the interpersonal function into: "'identity' function – text in the constitution of personal and social identities – and the 'relational' function – text in the constitution of relationships" (Fairclough 1995a, 133). All these domains contribute to the establishment and negotiation of identities of individuals, and the social and personal relationships between them.

In addition, Fairclough stresses an influential position of the mass media in contemporary societies and the multiplicity and variability of identities and relations in the mass media (Fairclough 1995b, 127). First of all, the variability of identities and relations in the mass media results from the ongoing changes in the macro-social context, the evolution of the mass media as institutions and of technologies that mass-communication makes use of. Secondly, Fairclough points to the relevance of institutional aspects of text production and reception in mass communication and the economics and politics of the mass media. Finally, he enumerates the following properties of mass communication that have implications for the negotiation of identities and relations: text production and reception involve major temporal and spatial disjunctions; a communicative situation consists of a chain of communicative events; the mass media redraw the boundaries between the public and private domains; and the mass media involve communication through various channels. In addition, the role of the audience is foregrounded, and such related aspects as the lack of immediate feedback on the part of the audience, or its size (Fairclough 1995b, 36). As the Internet is considered to be a mass medium (e.g. Morris and Ogan 1996), I find the above properties relevant for the purposes of my present work. A more detailed account of the characteristics of the Internet and computer-mediated communication as mass media is given in Chapter 3, Section 3.3.

It is also important to mention that the media reflect the cultural values of contemporary society, which, in turn, shape contemporary discursive practices. An interesting process related to the social changes in the contemporary world is the *aestheticization* of public identities (Fairclough 1995b, 183). The aestheticization of public identities means individuals' concern with their image, which implies the rather self-conscious construction of public identities. In addition, following a social view of language use, Fairclough (1995a, 136–140) points to other interconnected developments in discursive practices of contemporary society, such as a conversalisation of public discourse and its marketisation or commodification. Conversalisation is viewed as the infusion of private domain practices by the public domain, practices which are necessary for the complex processes of negotiating relationships and identities. The related aspects of discourse are its personalisation and the realisation of promotional objectives. In contrast, marketisation is linked to the commodification of contemporary culture. Discourse has become a vehicle for "selling" goods, services, organisations, ideas or people, which resulted in a greater instrumentalisation of contemporary discursive practices. Fairclough illustrates these developments on the example of public academic written discourse.

To conclude, in view of the above changes, negotiation of identity in the contemporary world involves more risk, but first of all more possibilities, which can be illustrated by the analysis of identity construction in electronic media. Before discussing the results of the empirical analysis of my material (Chapter 5), in the chapters that follow I will first give an account of the most important aspects of academic identity construction in speech and writing (Chapter 2). Then, I will present electronic discourse as a new language variety, making reference to the defining characteristics of computer-mediated communication (Chapter 3). Finally, I will address the individual and communal aspects of social interaction in electronic discourse relevant for the examination of identity construction (Chapter 4).

CHAPTER TWO

ACADEMIC IDENTITY IN SPEECH AND WRITING

The issues of an individual's identity in academic discourse are inseparably connected to the development of a social view of scholarly discourse. The area of academic discourse studies is an extensive field of research, so in this chapter I will focus on the issues directly related to the discussion of the discoursal construction of academic identity. First of all, I will contrast a traditional and a social approach to the study of scholarly discourse. My main emphasis will be on how this comprehensive approach, which integrates social and cognitive aspects of academic communication, brings into focus the interpersonal meanings in scholarly discourse. Consequently, academic discourse emerges as a site of complex interaction and can be analysed in terms of underlying human choices. I will also refer to the related points such as an academic discourse community and its values, power and authority.

2.1. The interactional character of academic texts

A traditional, anti-rhetorical approach to academic discourse views academic literacy as a set of fixed practices. Scientific text is the utmost authority and its main role is to disseminate the truth; and therefore, the need for objectivity and depersonalisation of scientific writing. As Duszak puts it, "the organisation of a research text is supposed to take place "above" or "beyond" the writing ego. It is believed to be governed by the internal requirements of scientific exposition and by the nature of the matter under analysis" (Duszak 1997a, 12).

Such underplaying of the human component in academic discourse has its roots in the Utilitarian discourse system of the 18th-century, directly responsible for the contemporary preference for the so called C-B-S style of professional communication, where C-B-S stands for "clarity", "brevity" and "sincerity" (Scollon and Scollon 1995; Swales 1990). The Utilitarian ideology is the achievement of the Enlightenment and its emphasis on reason and freedom, and the rise of science as the new authority. The Utilitarian ideals are found in the instances of Utilitarian scientific discourse, which is anti-rhetorical, positivist-empirical, deductive, individualistic, egalitarian and public, i.e. institutionally sanctioned (Scollon and Scollon 1995, 107). More specifically, scientific texts "should appear to give nothing but information (…), they should appear to be making no attempt to influence the listener or the reader except through his or her exercise of rational judgement" (Scollon and Scollon 1995, 108). The same point is made by Swales in relation to the research article: "(…) we find the research article, this key product of the knowledge-manufacturing industry, to be a remarkable phenomenon, so cunningly engineered by rhetorical machining that it somehow still gives an *impression* of being but a simple description of relatively untransmuted raw material" (Swales 1990, 125). The requirement for objectivity diminishes the authority of the individual and interpersonal relations, to the advantage of text, especially the written one. In other words, text should be "transparent" so as not to obstruct the readers' access to the transmitted information (Vassileva 2000, 9). At the same time, emphasis is put on the creativity and freedom of the individual, and an equal stance between the author and the reader.

The characteristics of academic discourse are also presented in Gotti's (2003) comprehensive account of specialised discourse. Gotti explains such characteristics of academic texts as objectivity, a non-emotive tone, conciseness and precision in a historical perspective, referring to the European tradition of the scientific language. However, as Gotti also admits, the characteristics of scientific discourse mentioned above cannot be generally applied to any field or speciality. "Every speciality displays pragmatic criteria, which, according to the author's communicative needs and disciplinary epistemology, result in an adaptation or a violation of its constitutive principles. Every surface variation is a consequence of specific choices made by the author in the semantic and pragmatic construction of discourse" (Gotti 2003, 309). For instance, authors often choose to violate the principles of scientific expression to enhance the persuasive force of their texts.

A traditional approach to scientific communication led to the studies which for long focused on the formal characteristics of academic texts, such as syntax, lexis, and text organisation (see e.g. Gajda 1982; Mikołajczak 1990; for overviews see also Biniewicz and Starzec 1995; Duszak 1998a). However, the assumptions of modern textlinguistics and discourse studies (de Beaugrande and Dressler 1981; van Dijk and Kintsch 1983) changed the focus of research from text properties to user properties, and initiated a "more human" approach to scientific discourse (e.g. Duszak 1997a, 1998a). The major advances were brought about by the change in the view of text as a process rather than a product. Text was considered as a communicative event, involving the participants of the interaction and a range of contextual features that influence the participants' discursive choices. These developments in textlinguistics made it clear that comprehensive investigations of scientific communication must recognise that there are interpersonal meanings at play. Textual variation in scientific texts is accountable in terms of authors' varying cultural and pragmatic motivations.

Given the above, there is some paradox and vulnerability about the nature of scientific style (Duszak 1997a; Vassileva 2000). On the one hand, the 18th-century foundations of modern science led to the development of a scientific style that is marked by a high degree of depersonalisation, formalisation and standardisation, reflected at all levels of its textual organisation. Such features are emphasised in the contemporary descriptions of scientific styles (see e.g. Biniewicz and Starzec 1995; Gajda 1990, 1993; Gunnarsson 1994; Mauranen 1993; Mikołajczak 1990). Formalisation and standardisation affect also the author's (self)-presentation in discourse and the author-audience relations. As already stated, the requirement for the objectivity of scientific text necessitates an unobtrusive and inconspicuous author representation. The author "is expected to remain hidden behind facts, research results, tables, formulas and the like" (Vassileva 2000, 9). On the other hand, a more "human", social approach to scholarly discourse draws attention to the interpersonal meanings in academic discourse, where particular discursive choices can be explained in terms of attitudes that authors assume in relation to themselves, their audience, the task at hand and knowledge in general. On the whole, the author's presentation in academic discourse emerges as a complex issue which must always involve some tension. Authors aim to convince the readers about the relevance and validity of the scientific facts and theories, and this is how they win recognition and prestige. However, they also respond to institutionally sanctioned conventions through the processes of accommodation, opposition and resistance (see the discussions of academic writing in Ivanič 1998; Vassileva 2000).

In the contemporary approach to academic communication, along with the interactional character of scientific text, emphasis is put on the relevance of the social context of academics' communicative activity (see e.g. Gajda 1996; Ivanič 1998). Taking as the point of departure the

Hallidayan distinction between context of culture and context of situation[4], Ivanič argues for the integrative approach to scientific communication, which takes into account both the immediate interaction between individuals and the cultural norms in which they operate (Ivanič 1998, 77). An important element of the social context is a general academic community (or scientific community), with its values and conventions. Although it might be argued that there is no such a thing as an academic community that can be clearly marked off from other communities, the term academic community is usually used to refer to a collectivity of scholars who share a range of values, assumptions and practices related to the pursuit and dissemination of knowledge, i.e. the scientific ethos. Valle (1994) considers the notion of the scientific community crucial for an understanding of modern science. She also stresses that a scientific community is to a large extent self-defining and self-regulating. "It is the community that (i) decides (…) what are the legitimate concerns of science and what kinds of questions can meaningfully and legitimately be asked; (ii) sets the criteria by which they validity of findings is to be evaluated; and (iii) defines the body of concepts, entities and propositions, which are accepted (…) as scientific knowledge" (Valle 1994, 76).

However, membership in a general academic community is not the only aspect of a complex social context of academics' scientific activity. As Gajda (1993, 174) emphasises, there is a number of factors that stand behind the subject whose aim is scientific inquiry and the pursuit of knowledge and truth. These include:

(1) society as a whole, whose general needs are a basic motivation for the development of science;
(2) an academic "micro-community" of a discipline, scientific school, specialisation, etc., with its specific research methodology and tools, assumptions, terminology, etc.;
(3) a scholar as an individuality that is determined biologically, mentally and socially (this brings about the relevance of such elements as an individual's cognitive style and organisation of his/her intellectual activity, his/her academic competence, intuition, creative imagination, etc.).

Thus, a scholar's cognitive-communicative activity is embedded in the context which appears to be a complex sum of cultural (every day life, art, politics, religion etc.) and academic aspects (the ideals and paradigms of science). Given the complexity of social context, the wide range of

[4] The distinction discussed within Halliday's social-semiotic view of language (Halliday 1978).

universal values that are shared, communicated and observed by members of academia on their way to knowledge include (see Gajda 1993, 175):

(1) heuristic values of knowledge and its inspirational power;
(2) praxeological values (i.e. values related to competence, efficiency, productivity);
(3) moral values;
(4) aesthetic values;
(5) instrumental values (i.e. economic and technical values, and also values related to academic career advancement and gaining academic prestige and authority).

As these values influence the nature of academic discourse, it might be expected that they will also affect the discoursal construction of academic identity. Members of an academic community negotiate their identity within the range of possibilities accepted by this community and inscribed in its communicative practices. Such practices are often locked in complex interpersonal relationships of changeable status and power, significant for the issue of identity construction in academic discourse (Ivanič 1998, 82).

The multiplicity of contextual parameters allows us to recognise the heterogeneity of scientific discourse. Gajda additionally points to the variation that results from scholars' distinctive personal styles (1996). He speaks of scholars' "individual styles" or "idiostyles"[5]. This term refers to: (1) the structure of text, where text is treated as a cognitive-pragmatic-linguistic whole, (2) which is produced relative to the cultural (historical-social-linguistic) and mental context, (3) through the individuality of the author as the subject who acts as the centre of the cognitive-communicative perspective (Gajda 1996, 251). Such a view of individual style allows us to analyse the scholar's textual activity through the prism of socio-cultural *codes* (i.e. conventions) and the individual's innovative behaviours. These codes enter into complex interactions and interdependencies, which is both limiting and stimulating at the same time. Once more, emphasis is put on the individual's decisions in which he/she oscillates between the observance of social and institutional norms and the satisfaction of his/her particular aims.

In relation to the purposes of this book, an interesting point is to find out to what degree scholars exercise the autonomy inherent in the Internet communication. On the one hand, the relative freedom and anonymity of

[5] Gajda makes also reference to other related terms that appear in the literature of the subject such as "individual style" or "linguistic persona" (Gajda 1996, 251).

the Internet may offer greater possibilities for innovation and self-realisation. On the other, the Internet has also such restrictive aspects as lack of stability of the electronic word, violation of privacy and copyright, lack of standardisation etc.

2.2. Interpersonal meanings in academic discourse: a discourse community view

The considerations of contextual factors lead us to the concept of an academic discourse community, which is essential to a social view of scientific discourse. The idea of a discourse community constitutes the basis of Swales' approach to the study of scientific communication (1990), and its main advantage is the focus on shared communicative purposes, values, assumptions and practices as the elements that decide about a community's cohesion. This approach allows us to recognise also further variation within academic discourse. The definition of the concept, its strengths and weaknesses, and the idea of a gradable membership were extensively discussed in Section 1.2.2 of Chapter 1. In this section, I would like to address further aspects of the heterogeneity of scientific discourse and those issues directly relevant for the discussion of the discoursal construction of academic identity, such as power and solidarity relations, where power is understood as a position in the social hierarchy, a form of social practice which may be negotiated by an individual (as discussed in Chapter 1 Section 1.2.5). In the final part of this section, I would like to discuss two other related approaches that enable us to tackle interpersonal meanings in professional and academic discourse, namely the model of metadisocurse (mainly the one advanced by Hyland 2005), and the model of interpersonal metaphors of mood and modality (Halliday 1994).

2.2.1. Interdisciplinary variation of scientific discourse

A social view of academic discourse allows us to recognise the heterogeneity of scientific discourse, not only on the individual level (see "individual styles" in Section 2.1 above), but also the variation resulting from such diverse factors as discipline-specific standards and methodologies, ideologies of science, cultural values and norms, intellectual styles (see e.g. Clyne 1987, 1994; Connor 1996; the volume edited by Duszak 1997; Duszak 1994, 1997a, 1998a; Gajda 2004; Hyland 2000; Mauranen 1993; Scollon and Scollon 1995; Swales 1990). This heterogeneity can be explicated in terms of underlying human choices, and therefore is pertinent to the discussion of author's identity in discourse. Also, I find the issue of variation in scholarly discourse relevant for the purposes of the present study, as the scholarly discussion list under analysis, although dominated by the English-speaking members, provides an intercultural setting. Therefore, in order to investigate (academic) identity and its construction in this context, it is crucial to be sensitive to the different intellectual and rhetorical styles of academics.

An important factor that is responsible for variation in scientific discourse is interdisciplinary diversity, which, in turn, results from the homogeneity of disciplinary communities and practices (Hyland 2000). In his discussion of social interactions in academic discourse, Hyland stresses the role of disciplinary cultures: "each discipline might be seen as an academic tribe with its particular norms, nomenclature, bodies of knowledge, sets of conventions and modes of inquiry constituting a separate culture" (Hyland 2000, 8). Socialisation into these cultures involves acquiring specialised discourse competencies that allow individual scholars to participate in their discourse communities. Disciplines develop institutionally sanctioned rhetorical conventions that result from shared beliefs, values and norms. Individuals are expected to comply with these conventions, and thus their textual choices are characterised by a certain degree of routine and uniformity. Still, the influence of disciplinary cultures is not deterministic: there is still space for individual diversity and innovation, depending on the communicative setting, purpose and audience, scholars' stylistic preferences, allegiances, commitment or the level of expertise.

It turns out, then, that disciplinary cultures play an important role in establishing the scholar's identity (see e.g. Breivega et al 2002; Dahl 2004; Fløttum et al 2006; Hyland 2000, 2005). As Hyland points out, on the one hand, disciplinary constraints on discourse are restrictive. On the other, the author's conformity to these constraints acknowledges his/her disciplinary authority and perceptions of community-shared values and norms such as an ideology of the discipline and the world, assumptions about the nature of things and methodologies, power relations, and doctrinal knowledge of external reality (see Hyland 2000, 10).

Apart from the diversity resulting from varying disciplinary cultures, scientific discourse reveals also variation linked to authors' national cultures and the intellectual traditions they have been brought up in. The support for the cross-cultural variation comes from the findings of contrastive rhetoric, discourse and genre analysis (see e.g. Clyne 1987; Connor 1996; the volume edited by Duszak 1997; Duszak 1994, 1997a, 1998; Mauranen 1993; Scollon and Scollon 1995; Swales 1990). Cross-cultural variation becomes evident on many levels of form and content organisation: e.g. in the global organisation schemata of texts (such as divisions within the text's space, their labelling, sequencing), in their degree of explicitness and metadiscoursal guidance, in their structural resources and rhetorical devices, etc. (see Duszak 1997a). As it might be expected, cross-cultural variation also concerns the authors' preferences in presenting their academic self-image and the image of others (see e.g. Breivega et al 2002; Dahl 2004; Fløttum et al 2006; Hyland 2002b, 2005; Koutsantoni 2005; Rowley-Jolivet and Carter-Thomas 2005; Vasslieva 2000).

Finally, I would like to point to the medium-bound variation of academic discourse (e.g. Duszak 1997a; Gajda 2004; Ivanič 1996). The communication channel proves important for identity construction, as individuals are additionally positioned relative to the practices and norms associated with a particular communication channel, whether that channel is speech, writing or CMC. In fact, as Gajda points out, the development of the Internet and the spread of electronicity have revolutionised scholarly communication and led to the emergence of the new order (2004, 53). This necessitates a new look at the linguistic means of building authorial presence in a new and complex communicative situation.

2.2.2. Power relations and authority: pronoun choice

Gradable membership in an academic discourse community implies that its members represent varying degrees of professional expertise and authority. Competing for academic credentials and recognition is viewed as a form of socializing into a new public role, a process that takes place through the adoption of community-approved discourse practices. Participation in knowledge exchanges, in turn, can be perceived in terms of face phenomena and power and solidarity relations, as it is rather impossible to separate intellectual pursuit from the individuals who embark on it (see e.g. Duszak 1997a; Tannen 2002; Ventola 1998a).

The construction of the scholar's authority proceeds for example through an adequate attribution of other researchers' work, references to and challenges of their claims, signalling authors' allegiances and through negotiations of their own claims (e.g. Hyland 2000; Teufel and Moens 2000; Ventola 1998a, 1998b). Although critical evaluation is usually very constructive for academic exchanges, attention has to be drawn to the destructive consequences of the "ritualised" (to use Tannen's term, 2002) expression of opposition and criticism in academic discourse, whether referred to as *bashing* (Ventola 1998b) or *agonism* (Tannen 2002). This ritualised adversativness in academic discourse means "conventionalised oppositional formats that result from an underlying ideology by which intellectual interchange is conceptualised as a metaphorical battle" (Tannen 2002, 1652).Tannen points to the underlying ambiguity and polysemy of power and solidarity. On the one hand, in conversational discourse, such linguistic strategies as the expression of disagreement, indirectness, interruption, silence vs. volubility etc. are effective means used to negotiate power and/or solidarity. On the other, dynamic opposition and verbal aggression can bring about a damaging effect on the exchange of scholarship (2002, 1653).

An important linguistic device that can be interpretable in terms of power relation is pronoun choice, which has already received considerable attention from researchers (for the analysis of pronoun use in written academic discourse see e.g. Breivega et al 2002; Fløttum et al 2006; Harwood 2005; Hyland 2002b; Ivanič 1998; Vassileva 2000, and in spoken academic discourse, e.g. Fortanet-Gómez 2004a, 2004b, 2006; Rowley-Jolivet and Carter-Thomas 2005). The research has usually been focused on the personal pronouns *I* and *we*, because of their relevance for the construction of individual and group identity and their boundary marking role, and less frequently, on the pronoun *you*, pertinent to the study of the author-audience relation. Two essential aspects of pronoun use are usually taken into consideration: reference and function. In terms of reference, there is no ambiguity as far as *I* is concerned, only a moderate diversity in the referential meanings of *you*, but a large ambivalence in the case of *we*. In terms of discourse function, the studies of pronoun choice in academic discourse reveal three major roles of personal pronouns: self-promotional, textual and rhetorical. Because of their rhetorical and discourse organisational role, the discussion of pronoun choice is necessarily related to the investigation of metadiscourse (see Section 3.1 below).

As regards the referential meanings of personal pronouns, an analysis of *I* and *you* can be found in Fortanet-Gómez (2006), and of *we* in Fortanet-Gómez (2004a) and Vassileva (2000). As for the personal pronoun *I*, the only possible referent is the writer/speaker; however, in her study of spoken discourse, Fortanet-Gómez (2006) differentiates between the "fixed speaker", i.e. the lecturer, and the "changing speaker", who participates in dialogue and reported speech and who usually needs to identify him or herself. The two referents are also assigned two sets of different discourse functions (see Table 2–1 below).

Referents	Discourse functions
Fixed speaker	Metadiscourse
	Attitude
	Subject of anecdotes
	Hypothetical *I* as an example
Changing speaker	Identification in dialogue
	Identification of other voices in reported speech

Table 2–1. Referents and discourse functions of *I* (adapted from Fortanet-Gómez 2006, 42).

Fortanet-Gómez also identifies two general referents of *you*, the "hearer" and "impersonal" *you*, and their corresponding discourse functions (for details see Table 2–2).

Referents		Discourse functions
Hearer	Audience (plural)	Metadiscourse
	Interlocutor in dialogue (usually singular)	Addressing the hearer
	Interlocutor in reported speech (usually singular)	
Impersonal *you*	They	Certain approximation of speaker/hearer
	People	
	We	Certain distancing of speaker/hearer
	I	

Table 1–2. Referents and discourse functions of *you* (adapted from Fortanet-Gómez 2006, 45).

Analysing the use of the most ambiguous pronoun, *we*, Vassilieva recounts the following referential meanings, most of which she finds relevant for the discussion of authorial presence in academic discourse (2000, 36):

- "institutionalised uses of *we*", referred to as "institutionalised exophora"; these include the so-called "royal *we*" and "editorial *we*"; the latter may be an exponent of a purposefully employed power rather than due to

conventions; this use of *we* may serve to enhance the position and power of both an individual and the institution he or she refers to;
- the so-called "pluralis modestiae" or "pluralis auctoris", i.e. *we* that refers to a single author; its use is rather infrequent in the discourse produced by recognised members of academia;
- the use of *we* to mark co-authorship;
- "inclusive *we*" to refer to the author and his or her audience; its use results from the author's assumption of the audience's engagement in the same endeavour; it also may serve as the author's invitation to engage the audience in the process of argumentation;
- "exclusive *we*", where the audience is deliberately excluded from the reference; instead, the author includes his or her professional community and/or immediate colleagues; as the English pronoun *we* does not distinguish grammatically between the "inclusive *we*" and "exclusive *we*", the interpretation is highly situation- and context-dependent;
- the use of *we* to refer to the human race; in Vassileva's view rather frequent in the social sciences; the distinction between the "eneral *we*" and "exclusive *we*" is not always straightforward, and also largely context-dependent.

Fortanet-Gómez (2006, 55–56) attempts to be even more specific about some of the referential meanings of *we*. Her categories for referential meanings of *we* identified in spoken academic discourse include the following categories:

- larger group of people (including speaker + audience) – it is used to represent other communities of people the speaker belongs to (e.g. Western civilisation as opposed to they – African tribes), humans, etc.;
- speaker + audience;
- *we* for *I*;
- *we* for *you* (audience);
- speaker + other people (audience is excluded);
- *we* for indefinite *you* or *one*;
- *we* for *they* (if the speaker is deeply involved in the situation described).

The variety of referential meanings of the pronouns in question reflects the complexity of the interpersonal meanings that can be mediated by means of pronoun choice. This increases the importance of careful and effective management pronoun use in academic discourse.

In terms of function of personal pronouns, the researchers note progressing personalisation of academic discourse, largely realised by the personal pronoun *I*, along with which comes an increase of self-promotion in academic texts (e.g. Breivega et al 2002; Harwood 2005; Hyland 2002b). The need for self-promotion and marketing of one's own research is linked to the growing competition within the academia and the commodification of scholarship and identity (see e.g. Duszak 2002b; Fairclough 1995a; Heller 2003). The research shows that skilful positioning by means of pronouns enhances the promotion of the author's scholarly competence, authority and acceptance of his/her work. Self-promotion is also carried out through self-citation: the choice of *I* allows academics to publicize their work as unique and worthy of attention. An important aspect here is that the degree of authorial presence and self-publicity depends on an academic's status within a scholarly community. Hyland's (2002b) cross-cultural, comparative investigation into the author's visibility in L2 student writing vs. research papers proves that personal pronouns are underrepresented in novice writing. One of the reasons can be that an individualistic identity may turn out problematic for the cultures where a more collective construction of the self is preferred.

Next to self-promotion, the findings about pronoun choice in academic discourse also reveal the textual (discourse organisation) and rhetorical function of personal pronoun use (see mainly Harwood 2005; Hyland 2002b; Fortanet-Gómez 2004a, 2006; Vassilieva 2000). The discourse organisation roles of personal pronouns aim at guiding the reader throughout the ongoing text and include: stating research goals/purposes, explaining procedures, stating results/claims, recounting the research process, etc. The rhetorical functions relate mainly to the process of scholarly argumentation and include: disputing with other researchers' claims, negotiation of one's own claims, elaborating arguments.

Moreover, as Ivanič points out, "particular discourse choices support particular ideologies of intellectual activity, of knowledge and of knowledge-making" (Ivanič 1998, 303). Correspondingly, the choice of pronouns is a type of discoursal positioning which merges with an individual's positioning relative to his/her role within the academic community and with their positioning relative to the field of study. In particular, the use of *I*, additionally accompanied by particular verb types, may be a measure of the subjectivity-versus-objectivity attitude towards knowledge-making. Following Bakhtin, Ivanič stresses that "there is a continuum from not using *I* at all, through using verbs associated with the process of structuring the writing, to using *I* in association with the research process, and finally to using *I* with verbs associated with cognitive acts" (Ivanič 1998, 307).

In general, the findings generally reveal that the discoursal construction of the author's self-image, authority and his/her relationship with the audience through personal pronouns is subtle and intricate, and that the use of a particular pronoun does not always render a straightforward interpretation, which holds true for both its reference and function. What is also important, the author's choice may depend on his/her personal stylistic preferences, understanding of current academic requirements, or compliance with discipline- and/or culture-specific standards (e.g. Breivega et al 2002; Rowley-Jolivet and Carter-Thomas 2005; Vassileva 2000). Moreover, authors' particular preferences in the use of pronouns are largely unconscious, although some researchers also note a growing awareness of the author's role in native academic writing in English, which becomes evident through an increasing personalisation of academic discourse (e.g. Vassileva 2000).

2.2.3. Metadiscourse

Another useful framework to study interpersonal meanings in professional and academic texts is metadiscourse[6]. Broadly speaking, metadiscourse signals are expressions which bring into focus the relationship between discourse participants (the text producer and audience), and the text producer and the evolving text, so, in other words, metadiscourse helps to relate the text to its context. However, different conceptualisations of metadiscourse vary as to the boundaries of the concept, and thus contribute to its fuzziness. The discrepancies also concern the functions of metadiscourse: in general, researchers point to its text-organising (e.g. Mauranen 1993; Dahl 2004) or attitudinal aspects (see e.g. the concept of *evaluation* in Hunston 1994 or *stance* in Biber et al 1999[7]).

Making reference to Halliday's functional view of language use, the text-organising aspects of metadiscourse refer to the textual component. This approach foregrounds the author's awareness of the text, as it refers

[6] The term *metadiscourse* was coined by Zellig Harris in 1959 to refer to the writer's language use representing his/her attempts to guide a receiver's perception of a text (see Hyland 2005, 3). In the literature of the subject, other related notions are alternatively used, but they are not always synonymous: see e.g. *metatext*, *text reflexivity* (Mauranen 1993), or *operatory metatekstowe*, *operatory tekstu*, *metatekstyzmy* in the Polish sources (see articles in the volume *Tekstologia Part 2* 2004).

[7] The most recent, comprehensive account of the language of evaluation and stance is offered by the Appraisal Framework (Martin and White 2005).

to his/her use of language about the progressing text, whether spoken or written. For instance, metadiscoursal signals provide information about the text, play a role in its segmentation and contribute to its cohesion; they modify and enhance propositional content (see the notions of *text reflexivity* in Mauranen 1993 and *locational metatext* in Dahl 2004; see also Wierzbicka 1971; Ożóg 1997; Labocha 1996; Winiarska 2001; Pluskota 1998). In relation to academic discourse, a rhetorical strategy which uses numerous reflexive expressions can be characterised as personal, explicit and helpful, but also authoritative, as "authority emerges from the sense of knowing what one is doing" (Mauranen 1993, 189). Mauranen also points to the potential dangers of excessive reflexivity, which may result in a text which is too didactic, interfering and patronising. Whether the effect is positive or negative, however, is culture-dependent, as Mauranen's research reveals cross-cultural differences in the degree of reflexivity in academic discourse.

Since text-organising metadiscourse facilitates navigation within the text, its use is also the explication of the author's awareness of his/her (imagined) audience. Metadiscoursal expressions aid the recipients in the processing of the text and reinforce rhetorical acts performed by the author (see the notion of *rhetorical metatext* in Dahl 2004). This brings in the relevance of the interactive aspect of metadiscourse and the prominence of its conative and phatic function (Pisarkowa 1974). As regards the research of textual metadiscourse and authorial presence in academic discourse, Dahl (2004) finds out that the author's use of textual metadiscourse is not only a marker of national culture but also of academic discipline.

Alternative approaches that give prominence to the attitudinal aspects of metatext in academic discourse include the concept of *evaluation* in Hunston 1994 (see also Hyland 2002a; Mauranen 2002) and that of *stance* in Biber et al 1999 (see also Fortanet-Gómez 2004b). The attitudinal aspects of metadiscourse relate to Halliday's interpersonal component of language use. Hunston considers linguistic expressions of evaluation to be an essential component of discourse: "for a text (…) to work as communication, there must be frequent indications of attitudes held towards information given in the text and towards the communicative value of the discourse itself" (1994, 191). Hunston links expression of evaluation to the persuasive function of academic discourse, and stresses that evaluation is frequently carried out implicitly, without reliance on the attitudinal language associated with interpersonal meanings in a text. Another important aspect is that evaluation not only entails personal judgement but is also based on the value system of an academic community. Finally, the three-partite model of evaluation[8] advanced by Hunston underlines the organisational role of evaluation in discourse: evaluation contributes to discourse structure by providing information about the progression of text.

Other approaches that investigate evaluative metatext in scholarly communication are offered by Mauranen 2002 for spoken discourse and Hyland 2002a and Starzec 1996 for the written one. In her study of academic talk, Mauranen takes a view of evaluation that approximates Hunston's evaluation of value, where evaluation "indicates the speaker's attitude to an entity on a good-bad scale, and which bestows quality on that entity" (Mauranen, 2002, 118–119; see also note 8 below). Once again, it is accentuated that expression of evaluation is community-based, evaluation being an essential element of socialisation. Focusing on such evaluative lexis as intensifiers and modifiers, Mauranen discovers that positive evaluation is a more explicit and emphatic characteristic of academic speech. Another major finding is a metadiscursive function of the evaluative commentary: an appraised element is frequently the progressing discourse. This serves to organise knowledge structures for interlocutors and to construct patterns of salience in the referential content under discussion (Mauranen 2002, 135).

Hyland, on the other hand, draws attention to the evaluative function of reporting verbs in the academic research paper (2002a). The focus of his research is academic attribution, which, apart from many rhetorical purposes, also serves to create a credible writer ethos; it constitutes a means of projecting the status of a reliable and competent member of an academic community. Hyland's categorisation of reporting verbs reflects an array of their evaluative possibilities. These allow writers to express, as appropriate, their supportive, tentative, critical, neutral, etc. stance towards reported claims. Reporting verbs prove an essential and delicate means of "situating one's work appropriately and communicating with one's peers effectively, a way of engaging with colleagues and of appealing to the epistemological and interactive understandings of one's community" (Hyland 2002a, 130).

In her discussion of evaluation, Starzec (1996) aims at showing the difference between popular-scientific and scientific articles in Polish. Her study reveals the prevalence of evaluative language and its greater range in popular-scientific texts. In contrast, scientific texts are richer in negative

[8] The three types of evaluation according to Hunston are: *status* – showing the author's perception of the relation between the proposition and the world, *value* – referring to the author's judgement of good or bad, and *relevance* – referring to the author's judgement of important or unimportant (1994, 194–200).

evaluation, but at the same time their authors tend to be more cautious in the expression of categorical judgements. Another discrepancy is that evaluation in popular-scientific texts is more explicit, intense and frequently emotionally-loaded, which is linked to the different rhetorical aims realised by popular-scientific discourse.

The expression of such non-propositional content as authors' personal feelings, attitudes, value judgements, or assessments is also referred to as *stance* (Biber et al 1999, 966). The expression of stance meanings can be realised by paralinguistic devices and word choice, but Biber mainly focuses on grammatical means. Grammatical stance devices include: adverbials, complement clauses, modals and semi-modals, stance nouns + prepositional phrases, and stance adverbs + adjective or noun phrases (Biber et al 1999, 969–970). An important point is that these devices form a cline in the extent to which they represent the grammatical marking of stance. In addition, Biber et al point to variability in the structural characteristics of stance markers and to ambiguity of their meaning. The semantic categories of stance markers are: *epistemic stance* – used to comment on the status of information in a proposition, *attitudinal stance* – used to report personal attitudes or feelings, and *style of speaking stance* – used to present the author's comments on the communication itself (Biber et al 1999, 972–975).

As regards the marking of stance in academic prose, relatively frequent grammatical stance devices are modals, complement constructions and adverbials. In comparison to other registers, it is adverbials whose distribution is relatively common in academic prose. As academic writing is expected to be devoid of first person involvement, personal attitudes and assessments of likelihood are quite commonly communicated by means of impersonal stance devices. In more detail, among the stance markers within the adverbial category, the most frequent are single adverbs, especially those indicating epistemic stance (e.g. *generally*; *perhaps*; in this respect academic prose is similar to conversation), and prepositional phrases (e.g. *in fact*; *in many respects*). Another finding is the prevalence of extraposed *to*-clauses, especially those controlled by adjectival predicates marking possibility, necessity/importance, or personal evaluations (e.g. *It is vitally important…*; *It may be possible to…*), and stance nouns controlling complements (e.g. *The fact that…*; Biber et al 1999, 979–986).

The above model of stance was applied to investigate aspects of evaluation in academic lectures (Fortanet-Gómez 2004b). Fortanet-Gómez uses for her analysis 5 lectures from the MICASE (Michigan Corpus of Spoken Academic English) corpus, lectures from the field of anthropology, economics and communication studies. I find this study particularly relevant for the purposes of the present study, because Fortanet-Gómez focuses on the pronoun *I* and the accompanying verbal group as potential co-contributors in the lexical and grammatical marking of stance. As far as lexical stance markers are concerned, the study reveals that the two most frequent categories accompanying *I* were affective or evaluative verbs (especially *think*) followed by *that*-clause, and modal verbs (especially *would*). The prevalence of *I* + *think* can be evidence for the speaker's consideration of politeness: it can function as a hedging device, an expression of hesitation or as a discourse marker. Also, the use of *would* can be linked to hedging. With respect to the semantic categories of stance markers, the research demonstrates the predominance of epistemic over attitudinal stance, but at the same time attitudinal stance markers reveal a wider range of devices (modal verbs and affective verbs following *I*). A general finding is that stance markers in the corpus under investigation are mainly used to express a relationship between the speaker and the proposition. The communication of the speaker's attitudes and feeling, on the other hand, contributes to the speaker-audience relationship (Fortanet-Gómez 2004b, 118–119).

A noteworthy account of metadiscourse from a cross-cultural perspective is given in Connor (1996), where metadiscourse is presented as a crucial aspect of persuasive academic writing. Connor emphasises both organisational and expressive or attitudinal roles of the use of metadiscoursal strategies in a text (1996, 48). She recounts the classification system for metadiscourse advanced by Vande Kopple (1985) and its revised version by Crismore et al (1993). Both these systems distinguish between textual metadiscourse, whose main function is to organise the text, and interpersonal metadiscourse, which is used to express personal feelings and attitudes and to interact with the audience (for details of both classification systems see Connor 1996, 49). The contrastive studies of metadiscourse in academic writing reveal the differences in the use of metadiscoursal strategies that can be explained by socio-cultural reasons. Connor points to the relevance of these findings in applied linguistics contexts (1996, 47–50).

Given the variety of approaches to metadiscourse, the concept appears fuzzy, however, with a big analytical potential to study interpersonal meanings in discourse (for more examples of analyses of metatexual and/or evaluative aspects of academic discourse see e.g. Breivega et al 2002; Duszak 1998a, 2002b). What the views discussed above share is a functional, community-based approach to metadiscourse, where metadiscourse appears as a relative and open category that communicates non-propositional content in a clause. The focus on metadiscoursal signals allows us to study authorial presence in discourse in relation to the communicative context, from the perspective of a social structure.

In this book I will speak in favour of an integrative view of metadiscourse which accommodates the textual and interpersonal function of metadiscoursal signals, as discussed in Hyland 2005. Hyland recognizes the limitations of his approach: the impossibility of reaching implicit indications of metadiscourse signals and their multifunctionality. The latter problem may result in blurring simultaneous meanings of metadiscourse signals, which, in turn, leads to overlaps between categories. Still, I find this approach more relevant for my present purposes, since it can offer a more complete account of the author's presence in a text. As Hyland argues, metadiscourse

> illuminates some aspects of how we project ourselves into our discourses by signalling our attitude towards both the content and the audience of the text. With the judicious addition of metadiscourse, a writer is able not only to transform what might otherwise be a dry or difficult text into coherent, reader-friendly prose, but also to relate it to a given context and convey his or her personality, credibility, audience-sensitivity and relationship to the message. (Hyland 2005, 4)

Hyland advances the classification of metadiscourse signals that reflects the complexity of the author/audience and author/propositional content relationships as mediated through discourse (2005, 49). In general, Hyland distinguishes two types of metadiscourse: *interactive resources* – text-organising resources whose presence is a consequence of the author's assumptions about the reader's expectations, capacities, etc.; and *interactional resources* – means of expressing the author's attitudes, opinions and engagement.

Hyland's classification of metadiscourse shows the multiple roles of metadiscoursal signals. However, his use of the terms *interactive* versus *interactional resources* deserves some reservation. This distinction may be misleading because of the multiplicity of the meanings in which both terms are employed (see e.g. Duszak 1998a or my discussion of interactivity in Chapter 3, Section 3.3). In particular, the term *interactive resources* fails to refer explicitly to the text-organising role of the resources included in this category: transitions, frame and endophoric markers, evidentials and code glosses.

As far as academic discourse is concerned, Hyland gives an account of the extensive research of metadiscourse in scholarly texts that reveals differences across scholarly genres, disciplines and national cultures.

Hyland's research points to the role of metadiscourse for academic persuasion: how it contributes to the rhetorical success of a text. More importantly though, the study of metatextual signals can offer insights into how authors discoursally construct their identity while managing their communicative intentions, whether through the spoken, written or computer-mediated medium.

2.2.4. Modality

Our understanding of how identities are constructed in discourse can also benefit from the analysis of modality. The domain of modality is an area which is considered to be difficult to delineate in semantic terms[9] (e.g. Nuyts 2006), and solving this notional problem is beyond the scope of my present work. Still, in my account of modality I would like to refer to a few aspects of the issue which I find relevant for the discussion of interpersonal meanings in academic discourse, namely the basic division of the semantic dimensions of modality (epistemic and deontic), the status of evidentiality as a modal category, and subjectivity/objectivity as a dimension used to subcategorise the expression of modal categories[10].

In the traditional categorisation of the domain of modality, the concepts of deontic and epistemic modality belong to basic semantic dimensions of modality[11], and they both have corresponding notions in Halliday's model of grammar. Deontic modality may be conceptualised in terms of permission and obligation, and so has much in common with the imperative (Palmer 1981, 153). It is concerned with the speaker's active relation to events. More broadly, deontic modality is "an indication of the degree of moral desirability of the state of affairs expressed in the utterance, typically, but not necessarily, on behalf of the speaker" (Nuyts 2006). In contrast, epistemic modality expresses the degree of commitment of the speaker to the truth of the proposition, or in other

---

[9] For instance, Palmer refers to modality as "the judgements we make about possible states of affairs" (1981, 43).

[10] For the most recent, comprehensive overviews of modality see e.g. Nuyts 2006, de Haan 2006.

[11] As Nuyts recounts, the third traditional category is dynamic modality, characterised as "an ascription of a capacity to the subject-participant of the clause (the subject is able to perform the action expressed by the main verb in the clause), of the kind expressed in the modal auxiliary in (a), or the predicative adjective in (b):

(a) That kid **can** sing like Frank Sinatra.

(b) Pete is perfectly **able** to solve this problem if he wants" (2006, 3).

words, the degree of probability of the state of affairs (e.g. Nuyts 2001, 2006; Palmer 1981). Epistemic modality is, then, concerned with the speaker's relation to propositions. Both kinds of modality can be construed as a scale, and both share the status of attitudinal categories.

While there is a relative agreement as to the core notions of modality, scholars differ about the status of the categories verging on the borders of modality. One of such notions is evidentiality, whose relevance for linguistic studies (also of academic communication) was foregrounded by Chafe and Nichols' work: *Evidentiality: the Linguistic Coding of Epistemology* (1986). Evidentiality indicates the speaker's source of information about the state of affairs expressed/postulated in the clause (see Nuyts 2006, 10; Saeed 1997, 133). As Nuyts relates, there are three subcategories of evidentiality: (1) *experiential*, information source is directly perceived through the speaker's own sense organs (e.g. *I've **noticed** that*), (2) *inferential*, information source is indirectly deduced on the basis of other, directly perceived information (e.g., ***Apparently***,...), and (3) *hearsay or reportative*, information source is obtained from others (e.g. *I **hear** that...).*

A problematic issue about evidentiality is its relation to modality, and whether it is even a modal notion at all. In general, there are three diverging approaches to the relation between evidentiality and modality: (1) the notions are conceptually distinct from each other (e.g. Fitneva 2001), (2) evidentiality falls within the scope of modality (e.g. Nuyts 2001, 2006), (3) the notions overlap (e.g. Plungian 2001; Verstraete 2001). One of the reasons for this discrepancy is the empirical fact that in the evidential systems of many languages there are linguistic forms which at the same time mark both the source of information and the speaker's attitude towards the reliability of that information (Dendale and Tasmowski 2001, 342–343). As regards the investigations of academic discourse, evidentiality can be studied by means of a category of evidentials included in Hyland's taxonomy of metadiscourse signals (2005).

A final conceptual problem related to the domain of modality that I would like to point to is subjectivity vs. objectivity as a dimension subcategorising modal categories (for various accounts see e.g. Nuyts 2001, 2006; Verstraete 2001). Although usually discussed with reference to epistemic modality, this dimension has relevance for both epistemic and deontic modality. In his overview of the issue, Nuyts recounts Lyons' distinction between subjectivity and objectivity, where "objective epistemic modality expresses an objectively measurable chance that the state of affairs under consideration is true or not, while subjective epistemic modality involves a purely subjective guess regarding its truth" (Nuyts 2006, 13). Nuyts himself puts forward an alternative distinction within the dimension in terms of who is responsible for the modal evaluation (2001, 2006). For him, subjectivity involves evaluation belonging exclusively to the speaker, whereas *intersubjectivity* indicates evaluation which is shared by the speaker with a wider group.

In my analysis of discoursal construction of identity I use Halliday's model of interpersonal metaphors of modality (1994). This grammatical system refers to meaning choices that interactants make when engaging in a communicative act (see Chapters 4 and 10 in Halliday 1994). Halliday defines modality as "the area of meaning that lies between yes and no – the intermediate ground between positive and negative polarity" (1994, 356). In his narrower view, the system of modality comprises two types: (1) modulation ("imperative" type), which involves the speaker's obligation or readiness towards the action; and (2) modalization ("indicative" type), which refers to the speaker's assessment of probability or usuality (1994, 357).

With reference to the traditional core categories of modality, Halliday's probability corresponds to epistemic modality, whereas obligation – to deontic modality. The four categories of modulation and modalization express different degrees of polarity, i.e. different ways of rendering the semantic space between the positive and negative poles. The linguistic realisations of modality can be more narrowly subclassified according to two variables: orientation, which can be subjective or objective, and explicit or implicit; and value, which can be high, median or low (Halliday 1994, 357–358). These parameters, if combined, generate as many as 144 categories of modality that allow speakers to express numerous modal meanings.

As far as investigations of aspects of modality in academic discourse are concerned, it is mainly epistemic modality that has become the focus of the researchers' interest. The studies of linguistic realisations of epistemic modality in scholarly written texts can be found in Gabrielatos and McEnery 2005; McEnery and Kifle 2002; Ventola 1997, and in spoken register – in Carretero 2002. The research mainly centres on cross-cultural differences in the expression of epistemic modality in native and non-native academic writing in English, on the example of students' MA dissertations (Gabrielatos and McEnery 2005), students' argumentative essays (McEnery and Kifle 2002), and research papers (Ventola 1997). The papers stress the usefulness of effective modality choices for academic argumentation and persuasion. This proves essential both for novices and experts, as learning to make right rhetorical choices is part of the socialisation into the role of an academic.

Carretero's work (2002), on the other hand, reveals the dependencies of epistemic modality choices on such factors of genre and register as: the overall purpose of the text and the individual purposes of the participants, the degree of planning, the need for accuracy, the topic of the text (field), and the social relationships between participants (tenor). She also links particular realisations of epistemic modality to the persuasive aims of an academic conversation (predominance of strong epistemic expressions), fulfilling speakers' individual purposes, such as communication of opinions (predominance of subjective expressions, especially belonging to the high and median degrees), or presentation of factual information (low incidence of epistemic expressions). Carretero's findings also point to the link between the employment of particular modality choices and speakers' concern with politeness, and the link between epistemic modality and the degree of speakers' spontaneity. It turns out, then, that the study of modality contributes largely to uncovering important interpersonal meanings that underlie scholarly discourse.

The discussion of the interpersonal meanings in academic discourse shows its heterogeneity and dynamism, which results from cross-cultural and individual variation. The variety of the perspectives that can be used to study interpersonal meanings in academic discourse allows to capture this dynamism of identity construction in discourse. The investigations discussed above show that an individual's identity appears as a complex interplay of positionings relative to his/her set of values and beliefs about reality, his/her status in relation to others, and, what proves particularly relevant for the purposes of the present work, the practices and norms associated with a particular communication channel, whether speech, writing or CMC. In the following chapter I will focus on the linguistic and technological aspects of CMC. My intention will be to present the electronic medium as an interesting and challenging context for academic identity construction.

CHAPTER THREE

ELECTRONIC DISCOURSE: LINGUISTIC, SOCIAL AND TECHNOLOGICAL ASPECTS

The aim of the present chapter is to present electronic discourse as a new, interesting site in which identity work may be accomplished and investigated. First, in order to characterise verbal expression in the electronic age, I will address the relationship between orality and literacy. This discussion will allow us to better understand the nature of both the changes that verbal expression has undergone and the relationship between orality and literacy. In addition, the technologies of the electronic age have transformed the classical writing-and-print-based literacy, leading to the emergence of a new kind of literacy. The chapter will survey some attempts to theorise this new literacy. First of all, I will discuss the most influential conception of *secondary orality*. Then, I will proceed to alternative conceptions that emphasise an increasing role of oral expression in the contemporary world: *literate orality*, *visual literacy*, *teleliteracy* and *electric rhetoric*. Finally, I will argue that electronic discourse (e-discourse) is a new language variety, because it possesses characteristics belonging to both sides of the speech-writing divide.

3.1. Orality versus literacy: the speech-writing divide

The analysis of the nature of verbal strategies in the electronic age must involve a discussion of the orality/literacy opposition. Notably, an accurate understanding of the relationship between orality and literacy as cultural processes was enabled only by the onset of the electronic age, as "the contrasts between electronic media and print have sensitised us to the earlier contrast between writing and orality" (Ong 2002/1982, 2–3). Thus, with regard to the transformation of the word brought by the new communication era, the nature of oral and literate cultures has been extensively re-examined within linguistics (e.g. Bartmiński 1989; Biber

1988; Baron 2000; Welch 1999), anthropology (e.g. Mizrach 1998; Ong 1982), and media studies (e.g. Loska 2001; McLuhan 1964, 2001; Wilk 2000).

Orality (or *primary orality*, to be contrasted with Ong's *secondary orality*; see Section 2 of the present chapter) is where human communication begins: it is "a condition of society in which speaking and listening form the only or principal channel through which communication in language takes place" (Durant 1997). In primary cultures, in which writing is unknown, oral expression is not only used for instrumental communication, but also for the transmission of cultural values, norms and behaviours. In oral cultures consciousness is formed by reliance on oral discourse, which is marked by the presence of such discursive features as formulas, repetition, the addition of phrases (Welch 1999, 57). Orality is considered to be natural in terms of its acquisition and production (excluding pathological cases; e.g. Durant 1997; Gilson 1969). Orality has the power to foster a communal sense among interacting individuals, and at the same time is ephemeral. Only spoken repetition makes oral expression endure, but at the cost of precision.

Furthermore, scholars emphasise the inseparability of the spoken word from the sound (e.g. Bartmiński 1989; Ong 1982; Wilk 2000) and its immediacy to human thought, activity and body (Derrida 1999; Ong 1982; Wilk 2000). In Ong's view, the appreciation of the mnemonic base of the thought and expression in primary oral cultures furthers the understanding of other constituent characteristics of orally based thought and expression (Ong 1982, 36). Namely, Ong argues that orality is also (1) additive rather than subordinative (characterised by the presence of additive structures), (2) aggregative rather than analytic (refers to the use of formulas to implement memory, such as e.g. epithets), (3) redundant, (4) conservative (in the sense of inhibiting intellectual experimentation), (5) close to the human lifeworld, (6) agonistically toned (the context of the spoken word encourages conflict and struggle), (7) emphatetic and participatory rather than objectively distanced (related to the emotional tie between the speaker and listeners which hinders the objectivity of expression, (8) homeostatic (related to the balance between the past and the present, designated by real life situations), (9) situational rather than abstract (oral expression is marked by the "use of concepts in operational frames that remain close to the living human lifeworld"; Ong 1982, 37).

The complexity and multidimensionality of oral expression is also stressed by Bartmiński (1989), who views orality as a set of characteristics that may co-occur in varying configurations and intensities. Therefore,

Bartmiński concedes, the only classifying feature of orality is its sonic character, as opposed to the graphic character of writing (1989, 431).

The nature of orality can be best elucidated by showing its relation to literacy, the second kind of consciousness, which began with the invention of writing. In contrast to oral expression, writing is artificial as it requires a tool and material to write on. Moreover, writing is artificial as some craftsmanship is involved in the expression of human thought in the written form (Gilson 1969). The process of transferring the spoken word into the written form is a strenuous activity, as consciously contrived rules of writing must be followed (Gilson 1969; Ong 1982). This, in Ong's view, is not a drawback, since writing more than any other artificial creation is essential for the realisation of fuller human capabilities (1982, 81). Gilson considers writing as an artefact: the "requirements" of the writing process influence the shape of the written thought, which is not a mere imitation of the spoken thought; it is transformed and subject to the rules of the written form of expression. In this way writing is a technology that was capable of transfiguring human consciousness and thought, transforming both individuals and societies, and thus making literacy one of the major cultural achievements of civilisation (see also Baron 2000; Biber 1988; Gilson 1969; Mizrach 1998; Ricour 1976; Welch 1999; Wilk 2000).

The cognitive effect of writing was enabled by "the separation of the word from the living present" (Ong 1982, 81): people gained access to an external and portable form of information storage, which resulted in the universalisation of the reception (see also Ricour 1976). This isolation of the word on the written surface, detached from any interlocutor, made the word in a sense more autonomous and indifferent to attack, uninvolved and self-contained. In addition, distance enabled a new degree of precision, abstraction and objectivity, and encouraged reflection and revision of the human thought. The consciousness-raising quality of writing, although much contested, is defended by much of linguistic and anthropological research (see e.g. Baron 2000; Biber 1988; Mizrach 1998 for extensive overviews). Although the representatives of the so called Toronto School (including Innis, McLuhan and Ong) viewed writing "as taking away from some of the spontaneity and variety of oralism", Ong somehow celebrated "the liberating power of the written word, and how it moved people from an "acoustic" space, bound firmly by community tradition and group norms, to a "visual" space where the individuated ego could take a detached "'god's eye' view of things" (Mizrach 1998). Literacy does foster metalinguistic awareness and intellectual and social development. Science, and the science of language in particular, would be impossible without the increased cognitive abilities of abstraction, decontextualisation, and objectification that literacy makes possible (Gilson 1969; Mizrach 1998 following Olson and Torrance 1991).

The discussion of the effects of literacy must involve the consideration of the emergence of the alphabet, and subsequently, the invention of print as means of "the technologizing the word". With regard to the cognitive effect of the alphabet, Baron's review (2000) focuses on two contrasting views. For one thing, scholars such as I. J. Gelb and D. Olson as well as the representatives of the Toronto School consider the emergence of alphabetic writing as a major cultural advancement in human history that enabled a kind of logical and historical thinking. For another, there is no real evidence for claiming that the alphabet is a superior representation of spoken language. Besides, Baron reminds of the imperfection of the alphabet to represent all vowels and consonants with individual sounds. Still, all in all, it is generally agreed that the major effect of the alphabet is the change it brought in the relation between speech and writing.

The invention of print, in Ong's view, continued in a more drastic and decisive way what writing had initiated (1982, 81). While writing had reconstituted the originally spoken word in visual space, print embedded the word in space ("typographic" space) more definitively, thus reinforcing the effects of writing on thought and expression. The examples of the spatially-entrenched word could be such development as indexes, lists, or the use of words (instead of iconographic signs) for labels (Ong 1982, 121).

As Ong continues, print encourages a sense of fixity, closure and finality of the author's word. What is more, print reinforces self-containment of the text through the possibility to enclose and duplicate thought in a number of identical copies (1982, 130). This brings the isolation of the thought from its author, the author from the reader, and the separation of the private and public sphere. Here, Wilk (2000) indicates a somewhat paradoxical nature of print: the effects are, on the one hand, the extended reception of the texts, and on the other, detachment of the audience.

In brief, although the humanistic value of orality is unquestionable, the social and cultural effects of writing and print are also substantial: the world of orality was transformed, human communication gained new forms of the materialisation of the word, and literacy became a mass phenomenon. Moreover, Gilson finds it essential to mention that the capability of writing to hold up the thought in time opened a possibility of its constantly renewable presence. Finally, writing, and print in particular, made it possible for a fully constituted human society to exist (Gilson 1969).

As regards the relationship between orality and literacy, indeed, the illumination was brought by the emergence of the technology of writing (and the invention of electronic media in particular). Ong concludes that writing can never dispense with orality, but orality can exist and mostly has existed without any writing at all, while writing never without orality. Moreover, from the very beginning, writing enhanced orality rather than demoted it (1982, 8–9).

An important point is that today the relation between orality and literacy is not understood in terms of binary opposition, a view which was shared by the so called the Great-Divide theorists (for an overview and discussion see Welch 1999). Rather, as the Consciousness theorists concede, the merger and interdependence view of the relation between orality and literacy has to be accepted (especially in view of the further changes brought by the electronic age). As for the Polish discussion of the issue, Bartmiński views orality and literacy more as characteristics of texts (1989). More specifically, texts can only approximate an ideal (prototypical) oral or literary text. Orality and literacy of texts can thus be adequately described according to approximation criteria to an ideal type rather than definitive criteria of the presence (or absence) of a specified set of categorial features (Bartmiński 1989, 431).

This, in turn, brings us to the relationship between speech and writing as two modes of communication, and reminds of the continuum view of the speech/writing divide. Biber notes that the cultures that have developed both a written and spoken form of communication exploit the two modes for different communicative purposes (1988, 8). Although both speech and writing are equally universal in meeting the communicative needs of language users, they are not used interchangeably but rather depending on the situational demands of the communicative task.

A review of anthropological and linguistic research on the relationship between spoken and written language reveals a number of conflicting approaches that concentrate on the superiority of one form of communication to the exclusion of the other (see e.g. Baron 2000; Biber 1988). As a result, on the one hand, a dichotomous relationship between speech and writing presupposes the opposition in the salient features of spoken and written discourse. According to Crystal, speech is typically time-bound (thus dynamic and transient), spontaneous, face-to-face, socially interactive, loosely structured, immediately revisable, and prosodically rich. Whereas writing is typically space-bound (thus static and permanent), contrived, visually decontextualised, factually communicative, elaborately structured, repeatedly revisable, and graphically rich (Crystal 1995, 2001; see also Baron 2000; Biber 1988).

On the other hand, the ethnographic and technological perspectives in linguistic research support the continuum view of the speech/writing divide. Given a substantial context-dependent variation of the linguistic properties between and within speech and writing, it is argued that writing may assume the characteristics of speech, as well as speech might reveal the prototypical traits of writing (see Baron 2000, 20, following the research of Deborah Tannen, Wallace Chafe and Douglas Biber). Therefore, currently, the continuum view is defended as more accurate, because it advocates the estimation of the spoken/written quality of texts along a spectrum of features determined by the conditions of actual usage.

To illustrate, to give an accurate and full account of linguistic variation among English texts, Biber develops a multi-feature approach to textual variation in which texts are compared along linguistic dimensions of variation (i.e. continuous scales or continuous quantifiable parameters of variation; Biber 1988). Namely, "each text can be given a precise quantitative characterisation with respect to each dimension, in terms of the frequencies of the co-occurring features that constitute the dimension" (Biber 1988, 19). The six dimensions that Biber uses in his model are: (1) Involved versus Informational Production, (2) Narrative versus Non-narrative Concerns, (3) Explicit versus Situation-Dependent Reference, (4) Overt Expression of Persuasion, (5) Abstract versus Non-Abstract Information, and (6) Online Informational Elaboration. Biber discovers that text types, both spoken and written, are not related in terms of dichotomous differences, but are disparate or similar to a varying degree with respect to each dimension. In other words, Biber's study proves the lack of absolute difference between speech and writing in English, and in effect, repudiates the polarisation of speech and writing as misleading. Moreover, the model can be used to develop an overall typology of texts, in which interrelations among texts will be defined in terms of their exploitation of linguistic features for functional purposes (Biber 1988, 206). Still, the study does not reject the interconnection between the two modes of language. To use the words of the great French philosopher, in literate cultures, human thinking is always accompanied, to a more or lesser degree, by the graphic representation of words in our consciousness (Gilson 1969).

3.2. The era of new literacies

The age of electronic and digital communication has not only furthered our understanding of the relationship between orality and literacy, but also, transformed the classical writing-and-print-based literacy, leading to the emergence of a new kind of literacy (see e.g. Baron 2000; Mizrach 1998; Ong 1982; Welch 1999; Wilk 2000). Attempts to understand and theorize this new literacy have resulted in a number of divergent approaches, terms and definitions. An important contribution comes from multimodal discourse analysis, as done within social semiotics (e.g. Kress and van Leeuwen 2001; Van Leeuwen 2005), or systemic-functional linguistics (e.g. O'Halloran 2004). Still, there is an agreement about how electronic and digital technologies have reinforced (not replaced) the "old" technologies, about the ensuing changes in consciousness and the emergence of a new form of communicative competence.

A significant theoretical basis for understanding and further theorizing of the new literacy was offered by Ong's (1982) theory of movement from (primary) orality to literacy to secondary orality. According to Ong, "the electronic transformation of verbal expression has both deepened the commitment of the word to space initiated by writing and intensified by print and has brought consciousness to a new age of secondary orality" (1982, 133). In Ong's third stage of consciousness (in which we continue to be), " there is a new emphasis on the ear and a change in the emphasis on the eye. The spoken word is now electrified, instantaneous, repetitive, and so familiar that we have normalized it (Welch 1999, 58). Notably, secondary orality depends on the previous stage of primary orality and the still enduring writing-and-print-based literacy. Ong claims that secondary orality does not expunge literacy, but depends on it epistemologically. As for orality, in Ong's view, it continues to live – in the form of secondary orality – because it has to (an argument recounted in Welch 1999, 65). Secondary orality shares with primary orality its magical aura, its encouragement of a communal sense, its concentration on the present moment, and the use of formulas (Ong 1982, 134).

Finally, in relation to the effects of electronic technology Ong finds it expedient to mention how the new technology (especially computers) continues the sequential processing and spatializing of the word (in post-typographic space), initiated by writing and intensified by print 1982, 134). This observation, however, must have necessarily referred to the earlier word-processing uses of the computer. Further transformations of verbal strategies resulting from the development of network and digital technologies encouraged non-sequentiality of texts, and challenged the idea of the traditionally understood spatializing of the word (see Section 3.4 of the present chapter).

Although Ong's theory of secondary orality was one of the transitional moments in the history of Western civilisation, it has been extensively criticised for its ambivalence (see Wilk 2000; also Loska 2001), its bias towards orality (see Welch 1999 for an overview), for its simple separation of the eye and ear, its underestimation of the role of television, and especially its neglect of the corrosive effect of the electronic media upon the social structures created by the print media (see Mizrach 1998 following Scheunemann 1996 and Meyrowitz 1985).

Still, the criticism that Ong's theory of secondary orality aroused resulted in a few new attempts to theorize the new literacy and the emergent electronic discourse. A number of alternative terms have been suggested. Wilk (2000) recounts Farrell's *literate orality*, whereas Mizrach (1998) mentions *visual literacy* and *mass media literacy*, the terms of limited adequacy, as the application of the term *literacy* in this context is as problematic as the use of the term *oral literature*. Mizrach's own suggestion is *teleliteracy*, a new form of communicative competence in the development of which Mizrach distinguishes two phases: Phase 1 - based on the electronic and audiovisual modes of communication and related to mass communication; Phase 2 (which teleliteracy has jus entered) – multimodal, interactive and non-linear, and related to the shift from analogue to digital media. Mizrach's focus is on the technologies of transmission and delivery of electronic information, and because of taking a media studies perspective, he purposefully, and regrettably, ignores the electronic technologies of interpersonal communication, such as the telegraph, telephone, fax, email, etc. This, in my view, is inappropriate, given the heterogeneity of the modern communication technologies, and the consequent fluidity of communicative situations, in which the borders between private and public get blurred easily. Finally, in Wilk's account of Mizrach's explorations of the new literacy, an interesting point is raised. Namely, the new electronic literacy involves also a new kind of reception (a new kind of "hearing"). Electronic media appeal to the holistic faculties of perception, not only to linguistic competence. They require new receptive predispositions because of the need to absorb a multiplicity of signals simultaneously and quickly (Wilk 2000, 37).

Another attempt to theorize the new literacy is Welch's *electric rhetoric*, grounded on Ong's theory of secondary orality, reconstructed pre-Aristotelian classical rhetoric, and contemporary literacy theories within rhetoric and composition studies, including gender and race issues. This, in Welch's view, "provides powerful strategies to help us explain the pervasive seductiveness of the current forms of electronic discourse, all of which are embedded in a merger of written, oral, aural, and visual structures of articulation" (Welch 1999, 7). The starting point for her explorations of the new literacy is the discussion of the dominance of screens in our everyday life and work (in the form of television, video, or computer), and its implications for our language interactions, consciousness and identity formation. Welch defines electric rhetoric as a new form of consciousness within discourse communities, "the merger of the written and the oral, both now newly empowered and reconstructed by electricity and both dependent on print literacy" (Welch 1999, 104). Welch emphasises that electric rhetoric is an extension of print-based literacy. It does not stay in opposition to literacy, but rather they are merged. In addition, electric rhetoric brings not only a new idea, but also a new performance. Therefore, Welch is concerned with the analysis of consciousness issues and their pedagogical implications.

Welch uses the theory of electric rhetoric to examine oralism of a television news programme and a website and finds Ong's features of oralism (see Section 3.1) relevant to both of them. Throughout the book Welch is mainly concerned with women's issues, but her theory and research can further the understanding and theorizing of the current literacy of the electronic and digital age.

Finally, the evolution of literacy till its present form is extensively discussed in Baron's *Alphabet to Email* (2000). Baron views secondary orality of the new communication age, rather dramatically, as the invasion of the norms of oral expression into the norms of the written word. She finds the continuum view of the speech/writing divide useful in understanding the current transformations of the styles of written English and the shape of the new literacy. Although her major interest is in the linguistic status of what she calls e-style (i.e. the style of the language in computer-mediated communication), and its influences upon contemporary written genres, Baron makes a few important observations about the new literacy. At the turn of the millennium many of the traits associated with the modern notion of print culture are increasingly being challenged as a result of the transformations brought by the new communication media, especially computer and network technologies. The major changes include: a blurred distinction between the notions of writer (author) and reader, the loss of the authoritative power of printed texts, the threatening of the traditionally conceived notions of individual authorship and intellectual property, changes in the experience of reading (non-sequential reading), and easy, technical modification of texts, which destroys the fixity and self-containment of the print-based verbal expression (Baron

2000, 91–94). The issues raised by Baron find particular relevance to the explorations of academic communication phenomena in cyberspace.

In general, the considerations about the profile of the new electronic literacy confirm the constant intermingling and interdependence of orality and literacy. In modern society, which is based on literacy, electronic media largely enhance the possibilities of learning how to read and write, extend access to literature, promote literary education and practising literature (December 1993; Godzic 2000). On the other hand, the prevalence of television and video draws people away from text-based entertainment and learning, and consequently the value and power of oral expression is rising (December 1993 following Lakoff 1982; see also Bartmiński 1989). In Bartmiński's view, the increased role of oral communication is the reflection of its humanistic value, and its deep relation to human personality (1989, 430).

3.3. CMC and its defining characteristics

When discussing the mechanisms of identity construction in CMC, emphasis should be placed on the defining, and often divergent, characteristics of the new medium that contribute to the complexity of the relation: (mass) media – social structure – individual (Goban-Klass 1999). These characteristics include (Barnes 2003; de Kerckhove 2001a):

- the hybrid nature of the electronic medium;
- interactivity (enabled by hypertextuality and connectedness);
- technological convergence;
- digitalisation, which largely contributes to the flexibility of the medium.

First of all, CMC supports multi-directional exchange of messages (one-to-one, one-to-many, many-to-one and many-to-many), and therefore is said to be a mixture of both mass and interpersonal communication. CMC is a medium that does not fit neatly into either category, because it can be used to foster interpersonal communication that does not require a face-to-face setting. In CMC the public and private spheres of communication continually intermingle, with obvious consequences for the character of social interaction. Interesting examples of this occur in the present study, where private exchanges between *Humanists* (i.e. members of the discussion group I investigated) were subsequently placed on the public forum.

The effect of the hybrid nature of CMC on how identity is negotiated in this new medium also becomes evident in how CMC combines such conflicting elements as impersonal and hyperpersonal linguistic expression, anonymity and highly controlled forms of self-presentation, disembodiment and re-embodiment, or uninhibited and depersonalised behaviour. One of the implications of the lack of physical contact between interactants is that senders of CMC messages may readily engage in selective and careful self-presentation. Asynchronous CMC enables users to reflect, edit and select the information and cues transmitted to recipients. Additionally, in intercultural CMC settings, the nature of the medium is likely to emphasise the differences between the interacting cultures and discourse communities (see e.g. Conoscenti 2004).

Another feature that is relevant for the issue of identity negotiation in CMC is interactivity, which is a defining feature for both the medium and CMC discourse. As a defining characteristic of the medium, interactivity refers to the capacity of the medium for interaction between a user and a digital environment, interaction which is enabled by the interconnected computer software and hardware[12] (Barnes 2003; de Kerckhove 2001a). In other words, interactivity facilitates a dialogue between users and a computer programme. Hypertextual links, encouraging navigation, constitute one of the most popular forms of interactivity. An important implication of "hypertextual interactivity" is that it gives users the opportunity to influence the shape and content of the text in a CMC situation. Thus, the new medium encourages active participation of the audience in the process of media consumption, to be contrasted with the passive reception of the media (Barnes 2003, 21)[13].

Media convergence denotes "the integration of all types of mediated communication into an electronic, digital format, an integration propelled by the widespread use of computers and networking systems" (Barnes

[12] I would like to point to the double use of the term *interactivity*. The term is applied in relation to the nature of the technology and as a characteristic of verbal expression. Therefore, I make reference to the concept twice in this chapter: when I discuss the defining properties of the medium (the present section), and when I focus on the properties of electronic discourse (Section 3.4). This use of the term may cause confusion, especially in view of other understandings of interactivity that have developed in linguistics, and discourse analysis in particular (for their discussion see e.g. Duszak 1998a; Sokół 2004).

[13] In her discussion of interactivity being a defining characteristic of the medium, Barnes refers to the distinction between *informational interactivity*, which refers to the processes of obtaining, navigating and locating data (e.g. through clicking on Web page links, filling in online forms, performing Web searches, etc.), and *human-computer interaction* (HCI), which involves users' interaction with computer hardware and software (e.g. the mouse, keyboards, graphical interfaces, voice recognition, etc.; Barnes 2003, 21).

2003, 29). This combining of various communication technologies to transmit information also allows the incorporation of interpersonal communication. Thus, the significance of media convergence lies in how it changes the patterns of interpersonal communication and information delivery to mass audiences. In addition, convergence facilitates the development of multimedia products that integrate various semiotic codes, enriching interpersonal communication and opening new possibilities for effective self-presentation.

As regards the implications of digitalisation, the storage of information in the uniform, computer-readable form eliminates the boundaries between communication media, equalises access to information, and renders digital documents more susceptible for modification and manipulation.

3.4. Verbal expression in computer-mediated communication: a new language variety?

CMC combined with network technologies has evidently transformed verbal expression. Given the heterogeneity of CMC communicative situations, the emergent and still evolving register manifests itself in a variety of styles and genres. A large part of the linguistic explorations of CMC discourse have concentrated on its precise characteristics in comparison with spoken and written modalities (see e.g. Baron 2000; Collot and Belmore 1996; Condon and Čech 1996; Crystal 2001; Dąbrowska 2000; December 1993; Yates 1996; Werry 1996). The analyses take into focus the language of particular synchronous and asynchronous types of CMC situations, and the emphasis is put on how users' linguistic choices reflect the tension between their expectations and purposes and the technological constraints and facilitations of the chosen situation.

To analyse the qualities of oral expression in CMC discourse, December (1993) studies Ong's features of orality in Internet chats and BBSs[14]. He advocates the existence of a tertiary form of orality, which results from greater time- and space-independence offered by the CMC situations under study, their flexibility in the choice of participant(s) of interaction, and their capability to combine text, multi-media and virtual reality message content. Consequently, the emergent verbal expression is marked by emotive, participatory, and expressive qualities, discernible in e.g. the turn-taking structure of a chat, the range and alternation of discussion topics, BBS's "cascades" (i.e. multi-authored speech acts

[14] BBSs = bulletin board systems, a form of asynchronous CMC.

whose meaning works through particular users additions-responses to the initial message[15]), or in the practice of quoting a previous author's message.

Similarly, oral aspects of a synchronous type of CMC are the subject of Werry's analysis of English and French IRC sessions (Werry 1996). Werry provides a useful taxonomy of features of IRC and enumerates ways in which participants reconstitute aspects of spoken language through graphic and orthographic means. Another example of the study that indicates the resemblance of synchronous CMC situations to direct spoken interaction is Condon and Čech's comparison of face-to-face and computer-mediated decision taking and planning (Condon and Čech 1996). Again, the authors stress the relevance of the contextual features of computer-mediated communicative events: these novel situations (dyadic "synchronous machine-mediated interactions" or "s-interactions") include such characteristics of direct spoken interaction as the possibility to specify the time and participants of interaction, the feebleness of the linguistic signal, and most importantly, the introduction of features of turn-taking and repair. Condon and Čech also point out some differences between synchronous CMC and face-to-face discourse related to decision making, such as the higher proportion of requests for information and action, of agreements and compliances with requests, and of elaborate metalanguage to express orientations (i.e. orienting phrases and discourse

---

[15] Here is an example of a 'cascade' given in December's article (see http://www.december.com/john/papers/pscrc93.txt):

Article: 435 of alt.culture.usenet
From: jchan@netlink.cts.com (Jim Chancy)
Subject: Re: Please Feed the Spooks
Date: 19 Jul 92 16:05:49 GMT
>>>>>>>>>>In article <2906@alpha.sdsu.edu> alex@alpha.sdsu.edu (Alex Frosh) writes:
>>>>>>>>>>>Er, please excuse my ignorance, but what are "cascades"?
>>>>>>>>>>hmmm...I too am lost, has anyone seen my shades ?
>>>>>>>>>uh, this is weird, do you think it will fade?
>>>>>>>>Has anybody here seen my old friend Darth Vader?
>>>>>>>AARRGGH I've cascaded and I can't get up!
>>>>>>FLARGH I've abraded and I can't get op!
>>>>>BLARGH I've dehydrated and I can't wet chops!
>>>>CHARGE! My brigade won't let me stop.
>>>BLAM! My gun just greased that cop!
>>BRAN! Colon rust ceased that slop!
>ZZAP! Just lost a MEGAFLOP!
RRIP! Take bonghits with a bop!

markers). In general, computer-mediated decision making is found to be more efficient than face-to-face interaction.

As regards the analyses of oral and written linguistic aspects of asynchronous CMC situations, Collot and Belmore apply Biber's multidimensional multi-feature model to analyse lexical and grammatical features of a corpus of postings to a Canadian BBS, and compare it with computerised corpora of spoken and written English (Collot and Belmore 1996). The set of situational constraints of a BBS allows to recognise it as a distinct variety of English. On the one hand, the BBS interaction is marked by an easy interaction of participants and alternation of topics, these being the characteristics of some varieties of spoken English. On the other hand, the interactants cannot see or hear each other. In addition, when considering the conventionally written aspects of a BBS, in BBS messages composed online, the use of planning and editing strategies is limited (Collot and Belmore 1996, 14). Thus, in Collot and Belmore's view, the unique situational features of a BBS are enough to assume that this "Electronic Language" embodies also a distinctive set of linguistic features. The language of BBSs, when analysed along Biber's six dimensions, proves to reveal some of the linguistic features characteristic for both written and spoken modalities, and resembles the genres of public interviews, and private and professional letters. The authors label the "Electronic Language" a hybrid variety of English to refer to its unclear linguistic identity. When considering the situational features of BBSs that explain the form of "Electronic language", Collot and Belmore note the importance of the degree of common interests and shared knowledge, the purpose of communication, the tripartite nature of participants' roles (including an addressor, an addressee and an audience), and the relationship of the speakers to the text (Collot and Belmore 1996, 26).

A corpus-based quantitative study is also used to investigate the linguistic aspects of another conferencing system, at the Open University in the UK (Yates 1996). Yates' comparison between spoken, written and CMC discourse follows a Hallidayan model that focuses on the textual, interpersonal and ideational aspects of language use. With respect to the textual aspect, which is measured in terms of vocabulary range and density, CMC corpus proves closer to writing than speech. This might result from CMC's greater technical opportunities to correct, revise and edit electronic text. Still, as Yates notes, these opportunities for greater variety in text production are frequently not fully exploited, which proves that not only mechanical aspects of the medium but also sociolinguistic issues operate in determining the production of texts (Yates 1996, 35). In addition, Yates observes that "users of CMC systems may be bringing their literate production practices to an interactive, social and orally-oriented interaction", rather than converting literate texts into oral ones (Yates 1996, 39).

When exploring the interpersonal aspect through the use of personal pronouns, Yates concludes that CMC is more akin to spoken language. Finally, with reference to the ideational aspect, CMC discourse reveals a significantly higher proportion of modal auxiliaries than either speech or writing, which could indicate a considerable presence of discussions that contain modalised statements.

An attempt to characterise synchronous CMC discourse in relation to speech and writing is also made by Dąbrowska (2000), who conducts a sociolinguistic analysis of personal emails in Polish in terms of their structural similarity (or dissimilarity) to the traditional personal letter. Again, to illustrate the uncertain nature of CMC discourse in email Dąbrowska points to its hybrid character: email reveals both the characteristics of more formal written communication, and of more casual and emotionally-loaded direct or telephone conversation (Dąbrowska 2000, 97). On the one hand, Dąbrowska's analysis demonstrates that an electronic letter preserves the formal requirements of traditional written communication: the body of an electronic letter usually contains such structural elements of a traditional letter as an opening (salutation), greeting, and farewell. On the other hand, the language of emails reveals a great deal of expressivity, directness and colloquialness of a casual conversation. This can be illustrated by the presence of code-mixing, unintended misspellings, the simplification of the Polish alphabet through the elimination of Polish diacritic marks, colloquial lexicon, chaotic expression, and more visually, through the creative use of punctuation (e.g. smileys, capitalisation).

The most comprehensive endeavour to specify the linguistic identity of CMC discourse is undertaken by Crystal (2001). To refer to the language of all CMC and Internet situations, Crystal uses the term Netspeak[16] and his main concern is its evaluation as a single language variety, emergent from the language use in a homogenous electronic situation. Like in the previous explorations of the language of various e-situations, Crystal's starting point is the consideration of the relationship between speech and

[16] Crystal uses the term of *Netspeak* in spite of its implied reference to oral communication, as a better alternative than cumbersome, in his view, *Netlish*, *Weblish*, *Internet language*, *cyberspeak*, *electronic discourse*, *electronic language*, *interactive written discourse*, *CMC* (Crystal 2001, 17). He finds *Netspeak* "succinct and functional enough", but stresses the term's wider application in the context of CMC and Internet linguistic studies.

writing, and subsequently, the application of spoken and written language criteria to Netspeak (following Crystal 1995). Crystal's main conclusion is that Netspeak relies on characteristics belonging to both sides of the speech/writing divide, but contrary to the prevailing impression, and in spite of the considerable presence of oral features, Netspeak remains closer to writing (see Crystal 2001, 42–43).

As regards the written characteristics of Netspeak, Crystal notes the presence of many varieties of written language which are just electronically adapted versions of their non-electronic counterparts that appear in digital libraries, archives and data services. This results form the medium's functions of e.g. databasing, reference publishing, archiving, advertising, which are known from traditional situations that use writing (Crystal 2001, 28). Moreover, the application of written language criteria to Netspeak reveals that out of all e-situations the Web is found to be the closest to written language, chatgroups[17] as most distant, and email and virtual worlds placed in between. However, the presence of the properties of written language in CMC situations is not straightforward. To illustrate, the space-bound nature of Netspeak can only seem temporary, given the possibilities of Web pages to get updated and of the text in them to move around, disappear, change colour or morph into animated characters, and the possibilities of easy electronic alterations of relatively stable email messages. The analysis of other features demonstrates a high degree of variation among particular e-situations, adding to an uncertain relationship of Netspeak to traditional written language (for details see Crystal 2001, 44–48).

Likewise, Crystal's considerations also reveal an ambivalent relation of Netspeak to traditional spoken language. Admittedly, the situations of email, chatgroups and virtual worlds are time-governed, expecting or demanding an immediate response, transient and full of energetic force and dynamism characteristic for face-to-face conversation. Still, even in these more speech-like situations there are many differences between Netspeak and direct conversation. Namely, Netspeak interaction is marked by the lack of simultaneous feedback, slower and more unpredictable turn-taking, and the lack of the formal properties of the spoken medium related to prosody, kinesics and proxemics. These characteristics correlate with the mechanical aspects of the interaction in the electronic medium, such as

[17] The Internet situations comprised under Crystal's "chatgroups" include both synchronous chats and asynchronous conferencing systems and discussion lists. Other researchers (e.g. Smith and Kollock 1999) choose the taxonomy of CMC and Internet situations that separates chats, conferencing systems (BBSs) and email discussion lists as too distinct e-situations.

e.g. time lag, unidirectional sending of relatively complete computer messages, inability to see all participants of interaction[18], the number of interacting individuals, bandwidth processing, traffic density on the host computer, etc. Additional limitations stem from the medium's large dependence on typing speed and ability, and the lack of reaction signals and comment clauses, i.e. factors that enable true spontaneity of direct conversation (for details see Crystal 2001, 30–41).

Clearly, the properties of the language found in CMC reflect the heterogeneity and variability of CMC situations. These characteristics of the new communicative situations, in turn, are responsible for the uncertain linguistic identity of Netspeak (Crystal 2001), and for the multiple interpretations of electronic text and its properties (Zwiefka-Chwałek 2002). The point that researchers generally agree about is the substantial, or even revolutionary, transformation of verbal expression and of the role and shape of the traditional forms of language (e.g. Burszta 2002; Chyła 2000; Crystal 2001; Wilk 2000; Zwiefka-Chwałek 2002).

Given the subsequent modification of the general role of language in social communication, resulting from the extended possibilities of verbal communication offered by CMC and the Internet, Wilk considers a potential change of the paradigm (2000, 49). A straightforward evaluation of this change in progress is complicated by the fact that, to use Bolter's argument, electronic text is the text in constant motion (Bolter 1991, quoted in Wilk 2000, 46). In Bolter's view, interaction with and through electronic text offers the multiplicity and potentiality of spatial and temporal experiences, in which an important role is played by the active reader. Thus, Wilk concludes, electronic text affords "a textual potentiality rather than a morphologically fixed message" (2000, 46; my translation). This makes electronic texts more accessible, anti-hierarchical and more democratic: the contexts in which electronic texts function question the axiological order related to the circulation of printed texts. CMC and the Internet enable new processes of text-creation, and consequently, the formation of social bond, and social and cultural order. New verbal expression is characterised by the lack of subordination to speech: it is organised according to its own, autonomous rules. Although more approachable, verbal expression in the new electronic contexts is

[18] This point does not apply to video conferencing. Moreover, currently, video transmission is incorporated into e-situations, which allows some degree of visual contact between participants of interaction (e.g. in chats). The speed of transmission, however, is insufficient to make CMC situations approximate direct spoken interaction.

also somehow devoid of its authority, submitted to immaterial audiovisual and multisensory experiences (Chyła 2000; see also Burszta 2002).

A central notion in the discussion of the new literacy and the properties of electronic text is hypertext, the term introduced by Theodor H. Nelson in the 1960s to characterize a new non-sequential way of text production and reception, dependent on the user's activity. Crystal quotes Jackson's definition of true hypertext, according to which it "entails the complete and automatic interlocking of text, so that all documents are coexistent, with none existing in a prior or primary relation to any other" (Crystal 2001, 202, following Jackson 1997). Today true hypertext does not exist, since links between documents are frequently not reciprocated, for such reasons as temporary unavailability of a link, refusal of access to a site or server, a link rot (caused by the removal of a page by its owner), etc. Still, the implications of text organisation based on hypertextual links, as Nelson predicted, have been significant: for literature, genre formation, perception of time and space, roles of the reader and author, and human thinking in general (e.g. Bardini 1997; de Kerckhove 2001a; Wilk 2000).

Drawing on the numerous attempts to characterize the nature of electronic text and hypertext, apart from orality, I choose to mention the following defining and interrelated properties: (1) dematerialisation of the word, (2) openness (the lack of delimitation), (3) decentring, (4) non-linearity, (5) intertextuality, (6) hypertextual reciprocity, (7) interactivity (which is both the attribute of the medium and electronic text – see note 14 in the previous section of Chapter 3), and (8) visualisation (iconicity) (e.g. Burszta 2002; Chyła 2000; Crystal 2001; Godzic 2000; de Kerckhove 2001a; Mitra 1999; Wilk 2000; Zwiefka-Chwałek 2002). According to Wilk (2000), the dematerialisation of verbal expression refers to its unstable and immaterial existence on the computer screen: electronic text is inaccessible until displayed on the screen. Wilk also points to the uncertain difference between the virtual presence of verbal expression on the computer screen and "real" presence of verbal expression on the pages of the book (2000, 44). In addition, Chyła's (2000) considerations of the consequences of dematerialisation of verbal expression centre around the technically mediated nature of human experience with the machine (i.e. the computer), and consequently with electronic text, which can be referred to as the effect of the simulation of the subject's interaction with the "text" machine. The dematerialisation of verbal expression could also be related to another property of the electronic word: its transparency. The electronic word becomes invisible because of the "looking-through" strategy of its examination[19] (Zwiefka-Chwałek 2002). The electronic word becomes in a sense invisible because the image displayed on the computer screen is just a way to reach what is behind and what is more significant. "Looking through" the word is characteristic for hypertext, which enables more fluid and natural cruising through electronic text.

This freedom of navigation, however not limitless, is afforded by the lack of delimitation of electronic text. Hypertext, which does not have any beginning or end is not an ultimately demarcated or formed structure. This feature shows how different this state of affairs is from the situation in which, in accordance with the semiotic tradition, an unequivocally determined and recorded text is a central reference point for the mechanisms of culture (Wilk 2000, 40). As regards hypertext, its unstableness, fluidity, ephemerality and lack of firm norms of text formation points to a different pragmatics of hypertext. Wilk recounts Bolter's argument that a constitutive feature of pragmatics of hypertext is the rhythm of text formation and reception, determined by the user's choice of links. Moreover, to refer to Levinson's observations, hypertext is not a rigidly pre-planned collection of words, but rather "a potentiality of multiple realisations, characterised by a large degree of openness and freedom" (Wilk 2000, 41; my translation).

The link-based structure of electronic text bears implications on its further defining properties, namely non-linearity, decentring, intertextuality and interactivity, and on the aspects of authorship and readership in electronic contexts. In CMC and Internet discourse, next to the large quantities of interrupted linear text, i.e. "text which follows unidimensional flow of speech, but interrupted by conventions which aid intelligibility" (e.g. the use of spaces between words and the division of a text into lines and screens), there are also large quantities of non-linear text (Crystal 2001, 196). The reception of non-linear text is multidimensional: in non-linear viewing there is no fixed order of experiencing the text. Different parts of electronic text (hypertext) receive varying degrees of attention, depending on the user's and text designer's choices. Clearly, the concept of hypertext linking challenges linear viewing and thinking, implies the transgression of space and time (e.g. Crystal 2001; Wilk 2000), a departure from logocentrism (Derrida 1999), and launching a new electronic culture based on non-linearity (de Kerckhove 2001a).

Although single instances of experiencing hypertext may result in the production of hierarchical connections, as already mentioned, hypertext by

[19] Zwiefka-Chwałek (2002) refers to Richard A. Lanham's (1993) distinction between "looking at" and "looking through" the word.

definition is non-hierarchical and decentred because it lacks a unanimous centre (e.g. Mitra 1999; Wilk 2000). When focusing on the attributes of WWW text, Mitra relates decentring to the property of hypertextual reciprocity thanks to which WWW pages gain discursive richness, strength and interactivity through reciprocal links to other pages. Also, the presence of hypertextual links influences the property of intertextuality, which refers to the way in which the texts connect with each other to produce unique discursive domains. Discursive domains, in turn, are defined as "specific hyperconnected interest areas to which the WWW texts point" (Mitra 1999). The navigation through decentred hypertext, although to some extent limited by the pre-programmed set of changes and links of the initial (primary) text, depends largely on the activity of the user: this makes the activity of the user another constitutive factor of hypertext. Other important consequences of decentring and hypertextual reciprocity are the changeability and merging of the roles of the reader and author, and the conscious abandonment of authorship, eventuating in questioning the authority of the author (Mitra 1999). Mitra argues that the effect of the decentred text is undermining the traditional centres of authority in discursive formations, built around the authors, texts and canons, and in dissolving the hierarchies of discursive power, which could be a necessary factor for sustaining the life of virtual communities.

Interactivity understood as the property of CMC discourse can be defined as "an expression of the extent that in a given series of communication exchanges, any third (or later) transmission (or message) is related to the degree to which previous exchanges referred to even earlier transmissions. (…) [D]efining interactivity as a variable relies on how much messages are based on the way preceding messages are related to even earlier ones" (Rafaeli 1988, 111). The significance of interactivity lies in its being an agent in the social dynamics of CMC group communication. Interactivity supports message interest and involvement, and thus is viewed as a network building mechanism. Being both a theoretical and practical construct, interactivity can be effectively used to measure e.g. the integrity and longevity of CMC-based groups, or the stability of membership (Rafaeli and Sudweeks 1997).

Finally, an important property of electronic text is its visualisation, also referred to iconicity or imagery (e.g. Crystal 2001; Godzic 2000; Zwiefka-Chwałek 2002). As already stated in Section 3.2 of the present chapter, electronic discourse is marked by the mixture of written, oral, aural, and visual structures of articulation (Welch 1999). The dominance of the visual code in electronic text becomes evident through such elements as smileys, acronyms and other creative uses of punctuation and spelling, graphic ways of organising expression into lists, matrices and branching structures, functional uses of colour, shape, and animation in hypertext, or play with parameters of simple text-editing, such as font size and type, background, shading, etc. To emphasise the significance of the visual in electronic text production and reception, Godzic notes that nowadays word-processing has actually transformed into image-processing. Since the user's initial contact with electronic text focuses on its graphic form rather than on its senses, senses communicated through words and images are substantially distanced from their physical representations. This also calls for a renegotiation of the word/image relationship (2000, 178), or can even mark the origin of a new visual code, which will give our culture a different post-alphabetic quality (Pękala 1997). In her discussion of the visualisation in the modern electronic text, Zwiefka-Chwałek refers to the concept of "hierogliphicons", i.e. "texts that combine a word with the plastic image, representing a given phenomenon by means of the sign connected with the designated phenomenon or denoting it conventionally" (Zwiefka-Chwałek 2002; my translation). In addition, Zwiefka-Chwałek argues that writing has always been the transformation of sound into the visual code, but the invention of the phonetic alphabet distanced a written message from the visual representation of its sense, and added an element of artificiality. The nowadays return to visual codes may result form their closer relation to reality, and their being more natural. The preponderance of the visual code in electronic media and the iconisation of writing reflect the general dominance of the audiovisual code in contemporary media discourse (Gajda 2000, 25).

In view of the liability, openness and equivocality of CMC situations and discourse, researchers are concerned with the search for stable and certain points of reference to uniformly define a new literacy, and determine the regularities of the linguistic properties of CMC. According to Wilk, in their attempts to ascertain how verbal expression is shaped in CMC, researchers must take the intratextual context (i.e. co-text) as the only proper point of departure (2000, 68–69). Influenced by de Kerckhove's (2001b) observations that "literate listening" is distinguished by paying more attention to words than to the context of situation[20], Wilk hypothesises that in CMC single words and expressions bear more significance than syntactically more complex structures.

---

[20] In his attempt to define a new electronic culture, de Kerckhove (2001b, 112–119) suggested a distinction between "oral" and "literate listening". Whereas "oral listening" refers to the components of the situational context, such as the topic of conversation, the speakers' intentions, etc., "literate listening" takes into focus words and their meaning.

Although CMC discourse is characterised by a large degree of heterogeneity and confusion, evidence can be found for its ordering and uniformisation (see e.g. Godzic 2000; Zwiefka-Chwałek 2002). Besides, since CMC situations share certain linguistic properties, a conclusion can be drawn that Netspeak is a new and genuine language variety that originated in a heterogeneous linguistic medium (Crystal 2001). The evidence for the ordering practices in CMC discourse is given by Zwiefka-Chwałek (2002), who mentions the hierarchical structures of threads in chaotic discussions of Usenet and Internet forums, which reflect how the ways of text organisation characteristic for writing influence the electronic word. Other manifestations of ordering practices could be Crystal's examples of graphic organisation of electronic text, such as lists, matrices and branching structures (see Crystal 2001, 197). Ordering and organisational routines indicate some degree of uniformisation in CMC discourse, which bears implications for determining the status of CMC language . For instance Godzic, on the one hand, acknowledges that the language of CMC and the Internet is distinguished by exuberant individualism and creativity; on the other hand, he notes such evidence for its uniformisation as the use of smileys and acronyms, signatures (and especially extended signatures which become mergers of ASCII art[21] and linguistic poetry), cybernauts' activity to preserve their language, which points to their high linguistic awareness (Godzic 2000, 180).

Crystal's engagement in the discussion on the uniformisation of linguistic practices in CMC results form his intention to determine the linguistic identity of Netspeak. Definitely an important element that contributes to some regularity of linguistic practices in CMC are forms of explicit guidance about the rules of netiquette, such as usage guides, dictionaries, style manuals, FAQ files (Crystal 2001, 71–81). While these guides could be an interesting manifestation of semi-prescriptivism, their main role is to introduce newbies[22] to CMC situations, and instruct about the rules of appropriate conduct and language usage. Although there is still a large degree of inconsistency and changeability in CMC and Internet usage, observations of the distinctive linguistic features which are typical of the Internet domain as a whole, along with the general characteristics of the medium, provide a solid ground for claiming that Netspeak is a genuine language variety, or rather a collection of distinct dialects (Crystal 2001, 92, 238). The distinctive linguistic features include: (1)

---

[21] ASCII stands for "American Standard Code for Information Interchange". ASCII artwork denotes artwork that is created by means of the symbols and characters that are available on the computer keyboard.

[22] A newbie is an inexperienced user of a CMC situation.

specific lexicon (e.g. lexicon that has emerged to talk about CMC situations, operations, activities, terms associated with the use of computer hardware and software, terms for various Internet users, etc.); (2) distinctive graphology (e.g. the use of capitalisation; smileys); (3) distinctive spelling practice (e.g. non-standard and deviant spelling, reduplication of letters to show emotions, the use of symbols borrowed from programming languages) (Crystal 2001, 81–91). Although there are still numerous uncertainties and discrepancies in the evaluations of the phenomenon of Netspeak, its significance cannot be doubted. As Crystal continues, the phenomenon of Netspeak is "a linguistic singularity – a new genuine medium", substantially different from other forms of communication:

> It is neither 'spoken writing' nor 'written speech'. (…) it is something fundamentally different from both writing and speech, as traditionally understood. It is, in short, a forth medium. In language studies, we are used to discussing issues in terms of 'speech vs. writing vs. signing'. From now on we must add a further dimension to comparative enquiry: 'speech vs. writing vs. signing vs. computer-mediated language.' (Crystal 2001, 238)

In conclusion, I find it necessary to point to some inconsistency in the use of the terminology with reference to electronic discourse, which may cause confusion. The area of CMC research is relatively new, but is developing very dynamically, so the systematisation of terminology is necessary. Having presented electronic discourse as a new language variety, in the chapter that follows I will continue to address social aspects of CMC. My focus will be the presentation of linguistic accounts of how individual and group identity is constructed in electronic discourse.

CHAPTER FOUR

VIRTUAL IDENTITIES, CYBERSPACE AND ACADEMIC COMMUNICATION

The aim of the present chapter is to focus on how the concept of virtual identity is theorised and empirically investigated. As discoursal construction of identity is both a matter of individuality and collectivity, I will look at the identification processes in cyberspace from the perspective of the individual and the community. Thus, I will also address the problem of defining and exploring virtual communities, and present an overview of the approaches to the study of communities in cyberspace.

In my discussion of virtual identity, I will underline its highly contingent and fluid character. I will give an account of the two opposing views on how identity is discoursally constructed in cyberspace. On the one hand, the analyses from a CDA perspective point to the restricting influence of the socio-cultural context on the individual's identity in CMC. On the other hand, there are findings that emphasise new, unlimited possibilities of identity construction, enabled by the medium's inherent properties. Then, having surveyed the most important conceptualisations of a virtual community, I will speak in favour of a discourse community approach, which allows us to focus on the members' shared linguistic practices and such aspects of social interaction in a community as the negotiation of individual and group identity. More importantly, being grounded in Swales' genre theory, a discourse community approach proves useful for the linguistic explorations of academic communication in cyberspace.

4.1. Computer-mediated communication and identity construction

New patterns of social interaction in CMC are argued to have made identity an even more complex, dynamic and unstable concept (e.g. Turkle 1996). Computer and network technology has enabled people to go beyond the limits of time and space, which, in turn, has intensified the fragmentation and dispersion of societies and individuals and undermined the settled bases of identity formation. CMC has also opened new opportunities for the (re-)negotiation of identity and proved beneficial for an understanding of the new decentralised sense of self. What I would like to particularly emphasise, thanks to its inherent properties, CMC has indeed enabled the revival of individuality.

The development of CMC has indeed necessitated a change in the individual's consciousness and transformed humans' perception of their mind, body and self (Turkle 2001). As it turns out, the character of digital technology and of the interhuman interaction in cyberspace has led to the formation of a dynamic self, which, in turn, has made identity a temporary and unstable choice. Consequently, understanding the digital world requires an effort on the part of what may be referred to as an "analogue human being" (Godzic 2001, 144; my translation) who is used to linear thinking. Human perception of the world is very much influenced by the fact that humans are beings with physical bodies, whereas in cyberspace, the necessary ingredients of identity – space and distance – as understood in the traditional senses of the words, are absent. Nevertheless, for Godzic, understanding the digital world proves extremely beneficial (Godzic 1999, 2001, following Negroponte 1997), particularly for the individual whose identity developed and was established long before the arrival of the new digital era, and who, in a way, was forced to become a "Cybernaut".

Following the postmodern view of identity, some linguistic accounts of the individual's identity in CMC emphasise the constraining and deterministic character of the electronic medium (e.g. Thoms and Thelwall 2005). Thoms and Thelwall's (2005) study focuses on the personal and institutional aspects of identity construction in academic homepages. Their analysis is based on 20 academic homepages, some of them university-constructed, and some self-constructed. Using a Foucaldian framework, the authors investigate identity construction through the use or disuse of the links within a particular homepage. Their main aim is to compare the relationship between an individual's identity and an institution, depending on whether or not a homepage is institutionally-based. Generally, Thoms – Thelwall observe a loss of individual identity in all the pages under study, either through the presence of the university server, or an academic's tendency to relinquish his/her power to the institution. The individual appears to have lost his/her autonomy, whereas the institution makes use of its employee's homepages to legitimise its own power and position.

Some researchers, though, despite admitting the lack of stability of identity, point to the new possibilities for self-presentation and the individual's agency (e.g. Aycock 1995). In his analysis of virtual identity construction, Aycock looks at the postings from a BBS related to chess playing. He relies on the Foucauldian concept of the "technologies of the self" and develops his own model of "self-fashioning", which emphasises that identity may be both imposed and freely chosen. Aycock's model includes four components: "(a) the private 'inner substance' that is believed to be the ultimate source of personal identity; (b) the degree and kind of commitment that is made to a given activity; (c) the personal routines or disciplines that are adopted to reshape one's identity; and (d) the eventual goal of the personal transformation that has been undertaken" (Aycock 1995). These components foreground the relevance of the private, public and communal aspects of the self, and of such issues as freedom, power, technique and privacy.

Communal aspects of identity construction are also emphasised by Benwell and Stokoe's study of how identity is negotiated by a new member (i.e. a *newbie*) on a message board (Benwell and Stokoe 2006). Benwell and Stokoe's (2006) analysis is based on Brown and Levinson's theory of politeness. It is a case study of a new member in an exchange on a message board, a synchronous type of CMC. Benwell and Stokoe find out that the process of initiation into the collectivity of the CMC is skilfully managed by both the newbie and "old" members. This provides evidence of the normative and polite behaviour characteristic for the functioning of a virtual community. Therefore, for a full account of the construction of virtual identity, it is also necessary to discuss the concept of a virtual community.

4.2. Defining virtual communities

The use of the term *community* dominates the literature about CMC-based social aggregations, but to what extent is the application of this term appropriate for the context of cyberspace? First of all, the question evokes the problem of defining the concept of community in general and its constitutive elements in the offline world. Thus, it proves useful to specify the character and role of online collectivities by relating them to traditional, real life communities. More specifically, attempts to define the concept of a virtual community focus on the key parameters of the community in cyberspace, i.e. its spatial (the community's location) and symbolic dimensions (the community's shared value system, interests, sense of identity, etc.).

Indeed, computer and network technology supports the formation of various collectivities that reflect the heterogeneity of CMC situations.

These collectivities can exist only in cyberspace or function as the electronic extensions of the real world communities. Online collectivities vary in size, social structure, their scope and reach, their frequency of interaction and level of formality, and the purposes for which they are created: i.e. the discussion of various topics, playing games, entertainment, work, etc. As regards the role of online collectivities in social interaction, researchers note two opposing views (Kollock and Smith 1999, 4). The positive view emphasises the benefits of CMC-based social structures for democracy, prosperity and renewal of the sense of community by strengthening social bonds globally and reversing the processes of social atomisation. The opposite view stresses the negative aspects of social networking in cyberspace, resulting from an uneven distribution of power on the Internet, and new opportunities for surveillance and control. Consequently, sceptics warn against the over-application of the term *community*, suggesting alternative names for CMC collectivities, such as e.g. “microcultures” (quoted in Q. Jones 1997), “socialising digital neighbourhoods” (Negroponte 1995), or “pseudo-communities” (quoted in S. Jones 1997, following Beniger 1987). However, “the kinds of interactions and institutions that are emerging in cyberspace are more complicated than can be captured in one-sided utopian or dystopian terms” (Kollock and Smith 1999, 4). What is needed then in this sphere of research is an objective and scholarly analysis of patterns of online social interaction and organisation.

One of the first proponents of the term *virtual community* was Howard Rheingold, a researcher known for the pioneering work on the cultural, social and political implications of modern communication media. Rheingold defines virtual communities as “social aggregations that emerge from the Net when enough people carry on those public discussions long enough, with sufficient human feeling, to form webs of personal relationships in cyberspace” (2000/1993: 5)[23]. Essentially, Rheingold's early definition of virtual communities evokes criticism for its lack of spatial dimension and the vaguely expressed “sufficient human feeling”. The problem stems mainly from the traditional understanding of community. The traditional concept of community encompasses both material and symbolic (ideological) dimensions. The material component refers to a range of social relations operating within specific – ethnic, religious, linguistic – boundaries or geographic localities. Ideologically, community refers to a sense of common character, identity or interests

[23] In the later edition of his popular book (2000/ 1993), Rheingold reconsiders his original definition and opts for a social network metaphor.

(Benschop 1997; Fernback and Thompson 1995; Fernback 1997). Traditional communities are characterised by direct social interaction, a shared value system, and a shared symbol system. Still, most frequently, the traditional approaches of social scientists to the study of community emphasise distinct geographic boundaries, within which events, artefacts and social relations can be effectively examined, and thus deem that communities should exist in shared physical space (e.g. S. Jones 1998a; Watson 1997).

To defend his view, Rheingold argues that in virtual communities, the space is a cognitive and social one, not geographic. For instance, computer conference conversations are dialogues that are situated in a specific "virtual place" (such as e.g. the conferencing system, the conference, the topic) and time. In virtual communities the sense of place requires an individual act of imagination, and what must be imagined is the idea of a community itself. He also recounts Licklider and Taylor's[24] predictions about virtual communities: "In most fields [virtual communities] will consist of geographically separated members, sometimes grouped in small clusters and sometimes working individually. They will be communities not of common location, but of common interest" (Rheingold 2000/1993, 24).

It must be noted, however, that the debate about the relationship between physical space and community, however problematic for the description of virtual communities, is not new (see Q. Jones 1997). According to Jones, as early as in the 1970s Bernard ushered in the notion of CMC-based virtual communities by arguing for the independence of the term *community* from the concept of physical space:

> The distribution of people in dispersed social systems is not only spatial but mental. Some people are in a planetary community; some are in a national community; still others are in a community bounded by their limited interests. The bodies of people might be in one spatial area, but not their social worlds. The concept of locale has little meaning in this context. The concept of communality was once proposed to refer to these locale independent relationships. Now the implications for the community of the independence from locale as shown by these new kinds of relationships are becoming overwhelming. (Bernard 1973, quoted in Q. Jones 1997)

---

[24] The research directors for the ARPA (The Advanced Research Projects Agency), an agency of the United States Department of Defence responsible for the development of new technology for use by the military. In 1968 they set in motion ARPANET (The Advanced Research Projects Agency Network), which was the world's first operational network, the predecessor of the global Internet, and for some, the first virtual community.

Clearly, in CMC physical space has been replaced by a medium of communication, by cyberspace, and this has necessitated a re-conceptualisation of the notion of space, and consequently, of community as well (Fernback 1997; Mitra 1997; Watson 1997). Virtual space has turned out to be "socially constructed and re-constructed space", "a repository for collective cultural memory", "a reconceived public sphere for social, political, economic, and cultural interaction", but also a place where "public" and "private" domains merge (Fernback 1997, 37). Consequently, communities have started to be considered not as products of shared physical or geographic space, but as products of shared relationships (Watson 1997, 120).

The considerations about the spatial dimension of community foreground physical presence as, apparently, a necessary component of a community. Admittedly, in the traditional sense, the notion of community has been confined to physical proximity (Mitra 1997). The critics of CMC-based communities question the authenticity of these communities by asserting that life in cyberspace can never be meaningful or complete because true communities rely on interaction on a face-to-face basis (Weinreich 1997). CMC cannot substitute for the sensual experience of meeting one another face-to-face, and therefore cyberspace can offer nothing more than just a technological ersatz for real life communities (see Rheingold 2000/1993; see also Baym 1998). Nevertheless, Rheingold asserts that the strong relationships that users develop through CMCs are, potentially, more valuable, as those individuals with whom one interacts are selected "more by commonality of interests and goals than by accidents of proximity" (2000/1993, 24).[25] Besides, just as other technologies (e.g. the telephone) have fragmented people's social lives and constructed new social spaces, CMC technologies have created a social situation for the formation of a new understanding of the term *community* (Cutler 1995, 12).

In addition, as CMCs appear to make the traditional condition of co-presence obsolete, the new understanding of community requires a new, extended sense of presence, larger than that tied to a geographic location (see also Benschop 1997). Both Cutler (1995) and Benschop (1997) argue that in the context of cyberspace, networks of social relations, as well as dyadic social relations, are understood in terms of social presence, because the presence of the communication partner is experienced as a social reality. This argumentation additionally supports the view that there is no

---

[25] Still, some researchers disagree that common interest is sufficient to generate a sense of community (see e.g. Baym 1998).

absolute need to include a spatial dimension in the concept of virtual communities.

As we could see above, the discussion on the spatial dimension of virtual collectivities discloses the confusion surrounding the term community, a confusion which existed even prior to the advent of group-CMCs and which brings us again to the definition of "traditional" communities (Fernback and Thompson 1995; Fernback 1997; Wellman and Gulia 1999). Fernback acknowledges that "community is a term which seems readily definable to the general public but is infinitely complex and amorphous in academic discourse" (1997, 39). When referring to the distinction between material and symbolic dimensions of the concept of community, it seems that symbolic values, such as shared interests, norms, beliefs, etc., are a sufficient binding force for a virtual community. This could also be expressed with reference to Tönnies' distinction between *Gemainschaft* vs. *Gesellschaft*, with Rhinegold's community functioning as a traditional, Gemainschaft-like community. Still, Fernback reconsiders his idea that in cyberspace shared interests alone are likely to generate enough communal spirit and social bonding (see also Baym 1998; Watson 1997). Although communities of interest do not command full engagement on the part of interacting individuals, users still can profit from their shallow membership at a relatively small cost. Watson holds that even the terminology of the medium, such as e.g. *user*, *information retrieval*, etc., implies that no commitment is required to participate in a group interaction. Watson invokes Postman's (1993) emphasis on common obligation as a central component of a community. Online communities lack the consequences of participating in common obligations, and thus the application of the term community to online formations pollutes this concept (Watson 1997, 122). Besides, formations organised by interest (i.e. on similarity) may be accused of homogeneity, as their participants do not have to deal with diversity (Baym 1998, 36).

When defining the concept of a virtual community, researchers also find it useful to compare online collectivities to their modern offline counterparts. At the same time, attention is drawn to the contemporary conceptions of community, in which priority is given to the symbolic or ideological dimension of the community. Namely, the emphasis is put on the factors that bind individuals culturally, i.e. solidarity and social interaction, the production and consumption of goods, the collective formation of goals and implementation of policy, and their shared experiences and symbolic constructions (Fernback 1997, 40). Thus, as Watson argues, the application of the term *community* to the context of cyberspace may be based on the conviction that the seemingly continuous presence of people in CMC interaction and their knowledge capital as a collective good are sufficient criteria of a community as known from the offline world (Watson 1997, 105).

In addition, the eagerness to refer to online collectivities as virtual communities may result from the present day nostalgia for the so called lost, "true" sense of community in modern life (S. Jones 1997, 11). It could make people particularly responsive to the emergent opportunities and evoked hopes that the Internet would recreate such a community, overcoming the constraints of time and space. Similarly, Fernback holds that "we tend to think of communities in the somewhat romanticized terms laid out by Ferdinand Tönnies and George Simmel during the late nineteenth century – as places where social interaction, shared value systems, and shared symbol systems governed the sense of community characterised by an organic notion of fellowship, custom, understanding, and consensus" (1997, 39).

The conceptualisation of the term *virtual community* poses fewer problems when virtual communities are compared to their modern real life counterparts. According to Wellman and Gulia (1999), community networks have for long been affected by technological changes. Thanks to cars, planes or phones, community networks are already possible over long distances. Thus, communities do not have to exist as "solidary, densely knit groups of neighbours", but rather "as social networks of kin, friends, and workmates who do not necessarily live in the same neighbourhoods" (Wellman and Gulia 1999, 169).

It must be also stated that most contemporary communities in the developed world (i.e. in technologically saturated societies) are just aggregations of atomised individuals organised into discrete geographic-legal units (Fernback and Thompson 1995). According to Wellman and Gulia, post-industrial societies are socially diverse, sparsely knit and well connected to the outside world. Modern real life communities are only partial communities which do not command a person's full allegiance: rather each person is a limited member of multiple, heterogeneous and low-density communities such as kinship groups, neighbourhoods and friendship circles. Community ties are geographically dispersed, sparsely knit, connected heavily by telecommunication and specialised in content (Wellman and Gulia 1999, 187). It seems then that the development of CMC has only reinforced the evolution of human communities into partial communities, which, however, are communities that offer a form of efficient social contact (see S. Jones 1998a).

As regards interpersonal relationships developed in CMC-based communities, the Internet supports a diversity of both strong and weak ties. As Wellman and Gulia (1999, 186) argue, the relationships people develop and maintain in cyberspace resemble their modern real life counterparts: they are intermittent, specialised and varying in strength to enable individuals to obtain a wide variety of resources. In addition, Baym (1998, 38) advances a hypothesis that virtual communities do not really serve as a substitute for off-line communities. On the contrary, online communities can be used to enhance or extend geographically local communities, as frequently people enter CMC interactions with pre-existing face-to-face relationships. Thus, apart from reinforcing the fragmentation of public life, cyberspace has the potential to integrate society, which validates the argument that virtual collectivities support contradictory phenomena (see Davis 1997). "Specialised newsgroups, discussion lists and the like foster multiple memberships in partial communities. At the same time, the ease of group response and forwarding can foster the folding-in of formerly separate Net-participants into more all-encompassing communities" (Wellman and Gulia 1999, 187). Besides, the ties that cut across various social groups enable the creation of cyberlinks between groups that otherwise would be socially and physically dispersed.

In conclusion, research on virtual community, indeed, discloses its problematic character and suggests that some re-conceptualisation of the notion *community* is needed, so that it could better apply to the types of contemporary social collectivities that are in existence, also in cyberspace. At the same time, however, the above discussion shows that the concept of a community is dynamic in nature, and that, as society and communication technologies evolve, it evolves concurrently (see Benschop 1997; Fernback and Thompson 1995; Fernback 1997; Mitra 1997; Q. Jones 1997; Watson 1997; Wellman and Gulia 1999). As Watson contends:

> Just as the emergence of nation-states transformed the meaning of "community" in our collective consciousness to fit a new world situation, so the rise of CMC technologies is operating to alter the meaning of this term again. (…) [W]e have seen our understanding of "community" shift from simple geographic proximity to communication and intimacy as social organisation grew with the Industrial Revolution. (Watson 1997, 123)

Evidently, the structure of cyberspace and CMC situations fosters significant alterations in the size, composition and structure of communities. As already stated, virtual communities appear to be groups affiliated around mutual interests rather than based on social characteristics, geographic proximity, or historical or ethnic origins. Thus, virtual communities are probably relatively homogenous with respect to participants' interests and attitudes, and relatively heterogeneous in participants' social backgrounds. In addition to shared interests, virtual collectivities must develop shared norms, collective beliefs, shared language and meanings, to be truly cohesive communities.

The tendency of CMCs to foster participation in multiple partial communities results in the construction of communities which are less stable than traditional, geographic, historic or ethnic communities, allowing a rapid and frequent fluctuation of members. Participation in virtual communities is well illustrated by Cutler's concept of the fluid forms of community. In his view, in virtual communities, a sense of community is achieved through the flexibility of distributed presences and selves, and the new social situations of cyberspace:

> Our distributed selves lead fluid existences that need distributed points of contact. A variety of media supply 'places' to become not merely audiences but presences acting for personal and public benefit. Privately we create a 'networked' sense of self. Publicly we find places to express ourselves, form our fluid identities, and receive the support to help us keep a sense of self-cohesion. (Cutler 1995, 27)

4.3. Approaches to the study of virtual communities

The analyses of CMC-based communities reveal the problems related to the currently existing methodology of research: how to study the symbolic inter-human connections that are allowed and structured by new technology? Evidently, the study of social collectivities in cyberspace questions the classical dimensions of scientific research in the disciplines that address the relationship between the individual, the community and its communicative practices. Similarly, modern linguistics faces a challenge of how to study individuals' linguistic behaviour in CMC situations, which are not only complex sites of social interaction, but also hold the potential of being effective analytic tools. They may offer possibilities of flexible and inexpensive collecting, organising and exploring digital data. However, there is still little understanding about how these tools might be used. For instance, the tools give an excellent possibility to fix electronic discourse by capturing text and information, but "does the very ability to record it [electronic discourse] in some fashion make us feel more certain we can put it under a microscope?" (S. Jones 1998, 4).

Ample research on CMC-based collectivities has concentrated on the discussion of various approaches and methodologies (e.g. Benschop 1997; Kollock and Smith 1999; Paccagnella 1997; S. Jones 1998; Preece and

Maloney-Kirchmar 2005)), on virtual communities' success (e.g. Mitra 1997; 1999; Rheingold 2000/1993; Watson 1997) or failure (e.g. Kolko and Reid 1998), and on their social dynamics (e.g. Reid 1991, 1994, 1999; DuVal Smith 1999; Watson 1997). In the discussion that follows I will focus on those approaches that foreground the relevance of linguistic practices for the functioning of virtual communities. My intention will be to show how linguistic explorations of communities in cyberspace can profit from the approaches and methodologies offered by other disciplines that address the social context of language use, such as ethnography, sociology and CMC research.

4.3.1. A virtual community as an *imagined community*

An interesting conception of a virtual community is built around Anderson's (1983) idea of an *imagined community* (see Baym 1998; Mitra 1997; S. Jones 1997). The model of an imagined virtual community draws on Anderson's argument that "all communities beyond the primal face-to-face interaction are imagined, a process enabled by mass media" (Baym 1998, 38). The essential elements of the conception of imagined communities are the following: (1) communities (as well as nations) are imagined around shared cultural practices, which allows to transcend a historical and geographic characterisation (see Mitra 1997); (2) the genuineness of communities lies in the style in which they are imagined; (3) in one way, online communities "are forged from the sense that they exist", because "we think, and sometimes feel, we belong to Internet communities" (S. Jones 1997, 17); (4) in another way, according to Jones, communities are imagined as "parallel groupings", i.e. groupings of people that are bound by the same goals.

Mitra finds the conception of an imagined community useful for the study of the presence of diasporic Indians in an electronic forum. Her intention is to look for the community's image or "imaging", i.e. "thc ways in which a community can textually produce itself, thus imagine itself – as well as present itself to the outside world" (1997, 55). The construct of an imagined community helps to understand how diasporic people construct their image of their community by means of the computer and Internet connections, the medium which allows the shared system of culture, beliefs and language to be spread across large distances.

In her search for the style in which a virtual community can be imagined, Baym claims that a virtual community's style is shaped by a set of pre-existing structures that include external contexts, temporal structure, system infrastructure, group purposes, and participants' characteristics

(1998, 38). Participants of a group interaction exploit these structures as the resources to construct shared social meanings, out of which the most significant are the emergence of group-specific forms of expression, identities, relationships, and normative conventions. This "dynamic set of systematic social meanings" enables participants to imagine themselves as a community. Baym applies her conception to the study of community in a Usenet group and manages to discover the manifestations of an emergent online community. The participants of the group under study develop forms of expression that allow them to codify and transmit group-specific meanings, negotiate group-specific identities, build a range of relationships, and establish norms that serve to regulate group interaction and organisation.

4.3.2. A virtual community as a social network

The conceptual revolution that moved from defining community in terms of space to defining it in terms of social networks (Wellman 1997; Wellman and Gulia 1999) encouraged the application of a social network approach to the study of online collectivities. S. Jones (1998a) argues that the focus on social networks is particularly suitable for defining social formations in cyberspace, as it redirects an analyst's attention from place to interactions that create communities. "In media that shift not only the sense of space but the sense of place, decentering (though not removing) the consideration of territory is necessary to permit entry of notions of power and its analysis" (1998, 20). The recognition of a social network approach for the impact of online socializing appears also in Rheingold's "Rethinking Virtual Communities", the chapter added to the later edition of *The Virtual Community. Homesteading on the Electronic Frontier.* "Social network analysis (…) counters the critique of virtual communities as alienating, dehumanizing substitute for more direct, less mediated human contact" (Rheingold 2000/ 1993, 361).

Paolillo (1999) proves the feasibility of a social network approach to the study of language variation and change in IRC, but also revealing some shortcomings of the current linguistic research. Through qualitative and quantitative analyses of logfiles of IRC interaction, Paolillo aims to find out CMC's impact on social contact among interacting individuals, and the kinds of transmitted linguistic features. To examine how the users' linguistic practices are established on IRC channels, Paolillo focuses on the study of both the network of participants' social interactions and the relationship of those social patterns to the distribution of the chosen linguistic variables. The logfiles of users' interaction can serve to directly measure the frequency of interaction, which, in turn, will enable to identify strong and weak network ties, but the formation of these on IRC channels will be different. Paolillo manages to discover network tie strength among the participants of interaction, and the correlation of tie strength with the linguistic variables. In this way, he obtained a picture of the function of linguistic variables as markers of social position, which, as Paolillo admits, cannot be readily obtained through other means. In addition, his findings prompt further research on how linguistic variables are disseminated through social networks in online environments.

4.3.3. A *virtual settlement* approach

The appeal of a *virtual settlement* theory (Q. Jones 1997) lies in its concentration on cultural artefacts of virtual collectivities, as these artefacts can provide an integrative framework for a community life. For me, the theory's additional advantage is its relation to a discourse community approach, advocated in this book (see Section 1.2.2 in Chapter 1 and Section 4.3.5 of the present chapter), as it encourages the focus on the analysis of the "material" aspect of a virtual community, i.e. produced text, and thus, contributes to the study of genre formation.

In his theory, Q. Jones takes an archaeological approach and argues that *virtual settlement* (i.e. cyber-place, or the environment of a particular CMC situation) is a prerequisite condition for the emergence and sustaining of a virtual community, and consequently, a proof of its presence. To be considered a virtual settlement, it is necessary for a cyber-place to meet a set of 4 conditions: (1) a minimum level of interactivity; (2) a variety of communicators; (3) a common-public-space where a significant portion of a community's interactive group-CMC occurs; (4) a minimum level of sustained membership. Once identified, a *virtual settlement* can by characterised by means of an empirical description of its CMC-message system, based on such variables as the number of subscribers, the number of active posters, the density of posting, the number and longevity of topics over a particular period of time, the average length of postings, etc. These will also be the variables I will use to build the context of interaction in the academic discussion list under my study.

Jones' theory was adopted to test for the existence of virtual community in an IRC[26] channel (Liu 1999). Liu adapted Jones' list of 4 conditions to the technical context of IRC, and extended the list by additional factors to account for particular characteristics of IRC-based

---

[26] IRC stands for "internet relay chat", a synchronous form of CMC.

group communication. In general, Liu's research proves that: (1) it is possible to test empirically for the existence of a virtual community; (2) the stability of membership can be accurately examined in terms of the sustained level of participants' co-appearance; (3) nickname stability should be included as an additional condition of virtual community existence in IRC; (4) the analysis of interactivity should focus on verbal and action-simulating messages, and on message content as well as on message directing; (5) the time difference between a referring message and the referred-to message should be incorporated into analysis and coding of message references.

4.3.4. A *structuration* approach

Watson's (1997) *structuration* approach focuses on the development of social norms and internal values as markers of a virtual community's presence and its boundaries. This approach is based on Gidden's (1984) theory of structuration, where structuration refers to the communicative processes all communities establish their borders and build their internal values. Watson argues that the success of the community he studied (i.e. the Phish.net) comes from its ability to develop tools for the maintenance of intimacy, behavioural norms, and values in order to preserve its integrity, especially in the face of the population's growth, which could endanger the collectivity's intimacy (Watson 1997, 116). In Watson's view, the processes of attaining and maintaining group intimacy are the factors that have to be measured in order to evaluate the genuineness of an online formation as a community. What is also important, the emergence of values, behavioural norms, and other such structures must derive from within community rather than be imposed externally: it must stem from a collectivity's needs and goals.

Watson observed that Phish.netters form a "true" community because they use both internal and external communication to proclaim their internal values, strengthen the borders of their community against outsiders, and legislate behaviour outside of the community according to the norms and values established within the community (1997, 110). This can be achieved through such means as: organisation of off-screen actions, attempts to subdivide the community (to isolate the place for the most dedicated members of the community), increase in the use of in-group language to protect from outsiders or "false" fans. Watson concludes that the Phish.net collectivity succeeded as a community because "structuration of normative behaviour within Phish.net community has been also the result of a repeated and continued need to affirm the foundational values of the community in the face of threats to those values" (1997, 119). Watson's observations confirm the importance of community values and norms for the community emergence and maintenance, and, just as the previously mentioned research did (Baym 1998; Mitra 1997), indicate an essential focus of analysis in the research on virtual communities.

Similarly, the significance of social conventions and shared symbolic meanings as elements of a community's culture is ascertained by Reid's research on virtual community (see Reid 1991 for the analysis of internet relay chats and Reid 1994, 1995 for the analyses of text-based virtual worlds). Reid argues that in the communities she studied, freedom from traditional social conventions necessitated the establishment of new conventions for the community to become cohesive. Thus, these online formations have proved to develop systems of unique symbolism and textual significance which enable them to achieve understanding, and which define these communities as distinct cultures. Here, culture is understood as a set of behaviours and rules which give a significance to common experiences and problems (see Reid 1994). Reid establishes that an online community is a self-regulating, hierarchical structure, whose integrity is kept through the cultivation of shared rules and rituals, and the implementation of controlling procedures, such as e.g. the punishment of transgressors who violate the shared system of values.

4.3.5. A discourse community approach

The concept of a discourse community has already proved an efficient tool in the analysis of linguistic behaviour in general, and of individual and group identity (see Chapter 1, Section 1.2.2.). It has also become an attractive conception for the explorations of individuals' communicative practices in cyberspace.

For instance, the reference to the notion of a discourse community[27] (as well as to the related notions of Foucault's (1972) discursive formation and Fish's (1980) interpretive community) appears in Mitra's (1999) attempt to conceptualise the notion of a virtual community, where she is concerned with the investigation of community presence among diasporic Indians on WWW. Mitra argues that in the study of virtual community, a point of departure should be the analysis of text. More specifically, the discovery of how members of a collectivity appropriate the textual and discursive opportunities provided by the medium will lead to a better understanding of the community of the texts' authors.

---

[27] As defined by Bizell (1982).

The essence of this approach is "the connection between discourse and community where it is suggested that communities are produced around discourses and the existence of communities is predicated upon the way in which network of texts are able to signify meaning to the community while the texts become signifiers for the communities as well" (Mitra 1999). Thus, the shared discursive practices, which concern the ways texts are understood, read and produced, can disclose the characteristics of the discourse community formed around the texts. An important element of a discourse community approach is the recognition of the existence of a priori conditions that constitute the community by providing a context for the formation of the community (see also Baym 1995). Among members of an academic community part of this context could the shared concern for the dissemination of knowledge.

Another example of the recognition of the usefulness of a discourse community approach for the study of virtual communities is Erickson's genre situated theory (1997). From the perspective of a designer of the infrastructure for supporting online discourse, Erickson encourages the focus on the instances of genre (i.e. shared artefacts) rather than on the assumed relationships among participants. Erickson stresses the following benefits of a genre–oriented analysis: (1) a possibility to analyse CMC discourse from the perspective of genre: identification of a communicative purpose, regularities of form and substance, and the situation, i.e. the institutional, social and technological forces that underlie the regularities of form; (2) a focus on the medium within which the discourse is embodied: how the digital medium supports the regularities, and how it enables participants of interaction to establish and reinforce the underlying conventions of the discourse.

Erickson defines a genre as a patterning of communication, whose conventions are generated in response to socially defined, recurrent situations (see Erickson 1997, 1999). Genres serve multiple roles for a community: (1) they are means of accomplishing social actions and other social purposes in particular situations, such as e.g. the recruitment of new members, or the construction of group and individual identity through the maintenance of a genre's characteristics; (2) they shape communication by creating shared expectations about the form and content of interaction, thus facilitating the processes of text production and interpretation. Thus, the analysis of textual behaviour of a given community can provide not only means to discover the textual conventions of particular genres, but also the mechanisms of regulating a community's integrity, or the mechanisms of culture building.

As regards the focus on the medium of interaction, it is necessary to emphasise its role as both a site and context of communicative events, the role combined with CMC's great flexibility and a range of practical potentials of software supporting CMC, where electronic storage and form of a digital document contributes to this malleability. As a result, the digital medium becomes an effective tool for conducting efficient quantitative and qualitative analyses of discourse. For instance, the medium provides efficient methods of processing electronic documents, or, of mapping and counting interactions in forms of group communication. The digital medium allows to develop means of establishing a degree of participants' membership in virtual communities, through measuring a degree of their participation in interaction, e.g. on the basis of density of postings. In this way, the medium will allow to tackle multiple memberships in virtual discourse communities – an important, for the purposes of the present research, aspect of social being in cyberspace. Furthermore, as Erickson (1997) asserts, even in situations when participation in CMC interactions will prove insignificant, the analysis of electronic discourse will still be relevant for genre theory, discourse analysis, or computer infrastructure designing.

When developing a new, discourse-community-based conceptual framework for tackling social interaction in cyberspace, it is necessary to distinguish between a virtual community itself and its cyberplace (i.e. its *virtual settlement*, to use Q. Jones' term, 1997; see also Erickson 1997). As Jones argues, only if a community is discerned from its material (i.e. messages or postings and the properties of a particular CMC system), it is possible to determine when a series of group-CMC demonstrates the existence of a virtual community. For Q. Jones, this distinction can provide a basis for what he terms "cyber-archeology", focusing on cultural artefacts that determine an integrative framework for a community's life. Whereas in Erickson's situated genre theory, the need for the same distinction results from the focus on a CMC system itself. According to Erickson, a CMC system can be viewed as an ecology of genres, "in which the various genres are interdependent and act to support the functioning of the system as a whole" (1999). The idea of genre repertoires owned by a community, combined with the notion of interdependence expressed in the concept of discourse systems, may serve to provide a useful conceptual framework for talking about CMC-based communities.

Lastly, in relation to the application of a discourse community approach to the context of cyberspace, Erickson points to the fact that textual conventions are shaped, reinforced, or renegotiated much more rapidly in the flexible digital medium (Erickson 1997, 1999). On the one hand, in the fluid and heterogeneous context of CMC, text can serve as a relatively secure research ground (see Wilk 2000). On the other hand, the malleability of the medium affects text not only on the level of individual documents, but also more globally, on the level of genres, which shifts the burden of stability from the technical to the institutional sphere of CMC-based communities (Yates and Summer 1997). In addition, the fluidity of the digital medium, and the potential for a strengthened connection between a genre (or a repertoire of genres) and its discourse community, will accelerate the processes of genre formation, modification and enactment, and consequently, the evolution of genres in general.

A discourse community approach developed primarily as a method of analysing text-based discourse in institutional or disciplinary contexts (see e.g. Swales 1990; Mauranen 1993; Scollon and Scollon 1995), and thus I find it useful for the study of academic communication in cyberspace. Yet, new issues emerge when a genre-oriented analysis is applied to the digital medium, which calls for a need to redefine, or extend, the notion of a discourse community. As I argued in Sokół (2004), a discourse community approach can provide an effective framework for the study of a virtual community, but a set of parameters needs to be established for measuring and evaluating the properties of textual and interactional behaviour in CMC-based communities. Only then, the fuzzy (see Swales 1990; Duszak 1998a), and perhaps "esoteric" (Swales 1993), notion of a discourse community can stand a chance of becoming a more settled notion, thus offering a basis for a more efficient empirical analysis and description of linguistic and social phenomena in cyberspace.

Virtual communities are mainly text-based groupings, in which textual conventions are created in response to specific institutional, social and technological elements of CMC systems. Therefore, being grounded in Swales' genre theory, an extended conceptualisation of a discourse community that focuses on shared textual practices, may be used to study academic communication phenomena in cyberspace. A discourse community approach holds the potential to capture an increasing complexity of contemporary scholarly exchange, that cuts across the multiple affiliations, disciplines and communicative contexts.

4.4. Computer-mediated communication and academic exchange

The spread of CMC and network technologies has necessarily, and substantially, transformed formal and informal scholarly communication, both globally and locally. In general, the changes include: (1) the restructuring of scholarly networks, and of informal scholarly networks in particular (see the "etherisation" of academic networks, "glocalisation", the transformation of the "invisible college"; (2) the emergence of new modes of scholarly communication, and work and research tools; (3) the alterations in work patterns; (4) the evolution of academic genres, forms of scholarly publication and knowledge storage.

As Koku et al argue (2001), also an academic community, which has expanded into cyberspace, has been affected by an ongoing paradigm shift in the organisation of social structures and institutions, a shift largely facilitated by the growth in the use of CMC and the Internet. Namely, social and institutional connections are being built through social networks – more flexible structures with permeable boundaries, rather than through hierarchically structured and clearly demarcated groups. In effect, the networks of scholars emerge as structures which are strongly connected, though spatially-dispersed and loosely-delimited. Moreover, the transformed scholarly networks reveal the ongoing "glocalisation", where CMC supports the consolidation of local interconnections, simultaneously enhancing their global expansion.

The reconstruction of scholarly networks is frequently viewed as the transformation of the "invisible college", and the related "etherisation" of scholarly networks (see Gresham 1994; Matzatz 2001; 2004; Koku et al 2001). The term "invisible college" originally refers to an informal network of scientific specialists "who function as the scholarly in-group within a given specialization" (Gresham 1994, 38). The main role of an invisible college is to disseminate knowledge and facilitate research within the specialisation through informal information exchange in conference and research centres. Gresham's review of research also indicates other significant functions of invisible colleges: supporting group identity and purpose, offering current and specialised information within a given area, sharing and testing new ideas, exchanging practical information about research and funding opportunities, contributing to interdisciplinary diffusion of ideas. As regards the drawbacks of invisible colleges, Gresham recounts their elitist and restrictive nature (limited size and restricted access opportunities) and high costs (e.g. resulting from high costs of participating in conferences; Gresham 1994, 38).

The growth in the use of CMC among scholars, particularly of email and discussion groups, have moved invisible colleges into cyberspace and extended research networks in general. In Gresham's view, the major benefit of the emergent "cyberspace college" is its potential to equalize the distribution of communication possibilities among scholars, irrespective of their status, experience or level of expertise. A "cyberspace college" reinforces the capacity of an invisible college for an informal scholarly networking, through overcoming the boundaries of geography, access and social barriers. Gresham notes the following scholarly and social benefits of discussion groups[28] as "cyberspace colleges": (1) communication with an international community of scholars; (2) communication with scholars within and outside one's specialization; (3) searching out and learning about "traditional" and electronic academic resources; (4) reviewing and debating new publications in the field; (5) meeting and interviewing experts for research; (6) exchange and critique of pre-publication papers; (7) doing collaborative research and writing; (8) sharing teaching tips and materials; (9) seeking advice for research and fieldwork from more experienced scholars; (10) gathering advice and bibliographic suggestions for dissertation research; (11) observing and/or participating in discussion beyond academia; (12) following up-to-date accounts and evaluations of new discoveries; (13) learning about research and publication opportunities; (14) receiving feedback on new ideas; (15) creating new contacts and maintaining relationships with distant colleagues; (16) chatting; (17) becoming part of a virtual community (18) overcoming the ephemeral nature of information in invisible colleges through offering searchable records of information exchanges (Gresham 1994, 44–45, 47). The only shortcomings of computer conferencing mentioned by Gresham are problems related to the transmission of trivial or irrelevant information (cf. information overload).

Similar advantages and disadvantages of the use of electronic discussion groups by members of academia are also mentioned in the analyses of academic electronic forums from the perspective of their owners and/or moderators (e.g. Berge and Collins 1993; McCarty 1992). McCarty emphasises the role of an academic discussion group as an electronic seminar (e-seminar), organised for the purposes of academic argumentation and collaboration, and whose main aim is to train the minds of interactants, to further an understanding of a given subject, and to facilitate community building. The cross-cultural context of an electronic seminar is a place where professional, intellectual, social and political purposes intermingle, as in any academic gathering. An interesting point is also the peripheral, although by no means insignificant, status of e-seminar in professional career development. A member's active participation in a discussion may support research and intellectual development, but is not a formally acknowledged measure of expertise and productivity. In

[28] To refer collectively to all kinds of discussion forums on the Internet, Gresham uses the term *computer conferencing*. Thus, he refers to both academic and non-academic discussion groups by members of academia.

addition, the peripheral status of an e-seminar allows for the introduction of humour, a factor which is favourable for learning, teaching and scholarly exploration.

Apart from the opportunities for professional advancement, networking and equality, Berge and Collins (1993) indicate the nominal cost of membership in a discussion group, and overcoming space and time dependence. While the drawbacks of moderated discussion forums include the possibility of censorship and the lack of standardised rules of conduct. However, much as being an obstacle in the free formation of ideas, gentle editorial presence of a moderator, as well as self-control and collegial pressure among members are sufficient factors regulating the norms of interaction in an e-seminar (see also McCarty 1992).

Other explorations into the role of the Internet and discussion groups for academia provide evidence primarily for changes in work patterns (Lubański and Matthew 1998), contact benefits and knowledge transmission and development (Ekeblad 1998, 1999; Matzatz 2001, 2004). Lubański and Matthew's (1998) concern is the socio-economic impact of the Internet in academic research environments, on the example of empirical researchers in economic and social sciences. The findings demonstrate the appreciation of Internet data services for the growth in productivity and quality of research. Empirical researchers under study use the Internet resources for the following purposes: (1) contribution to and exploitation of the data services; (2) distribution of research papers; (3) searching for teaching and learning support; (4) research collaboration and joint authorship. In addition, the researchers value the Internet resources, as they contribute to the increase in the quality of their research, e.g. through the integration of the Internet into research methods. At the same time, criticism is expressed against the uncertain quality of Internet publications. On the one hand, the Internet creates opportunities for quick and easy publication of research results. On the other, this easiness and lack of standards make researchers view unrefereed publications with scepticism.

In her analysis of the dynamics of a scholarly mailing list, Ekeblad (1998, 1999) argues that the conspicuous part of the activity on a list is the collective advancement of knowledge and understanding. This is enabled by the multilogical[29] features of CMC, which largely facilitate the processes of idea development and make a mailing list an efficient learning environment. Whereas Matzatz's (2001, 2004) analysis indicates

[29] To refer to the verbal interaction on a mailing list, Ekeblad uses the term *multilogue*, which ideally reflects the character of computer-mediated, multi-party exchange taking place on a list.

information and social benefits of discussion groups, but the evidence for gaining contact benefits surpasses the evidence for gaining information benefits. Admittedly, researchers under study find discussion lists valuable for (1) obtaining research information; (2) increasing the visibility of their research within and outside the discipline; (3) constructing contact links that facilitate the exchange of published and unpublished works. Matzat does not find clear evidence that participation in discussion lists among academia leads to the changes in the long-term collaboration networks of researchers. Moreover, although discussion groups offer more opportunities to access informal communication channels, especially for peripheral researchers[30], the findings do not support the equalizing effects of discussion groups. Academic discussion lists prove to contribute to the extension of researchers' communication network and become effective tools used for specific purposes.

The transformation of informal scholarly networks is also referred to as the "etherisation" of scholarly networks (Koku et al 2001). The "etherisation" of research networks signifies the intensified scholarly communication of findings and ideas, circulated through computer networks in the form of "ethereal papers" sent as attachments to email, or announcements, queries, debates or comments posted to academic discussion groups. The authors point to the general role of email in scholarly communication, and the integration of scholarly networks. Email's easy accessibility, ubiquity, velocity and multiple-message characteristics support the construction of weak ties and the flow of research information across diverse intellectual and social environments, between scholars on both the core and periphery. In effect, scholarly networks emerge as heterogeneous structures that do not demand total commitment, thus allowing unobtrusive and fluctuating membership in multiple groups. In addition, Koku et al argue that email has extended the possibilities of rapid and efficient exchange among networked members of academia, but by no means replaced FTF contact, nor determined how scholars communicate.

In the contemporary, globalised world, interaction in and through CMC has become almost a necessity for members of an academic community. Academics make use of various types of CMCs to realise various personal and practical aims. One of these aims could be using the new electronic media for self-promotion of one's name and academic

[30] The peripherality of a researcher implies a moderate number of contacts with other researchers relating to the regular exchange of written research papers. It is contrasted with the integration of a researcher.

activity. This, because of the possibilities offered by CMC, may become a powerful way of gaining recognition and building one's authority. In Chapter 5 I will present the empirical analysis of identity construction in an asynchronous type of CMC, an Internet discussion group, also referred to as an electronic seminar.

CHAPTER FIVE

ACADEMIC IDENTITY CONSTRUCTION IN AN E-SEMINAR: ANALYSIS AND DISCUSSION

Chapter 5 presents the empirical analysis of the linguistic cues of academic identity in electronic discourse, on the example of an e-seminar. In the initial sections of the chapter I will introduce the research subjects: the e-forum *Humanist* and its six active members, including the seminar's moderator. Having described the corpora used in my study, I will outline the theoretical framework of my research, its methodology, main objectives and the deriving hypotheses. Then, I will proceed to a detailed presentation of the analysis of my data. In general, my aim will be to specify the linguistic means of authorial presence on three levels of discourse organisation: the features of lexico-grammar, textual macrostructures and genres.

I will argue that the discoursal construction of academic identity in electronic discourse depends on such factors as the medium's defining properties, the lack of direct physical contact between interactants, on the norms and institutionalised practices of an academic community, but also on the needs and goals of the individuals. Most importantly, the analysis will demonstrate the individuating character of the medium, which has important consequences for how, in this context, scholars present their academic achievements and expertise, and construct a stable professional identity.

5.1. Presenting the *Humanist* discussion group

The discussion list under investigation is a moderated list established in 1987[31], whose main aim is to discuss a range of issues within the

---

[31] Detailed information about the *Humanist* can be found in McCarty 1992. Other data are also available on the *Humanist*'s Internet page, at:

multidisciplinary area of computational humanities (humanities computing) and the digital humanities. On the technical level, the *Humanist* is a distribution list, where messages from any member on the list are redistributed to other members, either automatically or with the mediation of a human moderator.

The *Humanist* is viewed by its moderator as an e-seminar, whose main aim is to facilitate intellectual self-development through interactive debates and to contribute to the dissemination of knowledge and the strengthening of an academic community (McCarty 1992). However, because of its cross-cultural context, this seminar is a place where professional, intellectual, social and political purposes merge. An interesting point is also the peripheral, although by no means insignificant, status of e-seminars in professional career development. A member's active participation in a discussion may support research and intellectual development, though it is not a formally acknowledged measure of expertise and productivity. In addition, the peripheral status of an e-seminar allows for the introduction of humour, a factor which is favourable for scholarly exploration. For the moderator's discussion of informality in the *Humanist* discussions and the forum's general role for members of academia see example (1) below[32]:

> (1) (…) what is electronic publication? how does it relate to other forms of "making public"? what are its inherent characteristics? Humanist's membership has shown that electronic mail and literate English are not incompatible. Humanists have done this by disciplining themselves to take some care with what they write. At the same time Humanist has evolved with the gradual discovery of what the medium is and what it is and is not good for. I would argue that although it may be used in a trivial way, there is nothing inherently trivial about it.
>
> Informality does seem inherent, however. In terms of formality, electronic seminars such as Humanist can, I think, be located somewhere between the written letter or essay and the spoken conversation or unprepared talk. Perhaps not less care but certainly less self-censorship or regulation goes into an electronic piece than into a written one, at least under such circumstances as ListServ provides. At the same time, we e-mailers are naturally more sparing with what we type into our computers that what we might speak into a telephone or at a convivial gathering.
>
> Apart from the exchange of raw information, things like Humanist seem to be particularly suited to free-ranging discussion, during which some truth emerges. A creative combination of watchfulness and relaxation

---

http://www.princeton.edu/~mccarty/humanist/.

[32] In all the quoted examples throughout the book, I have kept the authors' original spelling and punctuation.

allows for discovery that, I think, would not otherwise happen. We can and frequently do try out ideas in a way not possible elsewhere. Perhaps we like Humanist partly because such give-and-take of ideas is not something we can easily find among our face-to-face colleagues anymore, who are too busy being pressured and so cannot easily think slowly and generously about important matters the world has no time for. In any case, with e-mail "talking" one's way to understanding is possible. (MoA; 05.07.1989; Subject: informal and trivial)

The role of the *Humanist*'s moderator is crucial for several reasons. Primarily, he monitors or edits submissions to the list, and provokes and guides discussion. He cultivates a distinct editorial voice in order to indirectly indicate the language and style proper to the seminar. This decision results from the moderator's conviction that "an electronic seminar would gain respect and attract thoughtful people only if it were itself to embody what it sought: mindfulness, and love of language, including respect for spelling, grammar, style and accuracy of expression" (McCarty 1992). Indeed, the presence of the moderator constitutes a form of censorship and a gate-keeping mechanism. However, much as being an obstacle in the free formation of ideas, the gentle editorial presence of the moderator, as well as the self-control and collegial pressure among members are sufficient factors regulating the norms of interaction in the e-seminar. Here is a fragment from the posting in which the moderator comments on his managerial and editorial responsibilities within the *Humanist*:

(2) (…) Once again I think we need to take stock of what we're doing with Humanist and to impose on ourselves some restraint.

The long and very bulky discussion that began with "education and the universities", then mutated into physical and metaphorical "uncertainty", and has settled into variations on the theme of "anti-intellectualism" has become oppressive. As reader of Humanist I have felt the unpleasant weight of this discussion, and some others have told me likewise. Were we all sitting around a table in a seminar, we would doubtless have seen by now grimaces of discomfort at certain points, even perhaps heard the sorts of noises that people produce when they're impatient. E-mail makes for a semiotically deprived global village, so occasionally the headman (that's me) has to step in and say what would have been communicated much more effectively by subverbal means in person long ago.

Yes, I have been sloppy as editor, but sometimes with a purpose. When I have had a method in my sloppiness, it has been to encourage the experimental aspects of Humanist. Now in its third year, it does different things less often than in its first few months, but innovations happen, and these delight not just me, I think. We have recently developed, for

> example, an interesting query service for members with all sorts of questions. I don't see much wrong with that. Do you?
>
> Discussions, however, are another matter because they tend to be bulky. We simply must keep ourselves to our general topic, computing in the humanities, or like the creatures of fermentation, we will do ourselves in with our own most wonderful output. So, I call for a halt to the questions of anti-intellectualism (continue privately, if you will) and call again for increased awareness of what we're here for. (MoA; 26.07.1989; Subject: Enough)

Admission to the list is based on self-selection: those interested have to seek the moderator's permission to be accepted and are requested to provide their academic bio-note. The membership is truly international, but the overwhelming majority of members are from English-speaking countries (see membership statistics available at http://www.princeton .edu/~mccarty/humanist/membership.xls). The language of the seminar is English, but the use of other languages is encouraged. Actually, languages such as French, Spanish or German are only occasionally used. Finally, the size of the seminar's audience is difficult to estimate, because among the *Humanist's* subscribers, apart from individual members, there are also redistribution points such as research institutes and universities.

5.2. Describing the corpora and research subjects

Data collection for my research consisted of data retrieval from the *Humanist's* archives. The research material comprises a representative corpora of postings of six active members of the *Humanist.* As I combine diachronic and synchronic perspectives in my investigation, the selected corpora come from two periods of the members' participation in the *Humanist*: the first period covers the years 1989–1992 (period A), while the more recent period, the years 1999–2002 (period B). Given the assumption that the evolution of linguistic forms proceeds considerably quicker in the electronic medium (e.g. Erickson 1997), I decided that the span of 10 years would be sufficient to observe the changes in the discourse practices of the members under investigation.

The construction of the corpora used in the present research was preceded by the compilation of two general uncoded corpora of the *Humanist*'s selected volumes, downloaded from the list's server by means of the teleport programme (the *Humanist*'s archives are available in the Internet at http://www.kcl.ac.uk/humanities/cch/humanist/):

- General Corpus 1 of 9596 messages (3,022,470 words) from the *Humanist*'s Volumes 3–6 (the years 1989–1992);

- General Corpus 2 of 3842 messages (1,615,450) from the *Humanist*'s Volumes 13–16 (the years 1999–2002).

Because of the inconsistencies in the archiving of the *Humanist*, I pre-processed the downloaded files manually. The manual work aimed at standardising the structure of the postings so that each consisted of a header and message body, and involved the following procedures:

- removal of the unnecessary text inserted automatically by the archiving software;
- removal of any other text inserted as a result of the malfunctioning of the archiving software;
- ordering of the postings so that they all included the elements: "Date", "From", "Subject", even if these lines were not specified by the author of the posting; it would not be possible for the computer programme used for quantitative analyses to process the postings lacking in these items;
- removal of the multiple occurrences of the same posting.

Thus prepared, General Corpora 1 and 2 were subsequently processed by means of the computer software designed for the purposes of this research, operating in the Windows XP environment. The programme allowed an identification of the selected postings according to a number of tags such as date, author, and subject. The information about the postings was transferred to the MySQL[33] database and analysed quantitatively. The purpose of this macro-scale analysis was to identify the participants of the interaction during the selected periods and establish the frequency, size and topics of their contributions. My ultimate aim was to single out the most active members of the *Humanist*, who contributed to the discussions during the two selected periods. This focus on the interaction of the most frequent members allows a more efficient analysis of language variation and change at the micro-level. The most active individuals within a group are potential leaders of linguistic change, who by reason of their position in the group, their social background and patterns of behaviour accelerate the ongoing change most strongly (see Labov 2001, 34). In addition, I focus on the regular contributors to the interaction as their presence is one of the conditions of a successful scholarly seminar if its success is measured by high rates of message contribution and adoption (Rojo 1995). As Rojo argues, there is a correlation between the number of benefits

[33] The name of a popular open source database.

received by participants and the number of postings contributed to the exchange on a forum.

Six of the most active members of the *Humanist* agreed to participate in my investigation and gave their permission to use their contributions in the analysis. Thus, in effect, the investigated group consists of the *Humanist*'s moderator (hereinafter coded as Mo) and five ordinary *Humanists* (hereinafter coded as Hu1, Hu2, Hu3, Hu4 and Hu5 respectively). The biographical and/or academic data about the research subjects come from the Internet sources: their bio-notes which were posted to the *Humanist* group in fulfilment of a standard procedure encouraged by the moderator, and other messages contributed to the forum throughout the investigated periods, and personal web pages.

All the members under study are male and native speakers of English. They are established members of an academic community, affiliated to recognised academic institutions in Great Britain and the United States. At the time of conducting the research, five members were professors, and all six were holding important academic positions within their institutions. The academics under investigation all share an interest in the area of humanities computing. More precisely, they represent the following disciplines and areas of study: philosophy, religion and ethics, literature (one of them is also a recognised writer of fiction), computerisation of scholarly methodology and electronic text analyses.

5.3. Objectives, methods and hypotheses

The major aim of my research is to specify and characterise the linguistic expressions of academic identity in e-discourse. I attempt to pinpoint the linguistic cues that position a scholar as a member of an academic community, who is both a distinctive individual and part of a collectivity. My concern, then, is to focus on the manifestations of individual and group identity in scholarly e-discourse.

The theoretical-methodological basis of my research is an integrated model of discourse, and in particular, Swales' genre analysis (1990) and Halliday's systemic-functional grammar (1985, 1994). Swales' conception of genre analysis is an acknowledged system of analysis of professional genres (see e.g. Bhatia 1993; Mauranen 1993; Swales 1990), and therefore its application to study academic communication in an e-seminar can extend our knowledge about the role of this medium for members of academia. An advantage of Swales' conception of genre analysis is his application of a discourse community approach. A discourse community view allows a focus on the social dimension of the negotiation of group and individual identity in scholarly discourse, i.e. shared communicative goals, norms and discursive practices. As the individual's identity is constructed through their membership in the multiple communities he/she comes to interact with, their identification with a particular community's values is manifested through the adoption of the community's discoursal practices and genres (see Ivanič 1998, 83).

Halliday's distinction between the ideational, interpersonal and textual level of language use (1978, 1985, 1994) is important because these three levels contribute towards the discoursal construction of identity. For my present purposes, I focus on the analysis of identity construction in CMC discourse on the textual and interpersonal levels of language use. At the same time, in such an analysis, aspects of the ideational level of language use also become apparent. On the textual level, I investigate the rhetorical purpose(s) of the postings in order to establish their (sub-)generic status. I also analyse the selected elements of the generic superstructure directly related to the issue of identity construction, i.e. the header, opening phrase, closing remark and signature. On the interpersonal level I look at the linguistic manifestations of academic hierarchy, power relations and author-audience interaction through pronoun choice: the employment of the *I*- versus *we*-perspective and referential meanings of the pronoun *we*. I extend this lexical investigation by analysing the verbal group co-occurring with *I* and *we*. In the study of the verbal group co-occurring with *I* and *we*, I make use of the Hallidayan interpersonal metaphors of mood and modality.

The approach taken in the present study will allow me to offer a comprehensive view of how academic identity is constructed at three levels of linguistic description: lexico-grammar features, textual macro-structures and genres. Ultimately, I will be able to relate particular linguistic choices to social structures and practices, placed in the broad context of a specific socio-cultural reality (see Bhatia 2002, 21–22).

Although I focus my analysis on the individual (six frequent contributors to the *Humanist*) rather than the group, this is not inconsistent with the generally acknowledged view that language variation should be studied from the perspective of the collectivity/community. As Labov points out,

> it is true enough that when we examine a community closely enough, it will inevitably appear that each individual's pattern differs in some respects from that of everyone else. Yet, this unique object, the individual speaker, can only be understood as the product of a unique social history, and the intersection of the linguistic patterns of all the social groups and categories that define that individual. (Labov 2001, 34)

Thus, the study of language variation in a collectivity from the perspective of the individual allows us to identify the mechanisms and stages of language change[34], and its internal and external factors, such as specific language use, situational context, etc.

In my study of discoursal construction of academic identity in e-discourse, I integrate synchronic analyses with an evolutionary perspective. My aim is to observe language change with the stabilisation of the medium's use and growing e-competence of the *Humanists* under investigation. Moreover, the combining of diachronic and synchronic perspectives is considered essential for a reliable characterisation of functions that a given (sub)genre fulfils (Wilkoń 2004, 15). I conduct a comparative, corpus-based analysis which incorporates quantitative and qualitative investigations of my research material. The analyses are supported by the computer software, used to perform concordancing procedures, and the categorisation and calculation of the data.

My general research hypothesis assumes the evolution of the generic status of the e-forum and of the individual styles of the *Humanists* under study with the progressing stabilisation of the medium's use: from its transactional character to academic debate and information exchange. I also presuppose that the discoursal construction of academic identity in e-discourse depends on such factors as the medium's defining characteristics, lack of direct physical contact between interactants, the norms and institutionalised practices of an academic community, but also on the individuals' needs and personal goals. I expect that the hybrid character of the electronic medium, in which the public and private spheres of communication continually merge, is an unstable, and thus potentially threatening, communicative environment. This, on the one hand, results in the users' caution about their self-presentation and necessitates a more "conservative" reliance on the established, institutionally sanctioned norms and practices of an academic community, directly transferred from the offline world. On the other hand, the medium's relative freedom and anonymity may invite greater innovation and ingenuity in establishing one's professionally acceptable persona. In relation to the medium's characteristics, I also assume that since an e-seminar is a moderated asynchronous type of CMC, the discursive choices of the *Humanists* under study will reflect an individuating nature of the e-forum.

---

[34] Here, I draw on Labov's term "leaders of linguistic change", i.e. influential people within social networks who are capable of triggering language change (e.g. Labov 2001).

Finally, I think that the frequency of members' activity on the forum is crucial for the issue of academic identity construction in e-discourse. I anticipate that the generic status of the postings contributed by the most active members of the forum will give us a clue about which subgenres of a discussion list posting decide about a member's power and professional authority. Therefore, I postulate a hypothesis that there is a co-relation between the frequency of the *Humanists*' contributions to the forum and the subgenres employed by particular individuals.

5.4. Analysing interaction dynamics

One of my initial assumptions was that the discoursal construction of identity in an e-seminar related to the frequency of members' activity on the forum. Therefore, before focusing on the linguistic manifestations of individual and group identity in the corpora, I characterised the investigated *Humanists* in terms of the frequency of their participation on the forum and the size of their contributions. I computed the following quantities: (1) the total number of messages posted by each member during the investigated periods; (2) the total number of words produced by each member during the two periods; (3) the average number of words in a posting; (4) each member's average activity on the forum measured in the number of days' intervals between postings.

For the figures, see Tables 5–1 and 5–2. A and B refer respectively to the members' earlier and more recent participation in the *Humanist*. Tables 5–3 and 5–4 additionally include the comparison of the general information about the moderator's corpora and the frequency and size of his contribution, with the corresponding, average figures for the regular members.

	Hu1A	Hu2A	Hu3A	Hu4A	Hu5A	MoA	Average for all
Total number of postings	51,00	33,00	136,00	33,00	168,00	294,00	119,17
Total number of words	10570,00	5274,00	16702,00	6368,00	33488,00	62536,00	22489,67
Average number of words per posting	207,25	159,81	122,81	192,97	199,33	212,71	182,48
Average activity on the forum (measured in day intervals)	27,88	42,30	10,54	41,82	8,06	4,94	22,59

Table 5–1. General information about the corpora under investigation during period A.

	Hu1B	Hu2B	Hu3B	Hu4B	Hu5B	MoB	Average for all
Total number of postings	33,00	4,00	37,00	52,00	9,00	370,00	84,17
Total number of words	16469,00	3464,00	5626,00	7226,00	2353,00	117281,00	25403,17
Average number of words per posting	499,06	866,00	152,05	138,96	261.44	316,97	372,41
Average activity on the forum (measured in day intervals)	39,27	51,25	35,40	24,46	58,44	3,73	40,43

Table 5–2. General information about the corpora under investigation during period B.

	MoA	Average for regular Humanists
Total number of postings	294,00	84,20
Total number of words	62 536,00	14480,40
Average number of words per posting	212,71	176,43
Average activity on the forum (in days)	4,94	26,12

Table 5–3. General information about the corpora for all regular members versus the moderator (period A).

	MoB	Average for regular Humanists
Total number of postings	370,00	27,00
Total number of words	117 281,00	7027,60
Average number of words per posting	316,97	383,50
Average activity on the forum (in days)	3,73	41,76

Table 5–4. General information about the corpora for all regular members versus the moderator (period B).

Because of the moderator's position as the group manager and leader, in the general account of the dynamics of the interaction within the investigated group, I first established the pattern emerging from the analyses of the activity of the five regular *Humanists*, and then compared these results with the figures obtained for the *Humanist*'s moderator. To achieve this aim, I employed the methods of statistical analyses in terms of structure, dynamics and correlation (see e.g. Nawojczyk 2002; Sobczyk 2005). The investigation in terms of structure consists in the analysis of the statistical distribution of selected variables. Its aim is to synthetically characterise the selected group and to identify the emergent regularities. The study of dynamics enables a description of the changes of a given phenomenon throughout time. For the purposes of my research, I determined the short-term parameters of dynamics (i.e. statistical growth parameters). In the study of correlation, I used Pearson's coefficient of linear correlation, which allows an estimation of the interdependence between two given variables (see Biber et al 1998; Sobczyk 2005). In my research, I aimed to determine the correlation between the frequency of members' contributions and the total number of words they produced.

In order to extract the salient features of the data which specify the number and size of the messages posted by the five regular *Humanists*, I conducted a statistical investigation in terms of the structure, based on classic and positional parameters. Because of the number of observations in the sample (i.e. the number of individuals) and the character of the investigated variables, the following statistical parameters were determined: arithmetic mean x, standard deviation S(x), coefficient of variation relative to the standard deviation V(s), modal value D and mixed asymmetry parameter A_3[35].

As regards the earlier period, the values of the measures of central tendency x and D indicate that in the investigated group the average number of messages posted by the investigated individuals amounted to 84, and the average number of words used by them totalled 14480 (x; see Table 5–5). In contrast, the dominant individual (i.e. Hu5) posted 168 messages, producing the total of 33488 (D). The calculation of the variation measures reveals a high degree of disproportion both in terms of the total number of postings and in the words produced by the five members during the period in question. The values of S(x) show that the number of postings contributed by one individual diverges from the arithmetic mean by ±63, while the total number of words diverges from the arithmetic mean by ±11533. These deviations constitute respectively 75% and 80% of the arithmetic mean (V(s)), and thus further confirm a considerable variation within the investigated group. While the most productive individual generated 168 postings and 33488 words, the least prolific individual produced 5274 words (Hu2). Two of the investigated *Humanists* contributed the lowest number of postings, i.e. 33 (Hu2 and Hu4). Also, there are two *Humanists* (Hu3 and Hu5) who exceed the arithmetic mean, both as far as the number of postings and the number of words are concerned.

The level of average measures and measures of variation is reflected in the measures of asymmetry. The values of the mixed asymmetry parameter A_3 point to a strong negative skewness within the investigated group. This means that the dominant individual considerably exceeds the level of the arithmetic mean both in the number of contributed postings

[35] Also, the statistical parameters median M, quartile deviation Q and coefficient of deviation relative to the quartile deviation V_Q were determined. However, these values were not considered in the discussion, because of their convergence with the values of the classic parameters (The value of median did not contribute any essential information to the evaluation of the results. Likewise, the values of Q and V_Q pointed to the level of variation corresponding with the level indicated by the classic parameters).

and in words, which additionally proves the variation within the investigated group. As regards the comparison of the activity of the regular members with the activity of the seminar's moderator, the moderator outdistances the dominant individual contributing 294 messages of the total of 62 536 words.

Statistical parameter	Number of postings	Number of words
x	84,20	14480,40
S(x)	63,35	11533,48
V_s	75%	80%
D	168	33488
A_3	-1,32	-1,65

Table 5–5. The values of statistical parameters determined for period A.

With time, the overall activity on the forum declined: the number of postings fell by 68%, and the total number of words by 51%. Also, the statistical parameters did not improve. During the more recent period, the average number of messages posted by the investigated individuals fell sharply to 27, and the average number of words totalled 7 027 (see Table 5–6). The dominant individual (Hu4) posted 52 messages, and the dominant value for the number of words was 16469, contributed by Hu1. Although the values of S(x) diminished (±20 for the number of postings and ±11533 for the number of words), the investigated group continues to reveal a considerable variation as far as the number and size of the contributions go. The two least prolific members (Hu2 and Hu5) contributed respectively only 4 and 9 messages. However, during the more recent period, their membership in the e-seminar was substantially shorter than that of the other members. The values of the mixed asymmetry parameter A_3 also indicate the strong negative skewness within the investigated group, and thus its further diversification.

Statistical parameter	Total number of postings	Total number of words
x	27,00	7027,60
S(x)	20,09	5605,69
V_s	74%	80%
D	52	16469
A_3	-1,24	-1,68

Table 5–6. The values of statistical parameters determined for period B.

In general, during the earlier period, the members' participation on the forum was more frequent (on average every 26 days during the first period, and every 42 days during the more recent period). With time, on average the members contributed fewer postings, but their length extended (from 176 to 383 words per posting). Only the messages of one *Humanist* shortened (Hu4; from the average 192 to 138 words per posting), but their total number and the number of words increased (respectively from 33 to 52 postings, and from 6368 to 7226 words). Hu4 is also the *Humanist* whose contributions became more frequent (from 41 to 24 days on average between his contributions). The productivity of one more *Humanist* grew with time (Hu1): although the number of his postings decreased (from 51 to 33), they became considerably more lengthy (from 207 to 499 words per posting). As for the moderator's activity, his contributions become more frequent (from nearly 5 to 4 days on average between his contributions) and longer (from 212 to 316 words per posting). The total number of his postings and words increased, leaving the regular members even more behind (respectively the figures are: 294 and 370 postings, and 62 536 and 117 281 words).

In reference to the correlation between the frequency of members' contributions and the total number of words, the values of Pearson's coefficient (rxy) for the periods in question amount to 0,932271 and 0,47449 respectively[36]. The value of the coefficient for the earlier period indicates the lack of correlation between the variables involved. In contrast, the value of the coefficient for the more recent period points to the moderate correlation between the frequency of members' contributions and the total number of words. However, whether or not this correlation grows with the stabilisation of the medium's use requires a more extensive investigation, one that would involve more evidence from other members' interaction on the forum. In addition, the values of Pearson's coefficient may suggest that the frequency and size of members' contributions depends on other, external factors, such as individuals' personal purposes and needs, their interests in particular topics, their daily work routines, or degree of e-competence.

5.5. Identity and pronoun choice

For the analysis of the use of pronouns in the corpora under investigation I have selected *I*, *we* and *you*, as these are the pronouns that

[36] The calculation of the values of Pearson's coefficient for the two periods is included in Appendix D.

carry special status as far as individual and group identity construction is concerned. As I pointed out in Chapter 2, in traditional text linguistics, the person deixis has long been regarded as a linguistic manifestation of social relations and identities (see an overview in Vassileva 2000, 47–49; see also the volume edited by Duszak 2002). The pronouns *I*, *we* and *you* serve to set up interpersonal relations through an allocation of addressor/addressee roles to the participants of an interaction. In addition, they become linguistic exponents of the author-knowledge relationship.

The linguistic function of the semantically unambiguous pronoun *I* is to index a linguistic act and explicitly signal the agency (see Röska-Hardy 1998). In addition, first person claims appear to possess immediacy, transparency and salience, and give special relevance to the speaker's/author's linguistic act. In contrast, the pronoun *we* is the most complex pronoun category from a referential point of view (Helmbrecht 2002, 33). As Helmbrecht points out, the prototypical use of *we* pronouns is intrinsically connected to the linguistic establishment of social groups. More specifically, the use of the first person non-singular category serves the purpose of marking in-group/out-group distinctions, and thus is a forceful means of establishing and reinforcing social identities. The use of *you* is pertinent to the consideration of the author-audience relationship, and thus implicitly relates to the author's (self-)manifestation in discourse.

To investigate the management of individual and group identity in an e-seminar through the use of pronouns, I applied an evolutionary perspective and combined qualitative and quantitative analyses, which involved both electronic and manual processing of research data. First, it was necessary for me to process the corpora manually in order to remove any text whose authorship was not attributable to the subjects of my investigation (e.g. embedded messages, direct citations, etc.). Then, I applied concordancing procedures, which allowed me to single out the pronouns in question in their immediate linguistic context (obtaining the KWIC[37] files). The final stage involved the content analysis of the key pronouns with their adjacent verb structure and the computation of the quantitative results by means of the appropriate software, designed for the purposes of the present research. The software facilitated the analysis of the data and enabled an electronic registration of its results. Rather than rely on the available concordancing packages, I decided to use the software designed for the purposes of my research and fitting my research goals. The advantages of the use of such a programme included the possibility: to adjust the output of the analysis to suit my research needs

[37] Key word in context.

(e.g. removal of the irrelevant occurrences of the investigated items while the analysis proceeds, inclusion of additional coding categories), to adjust the KWIC files to include a sufficient amount of context for qualitative analysis, to calculate counts in raw, normed and percentage forms, and to analyse a corpus of an unlimited size (see Biber et al 1998, 254–256).

To achieve my aims, I adopted Vassileva's (2000) method of studying authorial presence in the academic research paper. In the analysis, I determined the overall number of occurrences of pronouns *I*, *we* and *you*[38] (for the discussion see Section 1.1), and investigated the referential meanings of the pronoun *we* (Section 1.2). The use of pronouns *I* and *we* directly signals authorial presence or absence, and the presence of the pronoun *you* is related to the relationship between author-audience.

5.5.1. I/we perspective and the pronoun you

The results of the overall occurrence of pronouns *I*, *we* and *you* in the corpora under investigation are interpretable in terms of power relations (for figures see Tables 5–7 and 5–8). First of all, I noted a higher frequency of the pronoun *I*[39] in relation to *we* in all corpora during the two periods (respectively, on average, 13,94 and 12,27 per 1000 words for *I*, and 5,04 and 6,48 for *we*). This may imply the members' need to mark their authorial presence in the group. Also, the prominence of *I* may result from the authors' roles of being expert and recognised members of an academic community. In the disembodied and pseudo-anonymous context of electronic medium, the members of an e-seminar may deliberately "transfer" their offline identities and use the medium for self-promotion. Admittedly, contributions to academic e-seminars are not a recognised measure of scholars' expertise. However, active and reliable participation in e-discussions may enhance members' career development and the propagation of their research and academic achievements.

As I recounted in Chapter 2, the preference for the employment of the *I*-perspective is also related to an individual's stance towards a particular ideology of knowledge-making. It draws from my data that the *Humanists* under study present themselves as independent knowledge-makers, responsible for the contents of their messages, and in effect, legitimate owners of the property rights over their contributions.

---

[38] Vassileva (2000) focused exclusively on the pronouns *I* and *we*.

[39] Frequent use of *I* in an asynchronous CMC is also noted in Davis and Brewer (1997).

	Hu1A	Hu2A	Hu3A	Hu4A	Hu5A	MoA	Average per 1000 words for all members
Total number of occurrences of *I*	120,00	50,00	237,00	161,00	442,00	871,00	-
Incidence of *I* per 1000 words	11,35	09,48	14,19	025,28	013,20	013,93	13,94
Total number of occurrences of *we*	34,00	21,00	51,00	032,00	121,00	421,00	-
Incidence of *we* per 1000 words	03,22	03,98	03,05	005,03	003,61	006,73	05,04
Total number of occurrences of *you*	08,00	20,00	35,00	029,00	153,00	196,00	-
Incidence of *you* per 1000 words	00,76	03,79	02,10	004,55	004,57	003,13	03,27

Table 5–7. The distribution of pronouns *I*, *we* and *you* in the corpora from period A.

	Hu1B	Hu2B	Hu3B	Hu4B	Hu5B	MoB	Average per 1000 words for all members
Total number of occurrences of *I*	105,00	6500	55,00	183,00	30,00	1432,00	-
Incidence of *I* per 1000 words	006,38	18,76	09,78	025,33	12,75	0012,21	12,27
Total number of occurrences of *we*	038,00	29,00	24,0/	016,00	11,00	0870,00	-
Incidence of *we* per 1000 words	002,31	08,37	04,27	002,21	04,67	0007,42	06,48
Total number of occurrences of *you*	031,00	14,00	36,00	022,00	-	0213,00	-
Incidence of *you* per 1000 words	001,88	04,04	06,40	003,04	-	0001,82	02,93

Table 5–8. The distribution of pronouns *I*, *we* and *you* in the corpora from period B.

During the members' earlier participation in the *Humanist*, the differences between particular members in the frequency of I perspective are rather insignificant, revealing a low degree of personal stylistic variation. Only Hu4 visibly stands out in this respect, with the frequency of I per 1000 words twice as big as in the other members' corpora (25,28, while the average for all *Humanists* is 13,94). With time, the incidence of I remained roughly on the same level in the postings of Hu4, Hu5 and Mo. It increased considerably in Hu2's postings (from 9,48 to 18,76), and decreased in the postings of Hu1 and Hu3 (respectively from 11,35 to 6,37 and from 14,19 to 9,78).

As far as the employment of *we* is concerned, its occurrence generally increased with time (from an average of 5,04 to 6,48 per 1000 words). The rise is noted in the corpora of Hu2, Hu3, Hu5 and Mo. This may indicate the development of the members' sense of group identity, and their growing commitment and awareness of their audience. Interestingly, the moderator's use of *we* stands out relative to the use of *we* by the regular *Humanists* within both periods of investigation (6,72 for Mo and 3,58 for the regular *Humanists* during Period A; 7,42 and 3,36 respectively for Period B), indicating his unceasing engagement and attachment to the e-seminar he moderates. Yet, during the more recent period, there is one *Humanist* (Hu2) whose use of *we* subtly exceeds Mo's use of this pronoun. Nevertheless, Hu2 contributed only 4 messages during the more recent period, as his membership was much shorter. In addition, all his postings represent the subgenre "voice in a discussion" (see Section 3.3 below), which makes me suspect that the employment of pronouns in question may also vary depending on the (sub)generic status of a posting, or even its inner structuring[40]. This calls for further empirical verification, necessarily supported by psycho- and sociolinguistic investigations.

Taking the pronoun *you* into account, its use is found rather infrequent in academic writing (Ivanič 1998), and is comparable to the frequencies of *I* in spoken academic discourse (Rowley-Jolivet and Carter-Thomas 2005). The consideration of the employment of *you* in e-discourse is interesting because of the hybridity of e-discourse between speech and writing. Also, the study of *you* may bring insights into the author's awareness of their audience. It must be remembered, however, that *you* is used with many intended referents (Biber et al 1999, 330).

In my data, I record a low incidence of *you* (the average values for the two periods are 3,27 and 2,93/1000 words respectively) relative to the incidence of *I* (13,94 and 12,27) and *we* (5,04 and 6,48). In addition, the data reveal a considerable variation in the use of *you* among the *Humanists* under study. During the earlier period, the lowest incidence of *you* is noted for Hu1 (0,76), while the highest for Hu4 and Hu5 (respectively 4,55 and 4,57). With time, the incidence of *you* increased for Hu1, Hu2 and Hu3, and decreased for the other three members. The employment of *you* is related to the authors' engagement in the ongoing discussions, and their

[40] Vassileva's (2000) investigation of the employment of the *I/we* perspective in research papers reveals differences in the distribution of pronouns depending on the research paper's section. This is related to the distinct functional roles of each section in the research paper.

responsiveness to others' requests, ideas, queries, etc. In such cases, *you* marks direct references to particular *Humanists* or the *Humanist* community in general, revealing the author's directness and the conversational character of an interaction. Less frequent is the so called generic use of *you*. The avoidance of *you*, on the other hand, indicates the author's distancing from their audience and employment of face-threatening acts. Again, the distribution of the pronoun *you* may also be (sub)genre-dependent, with its higher frequencies in more conversation-like and interactive subgenres such as "voice in a discussion" and "note" (see section 7 below). In general though, the low incidence of *you* brings the e-seminar discourse closer to written discourse.

Interesting findings are revealed by the juxtaposition of the pronoun use by the moderator and the regular *Humanists* (for figures see Tables 5–9 and 5–10). First of all, a very balanced distribution of the pronoun *I* in both periods of investigation indicates a non-imposing position of the moderator as the group leader. The moderator's employment of the pronoun *you* in the initial period is comparable to its average use by the regular members (3,13% vs. 3,38%), but it fell with time (to 1,82%, to be contrasted with 2,93% for the regular members). This shows a less direct stance towards the audience, despite the passing time and growing familiarity within the group. When addressing the audience, the moderator goes for the impersonal third person form "the *Humanists*", or the inclusive-*we*. For examples see (3) below:

> (3) Humanists have done this by disciplining themselves to take some care with what they write. (MoA; 05.06.1989)
>
> My thanks to those Humanists who immediately wrote in with supporting words for this global-e-village headman's halt-calling. (MoA; 27.07.1989)
>
> Humanists may be interested in the Vitruvius Project (Computer Science, Carnegie-Mellon, U.S.), whose goal is (…) (MoB; 30.07.1999)
>
> I have suggested to him that with a few alterations it would be a good thing for us humanists to circulate among our colleagues, especially those who might be tempted into the fold of networked academics. (MoA; 13.11.1989)
>
> Then we humanists view the quite significantly altered result through the altering lens of software, and we start thinking in new ways about the object of study (…) (MoB; 21.08.1999)
>
> As computing humanists our job (if I may say so) is to observe and understand that transformation; (MoB; 23.11.1999)

Finally, a considerable disproportion in the frequency of the pronoun *we* (twice as high use of *we* by the moderator), and its increased use in the more recent period demonstrate the moderator's growing sense of belonging to the group (see also the examples in (3) above and the analysis of the referential meanings of *we* in 5.2 below).

	MoA	**Average for all regular *Humanists***
Incidence of *I* per 1000 words	013,93	13,95
Incidence of *we* per 1000 words	006,72	03,58
Incidence of *you* per 1000 words	003,13	03,38

Table 5–9. The distribution of *I*, *we* and *you* for the regular members versus the moderator (period A).

	MoB	**Average for all regular *Humanists***
Incidence of *I* per 1000 words	0012,21	12,47
Incidence of *we* per 1000 words	0007,42	03,36
Incidence of *you* per 1000 words	0001,82	02,93

Table 5–10. The distribution of *I*, *we* and *you* for the regular members versus the moderator (period B).

5.5.2. Referential meanings of *we*

The pronoun *we* represents a wide variety of meanings and connotations, which consequently results in its ambivalence as far as the author-audience relationship is concerned, so essential for the author's (self-)portrayal in discourse. An exhaustive overview of the semantic meanings of *we* is given in Vassileva (2000, 50–52; see also Biber et al 1999, 329). The multiplicity of the interpretations of *we* is another proof for the subtlety and complexity of authorial (self-)presentation in academic discourse as mediated through the person deixis. In addition, the pronoun *we* proves a powerful tool in the management of the author-audience relationship, particularly relevant for academic discourse, whose essential aim is to persuade the audience to the presented argumentation. The author's use of *we* to include the reader makes the expression more personal, although in general the employment of *we* rather than *I* is considered to be impersonal: in this way the author may escape direct attention (Biber et al 1999, 330).

In my data, I identify three uses of the pronoun *we*:

- "*we*-represented academic institution"; this category includes the reference to the author and his/her academic institution, department or institute, or immediate colleagues and research partners; I find this category particularly relevant for the discussion of both individual and group identity;
- "general *we*"; by means of this label I refer to both "exclusive *we*" and *we*-the "human race" (see Vassileva's categories in Chapter 2), as the context in the concordances was insufficient to distinguish between the two; besides, the use of *we* without explicit referents is common among members of academia; it may also be the case that in such cases the referent is, rather unconsciously, taken for granted by an academic, or as Biber et al point out, authors may inconsistently switch between different uses of *we* (Biber 1999, 329);
- "*we*-members of the e-seminar"; this category of inclusive *we* is relevant for the discussion of the sense of group identity among the *Humanists* under investigation and their relationship with the e-seminar's audience.

As regards the last two categories, some occurrences of *we* in my data were clarified by means of an element in apposition, such e.g. *we at King's College London, we Humanists* (see examples below). The summary of the referential meanings of *we* as used in the corpora under investigation is included in Tables 5–11 and 5–12.

The category of *we*		**Hu1A**	**Hu2A**	**Hu3A**	**Hu4A**	**Hu5A**	**MoA**	**Total for all members (680)**
***we*-represented academic institution**	**raw occ.**	26	21	42	18	24	91	222
	%	76,47	100	82,35	56,25	19,83	21,62	32,65
general *we*	**raw occ.**	7	-	6	14	86	222	335
	%	20,59		11,76	43,75	71,07	52,73	49,26
***we*-members of the e-seminar**	**raw occ.**	1		3	-	11	108	123
	%	2,94		5,88		9,09	25,65	18,09

Table 5–11. Referential meanings of *we* in the corpora from period A. The figures indicate the number of raw occurrences of a given referential meaning of *we* in the corpora. The percentages indicate the frequency of a given referential meaning of *we* relative to the total number of occurrences of *we* in a given corpus.

The category of *we*		Hu1B	Hu2B	Hu3B	Hu4B	Hu5B	MoB	Total for all members (985)
***we*-represented academic institution**	**raw occ.**	18	21	20	8	-	86	153
	%	47,37	72,41	95,24	50,00	-	9,89	15,53
general *we*	**raw occ.**	19	7	1	6	7	473	513
	%	50,00	24,14	4,76	37,50	63,64	54,37	52,08
***we*-members of the e-seminar**	**raw occ.**	1	1	-	2	4	311	319
	%	2,63	3,45	-	12,50	36,36	35,75	32,39

Table 5–12. Referential meanings of *we* in the corpora from period B. The figures indicate the number of raw occurrences of a given referential meaning of *we* in the corpora. The percentages indicate the frequency of a given referential meaning of *we* relative to the total number of occurrences of *we* in a given corpus.

On the whole, the data reveal individual differences in the distribution of particular meanings of *we* that point to the authors' varying personal styles. Yet, some general patterns also become evident. First of all, the "general *we*" is the most frequent category in both periods of investigation. With time, its distribution remained on almost the same level: 49,26% and 52,08% for the two periods respectively. The "general *we*" in my data is mainly used to denote "*we*-the human race" or "*we*-academic community in general", i.e. the meanings which are commonly found in the academic discourse of humanist sciences. In practice, if not explicitly stated, the distinction between the two is indiscernible. This is even though, the use of "general *we*" creates the effect of an inclusion of the audience, and thus shows a closer reader-author relationship. In addition, such uses of *we,* if combined with verbs of mental and verbal processes, may indicate the co-operative ideology of knowledge-making, which recognises that knowledge is not the property of an individual, and that its pursuit is more fruitful if endeavoured collectively (Ivanič 1998, 311). For examples of the use of "general *we*" see (4):

> (4) Perhaps if a few more people had their wrists broken – **we**'d still be using horses? (Hu1A; 30.11.1991)
>
> The computerized display of new symbols should therefore allow us to affect the way **we** conceptualize our world. (Hu1B; 31.08.2002)

> The lofty and laudable goals of Michael's vision of the TEI have to be balanced by the fact that **we** do not live in the best of all possible worlds. (Hu2B; 07.05.1999)

> **We** should also INSIST on interoperability and portability when **we** talk to computer manufacturers. (Hu3A; 18.02.1990)

> About "could of" -- it is, of course, a spelled version of the perfectly reduction of "have" which **we** do not complain about in constructions like "you've". (Hu4A; 30.03.1993)

> **We** should have paper-bound books on cheap paper as the French do. (Hu4B; 30.08.2001)

> Machines do not think as **we** think, because **we** can desribe and program, or ordain their "thought," to use the French term for the computer. (Hu5A; 09.05.90)

> Though, even as **we** stand and muse, paused, **we** will be shoved from behind, or is it from the future...and end flat on our faces, the "gun" pressing behind our ear, and ...whose finger on the trigger? (Hu5B; 08.11.2000)

> Again, **we** ask, what do **we** want computers to do for us? (MoA; 12.05.1989)

> One answer is, of course, that **we** continue to use ordinary language in the traditional way with as much skill as **we** can muster but supplement it with hyperlinks. (MoB; 09.10.2000)

Secondly, I record a decreasing presence of the "*we*-represented academic institution" (from 32,65% to 15,53%), and a growing prominence of the "*we*-members of the e-seminar" (from 18,09% to 32,39%). The reverse distribution in the use of these two meanings of *we* provides important information about how academics validate their professional identity in e-discourse, and how they give it an institutional standing. The employment of the "*we*-represented academic institution" appears as an effective way of enhancing the authors' professional identity, particularly so in the initial period of their membership in the *Humanist*, while they were still introducing themselves to the group. The *Humanists* under study gain and reconfirm their scholarly authority, expertise and acclaim by presenting themselves as affiliates to offline academic institutions, members of conference organising committees, book and journal editors, co-researchers taking part in various academic projects and undertakings, etc. In this way also the collective identity of the academic institutions becomes strengthened, an identity threatened in the effect of the restructuring and de-stabilisation of contemporary, postmodern institutions (see Giddens 2001). As the authors' membership in the group solidified with time and their position settled, the use of "*we*-represented academic institution" declined correspondingly. Yet, the reliance on the authority of offline academic institutions remained a forceful and effective means of constructing a scholar's virtual identity. For examples of the use of the "*we*-represented academic institution" see (5):

> (5) More specifically, **we** are to develop "a theoretical foundation which recognizes the connectedness of all disciplines and achieves a more substantive integration of learning for our students"-- whether they are architecture or philosophy majors. (Hu1A; 22.05.1989)
>
> In keeping with the CAP format, **we** are interested first of all in presentations that will provoke collegial but critical discussion. (Hu1B; 18.08.1999)
>
> **We** need to strip out common non-French wordlists in lists **we** are using for a phonetic study. (Hu2A; 02.03.1990)
>
> **We** have been considering precisely this model when thinking about what **we** should do with PhiloLogic. (Hu2B; 14.05.1999)
>
> So far **we**'ve only run some tests, but **we** will be going into production mode this semester. (Hu3A; 29.06.1990)
>
> **We** have, at long last, scheduled the workshop on medieval manuscript transcription using the DTD developed by Michael Sperberg-McQueen, U.S. editor of the Text Encoding Initiative. (Hu3B; 01.07.1999)
>
> **We** have all the computer equipment we need for it: the University would have to pay a few hundred dollars for mailing the newsletter. (Hu4A; 11.01.1990)
>
> It took us several years of hard arguing before **we** got our administration and faculty committees to accept_writing computer programs_as tantamount to publication. (Hu4B; 15.10.2002)
>
> But he knows his stuff, and **we** have done lots of Persian translations. (Hu5A; 25.10.1989)
>
> I think **we** should take the title of the next ALLC/ICCH conference "The New Medium", quite seriously and try to understand what an adequate paradigm for it might be, instead of wondering how soon **we**'ll be able to curl up in bed with a good computer instead of a good book (MoA; 06.03.1990)
>
> Under this last sense **we** at King's College London refer to our "Seminar in Humanities Computing". (MoB; 28.02.2002)

The presence of the "*we*-members of the e-seminar" indicates a growing sense of group identity and cohesion within the *Humanist* community, and thus enhances and legitimises the position of individuals under investigation as the *Humanist*'s active members. Thus, the increased distribution of "*we*-members of the e-seminar" in the more recent period indicates also a shift in how the *Humanists* corroborate their professional identity. Again, as their membership in the e-seminar stabilised over time, it became a means of giving institutional validity to the individuals' virtual identity. For examples of the use of the "*we*-members of the e-seminar" see (6):

> (6) While **we**'re dreaming: 1. What have I missed in attempting to determine feasible and productive uses of computer technology for the next few years -- in the setting of a medium-sized liberal arts college with strong professional concentrations in business, architecture, pre-med, and communications? (Hu1A; 15.09.1989)
>
> rather, **we seek to address** both mind-and-body by taking up considerable amounts of computing resources to help the machine interface with an embodied knower - ultimately, through all of our senses. (Hu1B; 23.01.2002)
>
> Without Tom's knowledge -- sorry, mon! -- I propose that **we** move this discussion offline to Tom's ELTA site. (Hu2B; 28.11.1999)
>
> While **we** are all eagerly awaiting the draft TEI guidelines (hint, hint Michael Sperberg), I would like to know if there are any de facto standards for transcribing texts in the Romance languages, i.e., standards which have been used by large-scale projects and therefore which have a considerable body of already encoded material. (Hu3A; 01.08.1990)
>
> and as I know you are thinking right now, **we** Humanists are supposed to be the ones with open minds… (Hu4B; 12.08.1999)
>
> **We** are not talking about learning birdsong as chicks from our tribe: we are talking about theft. (Hu5A; 11.11.1989)
>
> Who and what is this "I"? **we** are talking merest fantasy here, are **we** not? (Hu5B; 28.10.2000)
>
> Once again I think **we** need to take stock of what **we**'re doing with Humanist and to impose on ourselves some restraint. (MoA; 26.07.1989)
>
> At the moment, however, as the year, the century and the millennium wind down to a close, I wish only to praise what **we** have made together, to celebrate it with you, to recognise that the ONLY reason why it is what it is and why it continues is that **we** wish it so. (MoB; 09.12.1999)

As regards the individual distribution of the referential meanings of *we* identified in the corpora, I record substantial discrepancies among the members under study. In both periods, the *Humanists* whose use of the "general *we*" exceeds 50% are Hu5 (71,07% and 63,64%) and Mo (52,73% and 54,37%). In the initial period, the lowest, zero level of the "general *we*" is noted for Hu2, and in the more recent period for Hu3 (4,76%). The distribution of the "general *we*" increased with time in the corpora of Hu1, Hu2 and Mo, and declined in the corpora of Hu3, Hu4 and Hu5. The presence of the "general *we*" might correspond to the distribution of "voices in a discussion" and "initiations of a discussion", the subgenres related to the purposes of argumentation and debate.

The highest distribution of the "*we*-represented academic institution" in the initial period is recorded for Hu1 (76,47%), Hu2 (100%) and Hu3 (82,35%), while the lowest for Hu5 (19,83%) and Mo (21,26%). In the more recent period, the reliance on the authority of offline academic institutions is still high for Hu2 (72,41%) and Hu3 (95,24%). Interestingly, Hu3 is the only one for whom I note an increase in the use of the "*we*-represented academic institution".

In the earlier period, the category of the "*we*-members of the e-seminar" is relatively frequent only in the moderator's corpus. With time, its distribution grew for the majority of *Humanists* under study, i.e. for Hu2, Hu4, Hu5 and Mo. For Hu1, the use of the "*we*-members of the e-seminar" remained roughly on the same, low level of less than 3%. A decrease to the zero level is recorded for Hu3.

The moderator, if compared with the regular members (see Tables 5–13 and 5–14), emerges as the *Humanist* with the biggest sense of group identity, and the lowest need to rely on his academic affiliation when presenting his online image. This becomes evident in the considerably higher proportion of the "*we*-members of the e-seminar" and its growing presence (25,65% and 35,75% for the moderator, to be contrasted with 5,79% and 6,96% for the regular members). Moreover, the moderator's use of the "*we*-represented academic institution" is substantially lower than by the regular members and reveals a declining tendency (21,62% and 9,89% for the moderator, to be compared to 50,58% and 58,26% for the regular *Humanists*). Finally, the moderator used more of the inclusive "general *we*" (52,73% and 54,37% for the moderator, compared with 43,63% and 34,78% for the regular members). Such a distribution of the particular referential meanings of *we* corresponds to the moderator's strong position as the group leader, manager and promoter, committed to the e-seminar he moderates and concerned with his relationship with the audience.

The category of *we*	MoA raw occ. (%)	Total for all regular *Humanists* (259) raw occ. (%)
we-represented academic institution	91 (21,62%)	131 (50,58%)
general *we*	222 (52,73%)	113 (43,63%)
we-members of the e-seminar	108 (25,65%)	15 (5,79%)

Table 5–13. The distribution of the referential meanings of *we* for the regular members versus the moderator (period A).

The category of *we*	MoB raw occ. (%)	Total for all regular *Humanists* (115) raw occ. (%)
we-represented academic institution	86 (9,89%)	67 (58,26%)
general *we*	473 (54,37%)	40 (34,78%)
we-members of the e-seminar	311 (35,75%)	8 (6,96%)

Table 5–14. The distribution of the referential meanings of *we* for the regular members versus the moderator (period B).

5.6. Identity and verbal group characteristics

As already stated, particular choices of lexico-grammatical features of discourse contribute to the authors' presentation in discourse. Thus, I find it relevant to investigate the verbal group co-occurring with *I* and *we* in order to search for explicit and implicit manifestations of authorial presence in academic e-discourse. To achieve my present purposes, I focused on the use of metadiscoursal verbs, these being an important element of the interpersonal level of language use. This approach follows from the social view of academic discourse (e.g. Hyland 2000). Admittedly, the use of metadiscoursal verbs is important because of the persuasive and argumentative functions of academic discourse. However, academic discourse is not only about the generation and transmission of knowledge, but also about social interaction. Although the use of metadiscourse is largely conventionalised, while making claims, academics express their allegiances and establish authorial voice.

My application of the term metadiscoursal verbs follows from the integrative approach to metadiscourse (see Chapter 2, Section 2.2.3 for a more detailed discussion), where metadiscourse signals serve to fulfil attitudinal and text-organising functions (Hyland 2005, 14). In this way, metadiscourse relates not only to the interpersonal but also to the textual level of language use. The investigation involved the content analysis of key words in context obtained through concordancing procedures. The linguistic context in concordances may be limited. Therefore, to increase the reliability of my qualifications, it was, occasionally, necessary for me to extend the context manually.

The first objective of my analysis of the verbal group co-occurring with the pronouns *I* and *we* was to determine the distribution of the metadiscoursal verbs in relation to the total number of the occurrences of the pronouns in question. In this way, I aimed to evaluate the degree of the authors' explicit participation in argumentation and academic debate. The results of this analysis are presented in Tables 5–15 and 5–16. In general, I noted a considerable proportion of the metadiscoursal verbs co-occurring with the pronoun *I* (approximately 40% in both periods of investigation), and relatively lower with the pronoun *we* (24,41% and 20,85% in the two periods respectively). These data indicate a large degree of the authors' engagement into direct argumentation and expression of their opinions, whether independent or shared. However, the prominence of verbs used with the *I*-perspective proves that the subjects of my investigation opt for emphasising their greater autonomy and individuality in leading scholarly argumentation and debate. This, in turn, enhances their authoritative and responsible stance in knowledge-making.

The second stage of my analysis of the verbal group characteristics was to focus on the use of private and suasive verbs, as defined by Biber (1988). "Private verbs (e.g. think, feel) are used for the overt expression of private attitudes, thoughts, and emotions" (Biber 1989, 105), while "suasive verbs (e.g. command, demand, instruct) imply intentions to bring about certain events in the future" (Biber 1989, 111). I find these verbs interesting for my investigation of the discoursal construction of identity, as the use of private verbs is speaker-oriented and assertive, whereas the use of suasive verbs is audience-oriented and directive (see Leech's semantic classification of speech-act verbs in 1983, 203–223). My major aim was to conduct a qualitative analysis of the verbal group that includes private and suasive verbs, to find out how the authors under study position themselves in relation to their audience – for the discussion see Sections 2.1 and 2.2.

		Hu1A (Total *I*: 120/ *we*: 34)	Hu2A (Total *I*: 50/ *we*: 21)	Hu3A (Total *I*: 237/ *we*: 51)	Hu4A (Total *I*: 161/ *we*: 32)	Hu5A (Total *I*: 442/ *we*: 121)	MoA (Total *I*: 871/ *we*: 421)	Total for all members (*I*: 1881/ *we* 680)
Incidence of metadiscoursal verbs in the verbal group co-occurring with *I*	raw occ.	41	19	95	59	197	360	770
	%	34,17	38,00	40,08	36,65	44,57	41,33	40,94
Incidence of metadiscoursal verbs in the verbal group co-occurring with *we*	raw occ.	10	1	6	10	30	109	166
	%	29,41	4,76	11,76	31,25	24,79	25,89	24,41

Table 5–15. The distribution of metadiscoursal verbs in the verbal group co-occurring with *I* and *we* in the corpora from period A. The figures indicate the number of raw occurrences of the investigated verbs in all instances of *I* and *we* respectively in the corpus. The percentages indicate the frequency of a given verb-type relative to the total number of occurrences of *I* and *we* respectively in the corpus.

		Hu1B (Total *I*: 105/ *we*: 38)	Hu2B (Total *I*: 65/ *we*: 29)	Hu3B (Total *I*: 55/ *we*: 24)	Hu4B (Total *I*: 183/ *we*: 16)	Hu5B (Total *I*: 30/ *we*: 11)	MoB (Total *I*: 1432/ *we*: 870)	Total for all members (*I* 1870/ *we* 988)
Incidence of metadiscoursal verbs in the verbal group co-occurring with *I*	raw occ.	35	41	23	83	19	597	798
	%	33,33	63,08	41,82	45,36	63,33	41,69	42,67
Incidence of metadiscoursal verbs in the verbal group co-occurring with *we*	raw occ.	10	6	3	3	3	181	206
	%	26,32	20,69	12,5	18,75	27,27	20,80	20,85

Table 5–16. The distribution of metadiscoursal verbs in the verbal group co-occurring with *I* and *we* in the corpora from period B. The figures indicate the number of raw occurrences of the investigated verbs in all instances of *I* and *we* respectively in the corpus. The percentages indicate the frequency of a given verb-type relative to the total number of occurrences of *I* and *we* respectively in the corpus.

I also carried out a quantitative analysis of the data: the results for the verbal group co-occurring with *I* are presented in Tables 5–17 and 5–18, and for the verbal group co-occurring with *we* – in Tables 5–19 and 5–20. As far as the comparison of the results is concerned, the most striking observation is a predominance of the investigated verbs with the pronoun *I*. Another important finding is that the use of suasive verbs is generally outnumbered by the use of private verbs. This is another indication of the individualisation of verbal expression in my data.

Finally, I analysed the verbal group with metadiscoursal verbs from the perspective of modality. As I recounted in Chapter 2, Section 2.2.4, the study of modality allows us to focus on the author's attitude to the proposition and his/her engagement in a communicative act in general.

		Hu1A (Total *I*: 120)	**Hu2A (Total *I*: 50)**	**Hu3A (Total *I*: 237)**	**Hu4A (Total *I*: 161)**	**Hu5A (Total *I*: 442)**	**MoA (Total *I*: 871)**	**Total for all members (1881)**
Private verbs	**raw occ.**	24	15	53	32	127	234	485
	%	20,00	30,00	22,36	19,88	28,73	26,97	25,78
Suasive verbs	**raw occ.**	8	4	15	2	6	32	67
	%	6,67	8,00	6,33	1,24	1,36	3,68	3,56

Table 5–17. The distribution of private and susaive verbs in the verbal group co-occurring with *I* in the corpora from period A. The figures indicate the number of raw occurrences of the investigated verbs. The percentages indicate the frequency of a given verb-type relative to the total occurrences of the pronoun *I* within period A.

		Hu1B (Total *I*: 105)	Hu2B (Total *I*: 65)	Hu3B (Total *I*: 55)	Hu4B (Total *I*: 183)	Hu5B (Total *I*: 30)	MoB (Total *I*: 1432)	Total for all members (1870)
Private verbs	**raw occ.**	25	25	16	40	14	397	517
	%	23,81	38,4	29,09	21,86	46,67	45,58	27,65
Suasive verbs	**raw occ.**	1	5	3	4	2	59	74
	%	0,95	7,69	5,45	2,19	6,67	4,12	3,96

Table 5–18. The distribution of private and susaive verbs in the verbal group co-occurring with *I* in the corpora from period B. The figures indicate the number of raw occurrences of the investigated verbs. The percentages indicate the frequency of a given verb-type relative to the total occurrences of the pronoun *I* within period B.

		Hu1A (Total *we*: 34)	Hu2A (Total *we*: 21)	Hu3A (Total *we*: 51)	Hu4A (Total *we*: 32)	Hu5A (Total *we*: 121)	MoA (Total *we*: 421)	Total for all members (680)
Private verbs	**raw occ.**	4	-	1	2	10	19	36
	%	11,76		1,96	6,25	8,26	4,51	5,29
Suasive verbs	**raw occ.**	1	-	1	-	1	6	9
	%	2,94		1,96		0,83	1,43	1,32

Table 5–19. The distribution of private and suasive verbs in the verbal group co-occurring with *we* in the corpora from period A. The figures indicate the number of raw occurrences of the investigated verbs. The percentages indicate the frequency of a given verb-type relative to the total occurrences of the pronoun *we* within period A.

		Hu1B (Total *we*: 38)	Hu2B (Total *we*: 29)	Hu3B (Total *we*: 24)	Hu4B (Total *we*: 16)	Hu5B (Total *we*: 11)	MoB (Total *we*: 870)	Total for all members (988)
Private verbs	**raw occ.**	2	1	1	2	1	33	40
	%	5,26	3,45	1,17	12,50	9,09	3,79	4,05
Suasive verbs	**raw occ.**	-	2	1	-	-	4	7
	%		6,90	1,17			0,46	0,71

Table 5–20. The distribution of private and suasive verbs in the verbal group co-occurring with *we* in the corpora from period B. The figures indicate the number of raw occurrences of the investigated verbs. The percentages indicate the frequency of a given verb-type relative to the total occurrences of the pronoun *we* within period B.

5.6.1. Verbal group and the *I*-perspective

5.6.1.1. Private verbs

The category of private verbs includes verbs of thinking, cognition and emotions, used with the aim of expressing a personal opinion. The presence of verbs of thinking, cognition and emotions strongly signals authorial presence and serves to personalise the authors' claims. To refer to Biber's (1988) MD-MF model suggested to study variation in discourse, these verbs are one of the indicators of involved or interactive focus in a text[41] (Biber 1988, 105). Thus, private verbs indicate a verbal, as opposed to a nominal style, particularly so if used in the present tense forms. In addition, the presence of private verbs points to the individuating character of academic e-discourse.

The lists of verbs identified in personal opinions differ from one individual to another, but in general includes the following lexical items: *think, find, hope, believe, anticipate, see, perceive, doubt, gather, guess, view, fear, feel, imagine, hate, dislike, expect, not mind, love, enjoy* and *regard*. The *Humanists* who use the widest range of private verbs are Hu5 and Mo. For examples of private verbs see (7):

> (7) as much as I welcome Willard's raising important questions for HUMANIST readers, **I believe** some greater precision in defining the questions would be helpful (Hu1A; 30.11.1991)

[41] A reference is made here to Dimension 1 in Biber's MD-MF model, namely "Involved versus nformational production".

In my mind, moreover, this work and its results fits reasonably well with what **I perceive** to be an emerging coherence to our working definitions of "humanities computing" (…) (Hu1B; 30.12.2002)

This is a glaring omission which **I feel** needs to be corrected. (Hu2A; 19.02.1993)

The rest of Michael's post, which **I think** is both very informative and intelligent, offers his approach to picking and choosing encoding to process. (Hu2B; 13.05.1999)

Thus **I see** the humanist workstation, right now, primarily as a productivity enhancer. (Hu3A; 06.02.1990)

This originally started, **I gather**, because of federal regulations which originated with NIH for recipients of NIH grants. (Hu3B; 09.02.2001)

I'm sorry, but **I think** "Desiderata" is not bunk, but junk. Badly written, low-level junk. (Hu4A; 15.02.1993)

I feel sorry for them but **I don't see** that as a reason to abolish meetings. (Hu4B; 01.06.2000)

No amount of computer teaching will change it, **I fear**. (Hu5A; 19.02.1990)

but it took time to think up some way of leveraging the power of the arm, and **I dont think** it came about because it was dreamed up. (Hu5B; 19.10.2000)

I'm fascinated by the number of people who think of the machine as neuter. There's almost nothing **I regard** as neuter. (MoA; 04.05.1990)

The Saul Bass page *stands out*, **I view** it as remarkable not just because of the obvious skill of the design and execution but also, perhaps even primarily, because it stretches the media (…) (MoB; 19.08.1999)

For considerations of politeness, the verbs are occasionally coupled with a hedging structure (usually a modal *would* or *might*) with the aim of mitigating the authors' views (see examples in (8)). Personal opinions may also be enhanced by adverbs of attitude (*frankly, truly, keenly, sincerely, oddly enough, keenly, sure, really, actually*) and degree (*much, very much, deeply, rather*), or the auxiliary *do* used for emotive emphasis. For examples of personal opinions see (9), (10) and (11) below. An interesting effect of the strengthening of a personal view is achieved through the use the new spelling conventions characteristic for e-discourse. In the

Humanist postings, underlining is commonly expressed by means of underbars[42] as in example (11) below:

Examples including hedging:

(8) if a choice must be made between available software and powerful hardware, **I would prefer** to have the software in hand and get to work, rather than become embroiled with the dubious joys of trying to create my own programs. (Hu1A; 03.08.1989)

I've worked with EMACS on Windows, and **I'm afraid that I didn't like** it at all. (Hu3B; 21.05.2001)

I should think that e-mail is more like mail, and less like books or writing. (Hu5A; 06.01.1990)

As an ignoramus in lexology, to coin a term? **I might think** first, of course, of asking to know the standard search and retrieve things, Boolean, etc. (…) (Hu5; 28.01.2000)

But **I would guess** that some digging would unearth many such cases. (MoA; 03.03.1992)

Examples including adverbs of attitude and degree:

(9) **I truly prefer** deciding what I want to do and then forcing the technology to do it, or failing that, gong ahead and doing it without the technology, even though that may slow my work down by factors of ten and prevent me from getting the job done for a year or so. (Hu4B; 13.12.2002)

I frankly think that far too many University Press people are trying to impress each other with binding, type faces, dust jackets, etc. (Hu4B; 30.08.2001)

I prefer that choice to what **I really think** and have suggested: that his position and statements are unworthy of history and of those many millions, tens and tens of millions, who have died because of positions like his that favor tyranny by disarming freedom, or would if they are given the license to. (Hu5A; 26.02.1991)

I sincerely hope that in many instances the e-info can be left to take its speedy journey into the void. (MoA; 04.07.1991)

But this time **I really don't think** it's much of a risk. (MoB; 24.10.2000)

I keenly appreciate Mark Wolff's comment, in Humanist 15.041, that academics quite understandably get annoyed at the extra-territorial

[42] In the corpora under analysis, underbars are also commonly used when quoting the titles of books, articles, etc.

demands which humanities computing can place on their attention. (MoB; 27.05.2001)

Perhaps now that research in the humanities is externalised via the computer, there is an intellectual object to be studied, and so we will be studied. **I sure hope** so. (MoB; 09.03.2000)

I doubt very much whether the "mother of all battles" has anything at all to do with the metaphorical concepts mentioned by Mark Turner and rather more to do with metaphorical expessions in Arabic based on kinship relations. (Hu3A; 04.03.1991)

I much prefer to find out what the other folks are doing (and papers in other fields never seem as disheartening). (Hu4B; 07.08.2001)

I rather like e-mail since it saves going to the postoffice and quickens conversation, when there is such, with distant friends. (Hu5A; 06.01.1990)

I urge you to look again at The Bed,
<http://www.acm.org/sigchi/chi97/proceedings/short-talk/cd.htm>,
formerly brought to your attention in Humanist 12.609, and meditate on why this provokes (**I very much hope**) a profound uneasiness. (MoB; 04.11.1999)

Examples including the auxiliary *do* used for emotive emphasis:

(10) **I do believe** that the dynamic text (ACH/ALLC 1989) was precisely about this, the delivery of electronic editions with software packages that would make them usable. (Hu3B; 23.05.2001)

I do think, though, that the chance that some CEO or other exec would be able to create a "real University" (or, from what I've seen of Colleges of Business including the one at my school) laughable and dismaying (…) (Hu4B; 07.12.2000)

Although I have great respect for handwritten notes, letters &c., **I do find** the transcribing of them from the travelling 3x5 slips to be highly problematic and frustrating (MoB; 04.08.2001)

An example with the use of underbars:

(11) **I _think_** mine is partly a humanist's reaction to any kind of "human engineering". (Hu4A; 30.11.1989)

5.6.1.2 Suasive verbs

The presence of suasive verbs enhances authorial presence, engagement and responsibility and directly addresses the reader (see examples in (12)). Among the examples with suasive verbs I have also distinguished instances of recommendation and request. Recommendations in the corpora under my study are realised by means of the suasive verb *recommend*, sometimes hedged through the use of a modal, or strengthened by an adverb of attitude, degree, or the emphatic auxiliary *do*. The presence of the suasive verb indicates overt expression of persuasion (see Biber's Dimension 4 in his MD-MF model; Biber 1988, 111) and demonstrates the author's professional competence and authority – for examples see (13) below:

(12) Without Tom's knowledge -- sorry, mon! -- **I propose** that we move this discussion offline to Tom's ELTA site. (Hu2B; 28.11.1999)

So, what **I propose** is this: daily to gather the non-computing "notes and queries" into one number of Humanist, label it "Notes and Queries", and publish it as often as the volume of mail requires. (MoA; 30.11.1989)

So, **I urge** those of you who are interested to arrange your schedules accordingly. (MoA; 21.05.1989)

I'd like to see a rigorous definition of what is meant by "information" before considering how much there might be. (MoB; 15.11.2000)

Examples of recommendations:

(13) In response to Willard's request... **I'd _strongly_ recommend** Myron Tuman, ed., _Literacy Online: The Promise (and Peril) of Reading and Writing with Computers_ (University of Pittsburgh Press, 1992) for a series of articles on hypertext. (Hu1A; 13.04.1993)

Along these directions **I would** also **recommend**: Hillis (1999) critiques Virtual Reality as resting on postmodern/Cartesian dualisms, one resulting precisely in the sort of schizophrenia that Kaltenborn discusses (see especially Hillis, ch. 6, "Identity, Embodiment, and Place VR as Postmodern Technology"). (Hu1B; 21.01.2002)

I would not recommend replacing WordPerfect 5.0 with Nota Bene. (Hu3A; 24.10.1989)

I highly recommend XTREE or its big brother, XTREE Professional, both of which are available from Executive Systems, Inc. (Hu4A; 31.10.1989)

I recommend for starters (and perhaps finishers, too) Lem's masterpiece, FIASCO (Hu5B; 10.10.2000)

I can therefore **heartily recommend** the following to you because it does more than descry, accurately, the signs of the times. (MoA; 14.04.1993)

I esp recommend to your attention the articles by the articles by Philip E Agre, H M Collins, Douglas R Hofstadter, the interview of Heinz von Foerster by Stefano Franchi, Gven Gzeldere and Eric Minch and von

Foerster's own keynote address for the International Conference, Systems and Family Therapy: Ethics, Epistemology, New Methods, held in Paris, France, October 4th, 1990. (MoB; 24.02.2000)

Having just finished the book **I can recommend** with fresh enthusiasm James D Watson's The Double Helix: A Personal Account of the Discovery of the Structure of DNA (New York, 1968) (MoB; 17.11.2002)

But **I do wish to recommend** the entire book in passing, hoping to solicit comments on it from others who know the work, while speeding to a particular question that he raises. (MoB; 30.11.2002)

In the requests, mental verbs are coupled with a modal *would*, which softens the request and indicates the author's concern for politeness. This is even though, the use of the *I*-perspective positions the author straightforwardly as a knowledge-seeker. On the other hand, requests as well as recommendations serve to engage the readers into performing some action. For examples of requests see (14):

(14) Two questions here, really. (1) **I would like** a relatively objective estimate of just how difficult such a task is (…) (Hu1A; 02.12.1989)

I would like your collective advice on type of machine (…) (Hu1A; 23.04.1990)

I wish to request information on doctoral programs which allow for combining philosophical studies with literary studies. (Hu1A; 03.09.1991)

In any case, **I would greatly appreciate** hearing from anyone who has either knowledge or strongly held opinions. (Hu3A; 13.02.1990)

I would very much appreciate your reactions to a terminological problem I face. (MoA; 13.02.1991)

With the indulgence of my fellow Humanists, **I would like to** keep the subject alive for a bit longer. (MoA; 11.12.1992)

I for one **would appreciate** having a reference or two to a critical methodological survey of what happens in the social sciences (MoB; 23.02.2000)

5.6.1.3 Modality

As I recounted in Chapter 2 Section 2.2.4, metaphors of modality are a type of interpersonal metaphors in the Hallidayan model of grammar relevant for the purposes of the present research. These include modalization and modulation, which in philosophical semantics are referred to respectively as *epistemic modality* and *deontic modality*

(Halliday 1985, 332–341). My intention was to investigate the realisations of modality in all the occurrences of metadiscoursal and mental verbs with the *I*-perspective. I generally aimed to investigate the *Humanists*' relation to their propositions (epistemic modality) or to events (deontic modality).

As far as epistemic modality is concerned, I have limited my analysis to the linguistic realisations of probability. My objective was to find out how explicitly the authors commit themselves to the truth of the proposition in their statements, i.e. to what degree they acknowledge the likelihood of the proposition. For this purpose, I use the taxonomy of the linguistic realisations of epistemic modality based on the Hallidayan model of modality choices:
- the choices of orientation: subjective vs. objective, and explicit vs. implicit – orientation designates the degree of subjectivity/objectivity encoded by the author in a projecting clause (Halliday 1985, 333, 336);
- combined with the choices of value: high, median, or low – value designates the degree of probability set on the modal judgement (Halliday 1985, 337–339).

At the same time, following the view that the domains of epistemic modality and evidentiality overlap (see e.g. Plungian 2001; Verstraete 2001; for a more detailed discussion see Chapter 2, Section 2.2.4), I aim to look at how the *Humanists* under study qualify the reliability of information through signalling its source. In other words, I assume that the realisations of epistemic modality may combine the author's attitude marking with the source-of-information marking. With reference to deontic modality, I search for the linguistic realisations of the author's active influence over the event or situation.

Given the fact that in this section I focus on the analysis of the metadiscoursal and mental verbs used with the *I*-perspective, the linguistic realisations of epistemic modality in the data are necessarily explicit and subjective, as subjectivity is encoded through the presence of the personal pronoun *I*. The use of the *I*-perspective additionally indicates the author as the source of the information: obtained through direct perception (e.g. *I can see*), direct experience (e.g. *I know*), inference (e.g. *I conclude*), or reasoning (e.g. *I understand*).

In the data, I also identified examples of the three choices of value. The choice of value, as Carratero suggested, is conditioned by factors of genre and register such as the overall purpose of the text and the individual purposes of the participants of an interaction, the degree of planning, the need for accuracy, the topic of the text (field; factual vs. speculative content), and the social relationships between the participants (tenor; Carratero 2002, 11). It draws from my data that the degree of probability placed on the judgement is also dependent on the inherent characteristics of the communication medium (channel).

The epistemic expressions of high probability indicate the author's certainty and firm knowledge of the truth of their proposition. Therefore, their use enhances the author's professional authority and competence, but is also self-imposing and potentially face-threatening. In my data, the linguistic realisations of high value include:

- lexical verbs: *know*, *not see*, *not find*, *assure*, or expressions with lexical verbs: *take it*, *see no reason*, *know with certainty* – examples in (15);
- adverbs of degree or attitude: *certainly, of course readily, obviously, completely* – examples in (16);
- the modal auxiliary *can/cannot* used to express logical possibility[43] – examples in (17);
- emphatic *do* – examples in (18);
- adverbials: *as I (well) know*, *as I say* – examples in (19).

Examples of expressions of high probability with lexical verbs:

(15) Positivists would like us to think so – but **I do not find** this to be true. (Hu1A; 29.11.1989)

Apparently, the Apple Color 12" monitor is especially bad in this regard -- **I take it that** we're discovering that low-level radiation from such monitors is carcinogenic? (Hu1A; 19.07.1990)

I know that it's not at Berkeley. (Hu3A; 11.01.1990)

I don't see that exposing students to other languages is any different than expopsing them to other music,painting, architecture, etc. (Hu4A; 19.09.1990)

But **I see no reason to** clear off the two feet of shelf space the print MED takes, and I would lose a lot of randomly accessed information if I did that. (Hu4B; 16.01.2002)

But, then as a practicing poet **I know** those metaphors are absurd. (Hu5A; 22.01.1991)

I wager some will think I've gone round some bend with this one, and that the question has nothing to do with computing in the humanities, but **I assure you that** it does. (MoA; 03.04.1990)

[43] The modal auxiliary *can* is especially ambiguous in academic discourse as it is used to mark both ability and logical possibility (Biber et al 1999, 491).

What particularly intrigues me are those times when I cannot say, even silently to myself, what the characteristics of the book I am remembering are, yet **I know with certainty** that there's a particular book I need, and its particularity is defined by a strong yet inarticulate sense. (MoB; 02.05.2000)

Examples of expressions of high probability with adverbs of degree or attitude:

(16) **I readily agree that** this is not revolutionary. (Hu3A; 19.09.1989)

The discussion in HUMANIST about concordances---whether they should be published (**obviously I agree** with you about this), lemmatization, etc (Hu4A; 22.06.1989)

Now this **I completely agree** with (Hu4B; 08.08.2001)

I agree of course it is a battle for funding, and the Humanities went to the wall about 1950, where they have remained, perhaps for good and sufficient reasons. (Hu5A; 26.09.1990)

I certainly agree with him that setting up stringent requirements for humanities computing is conterproductive. (MoB; 05.02.2001)

Examples of expressions of high probability with the modal *can*:

(17) **I can see** clear advantages to hypertext for linking up separate texts. (Hu3A; 15.02.1990)

I cannot imagine that spending the time teaching methods of critically judging Chaucer would have been a good substitute. (Hu4B; 20.03.2001)

You say I am a dreamer? This **I cannot deny**. (MoA; 25.10.1989)

Examples of expressions of high probability with the emphatic *do*:

(18) **I do believe that** the dynamic text (ACH/ALLC 1989) was precisely about this, the delivery of electronic editions with software packages that would make them usable. (Hu3B; 23.05.2001)

I do think, though, **that** some CEO or other exec would be able to create a "real University" (or, from what I've seen of Colleges of Business including the one at my school) laughable and dismaying, and I wish we could nail down the rights to the word, as if it were a wine variety.... (Hu4B; 07.12.2000)

Examples of expressions of high probability with adverbials:

(19) and **as I know** you are thinking right now, we Humanists are supposed to be the ones with open minds..... (Hu4B; 12.08.1999)

The same 10K$ can be found readily for an extra microscope in the blood lab, maybe, but not the geology lab, **as I well know** here at UCLA. (Hu5A; 13.01.1990)

As I say, Humanist is what you make of it. I invite any (MoA; 27.07.1989)

The most predominant and diverse choices of value in my data are the expressions of median probability. The median value is indicative of speculation, tentativeness and some degree of contingency. Their use may also result from the author's considerations of politeness, intensified by the potentially more threatening communicative context of the electronic medium. The linguistic realisations of the median value include:

- lexical verbs including verbs of tentative reporting, cognition or opinion: *anticipate, argue, assume, believe, consider, expect, gather, guess, hope, imagine, observe, perceive, presume, realise, regard, see, see something as, sense, suggest, suppose, suspect, think, view* – see examples in (20);
- adverbs of degree or attitude: *frankly, sincerely, very much, sure* – see examples in (21);
- the modal auxiliary *would* which is used to hedge an opinion – see examples in (22);
- *seem* and *be inclined to* – see examples in (23);
- adverbials: *oddly enough, as I understand/recall, as far as I know, as far as I can see, as a personal opinion, if I recall/remember correctly* – see examples in (24).

Examples of expressions of median probability with lexical verbs:

(20) **I anticipate that** responses to these questions will tell us something about computers and the humanities among faculty who find themselves with less than all the support they might ask for. (Hu1A; 02.12.1989)

In my mind, moreover, this work and its results fits reasonably well with what **I perceive** to be an emerging coherence to our working definitions of "humanities computing" - though, of course, it is a first marker of humane discourse that we may well want to debate that claim (smile)! (Hu1B; 30.12.2002)

The corrective, **I believe**, is to engage and exploit the developments in critical theory head on ("in your face") (Hu2A; 03.12.1992)

Trying to build that capability into a large scale text search and navigation engine would, **I fear**, be far beyond ARTFL's means. (Hu2B; 07.05.1999)

I don't think that the humanities scholar should have to become a computing specialist to do this kind of work, any more than he has had one in order to use a computer for word processing. (Hu3A; 31.05.1989)

Much of the material has **I suspect** been drawn from the D-LIB electronic journal. (Hu3B; 16.12.2000)

My University library had a copy and **I imagine** many others will as well. (Hu4A; 03.03.1993)

I regard that as a shortcoming of many of the to the List, not mine (so there). (Hu4B; 17.01.2000)

It was cold and clear: **I consider** Lakoff's arguments both insidiously UNreasonable, if reasoned, and full of simplistic nonsense. (Hu5A; 26.02.1991)

I think a bot might be devised to learn from all the threads of commentary upon and within and recursive in the Talmud, which is not the Library of Congress, but a small and finite number of volumes. (Hu5B; 28.06.2000)

More information is, **I presume**, available from the secretary of the convention, Fondazione IBM Italia, via Giorgione 159, 00147 Roma, voice: 06/54864568, fax: 06/54864964. (MoA; 10.09.1991)

The Saul Bass page *stands out*, **I view** it as remarkable not just because of the obvious skill of the design and execution but also, perhaps even primarily, because it stretches the media, which I expect will rapidly grow in the direction stretched, and so it will no longer have the particular distinction of being unusual. (MoB; 19.08.1999)

Examples of expressions of median probability with adverbs of degree and attitude:

(21) **I frankly** think that far too many University Press people are trying to impress each other with binding, type faces, dust jackets, etc (Hu4B; 30.08.2001)

I rather think Corre was expressing something else: the economics of it all. (Hu5A; 26.01.1990)

I sincerely hope it stirs up like passions in others, since further debate would at minimum indicate that concern for our field as a whole is not the solitary bent of a very few. (MoB; 22.05.1999)

Perhaps now that research in the humanities is externalised via the computer, there is an intellectual object to be studied,, and so we will be studied. **I sure hope** so. (MoB; 09.03.2000)

He will, **I very much hope**, remain in the virtual here after the physical move to a lovely part of that fine country, where our field is indeed prospering. (MoB; 14.11.2002)

Examples of expressions of median probability with the modal auxiliary *would*:

(22) **I would add that** the condemnation of positivism provided by the reading has been, to my understanding, strongly reinforced on an epistemological level by quantum mechanics, relativity theory, Goedel's theorem, etc. (Hu1A; 29.11.1989)

I would suppose that as his course is being offered by a department of Spanish, it will need to have all of its examples drawn from that disciplinary area. (Hu1B; 29.10.2002)

I would deny that humanities computing folk are not concerned about standards. (Hu2B; 14.05.1999)

I would argue that the web, in particular, allows us to get beyond that dichotomy because it provides, potentially, the possibility of actually measuring the impact of a particular web site on its discipline. (Hu3B; 08.04.2000)

In general, **I would say that** E-mail can sometimes lend itself to rather sweeping personality changes: not only for the good, as noted above, but for the bad. (Hu4A; 26.11.1989)

It began, **I would say** even before the Revolution. (Hu5A; 21.05.1990)

Doctorow is pulling the Humanist leg, I think, since his reversals have nothing to do, **I would suggest**, with how things in history actually happened. (Hu5B; 19.10.2000)

I would argue that although it may be used in a trivial way, there is nothing inherently trivial about it. (MoA; 05.07.1989)

I would assume that the practice called 'usability' would bear on the question raised here, though of course usability has quite another aim. (MoB; 23.02.2000)

Examples of expressions of median probability with *see* and *be inclined to*:

(23) **I seem to remember** reading good reviews of LXR Test, however, I can't recall having examined it closely. (Hu3A; 14.09.1989)

When Thoreau went to Harvard about 165 years ago there were **I seem to recall** its having been mentioned (by Matthieson, in AMERICAN RENAISSANCE, I think), that there were (after 200 years of Harvard's history) about 55,000 books, of which perhaps 54,000+ were collected sermons. (Hu5A; 28.09.1990)

I'd be inclined simply to think that her question came from her somewhat limited experience of the Web -- were it not for the fact that argumentation in a hypertextual medium is no simple matter. (MoB; 17.02.2001)

Examples of expressions of median probability with adverbials:

(24) The Racine is part of a corpus that was collected at Besancon and, **as I understand it**, is part of the Tresor de la Langue Francais. (Hu2A; 20.03.1990)

Oddly enough, I see strong points of contact between humanities scholarship and open source hacking, since both are motivated less by monetary reward (assuming, of course, that the scholar and/or hacker has a means of support) than love of the work itself and recognition of peers. (Hu2B; 14.05.1999)

Also, **if I remember correctly** there has been some work done a at Yale (Linguistics) using DOS. (Hu3A; 05.10.1989)

As far as I know course buyout of the sort described below is not permissable at Berkeley. (Hu3B; 13.09.2000)

No use trying to fight that fight again, but **as far as I can see**, the MLA is good for only one thing, the Annual Bib. (Hu4A; 14.02.1993)

As a personal opinion, I suspect that one example of MIS at work can be found in the hearings of the (U.S.) President's Commission on the Challenger disaster. (Hu4A; 30.11.1989)

Law is a manifestation of social concerns, in the action of controversy, **as I understand it**, with a vast and deep subtext, and tight rules of argument, which are not the same rules as rhetoric and debate. (Hu5A; 08.08.1990)

However, Beowulf refers t o hrothgar, **if I recall correctly**, as a "ring-giver." (Hu5A; 29.04.1991)

The interface isn't quite as trendy, but the program works. **As far as I know** it isn't infected. (MoA; 02.08.1989)

One such occurred in Oxford, **as I recall**, in the 17th century, or perhaps earlier. (MoA; 03.03.1992)

As far as I know these attempts have not been terribly successful, with the one exception of the Text Encoding Initiative. (MoB; 21.02.2000)

If I understand the import of what these fellows are saying, this would mean that people like us could build far more adequate scholarly forms (editions, commentaries et al.) online. (MoB; 29.10.2000)

The least frequent choices of value in my data are the expressions of low probability, which may be associated with the author's assertive and self-restrained stance. Their use may indicate the author's uncertainty, caution or tactfulness, and is considerably self-revealing – hence, most probably, their low incidence in public academic discourse. Still, as it is repeatedly proved, the communicative context of the electronic medium incorporates also the elements of private interpersonal communication and is largely individuating. This is proved by the examples of the low value from my data which combine the author's indeterminacy, self-disclosure and care for non-imposition. The linguistic realisations of the low value in my research material include:

- lexical verbs: *doubt, wonder, not know* – see examples in (25);
- the modal auxiliary *might* used to mark logical possibility[44] – see examples in (26);
- the adjectival expression: *not sure* – see examples in (27).

Examples of expressions of low probability with lexical verbs (28):

(25) If this disparity goes beyond that - **I wonder** if it would inspire a listing by HUMANISTS of similar tasks important to our teaching, research, and publication that, however important they may be and however well-suited they may be to computational algorithms, likewise remain under- or non-supported in the midst of the computer revolution? (Hu1B; 05.03.2001)

I don't know if this disparity between need and computational possibility, on the one hand, and software reality on the other, means anything other than indexing is something only a very few souls concern themselves with, and hence fail to constitute a robust market that would make software development commercially worthwhile. (Hu1B; 05.03.2001)

Unfortunately, **I tend to suspect that** we are at fault. (Hu2A; 03.12.1992)

I tend to see calls for patience as a way of evading the issues. (Hu2A; 03.12.1992)

[44] The frequency of the modal auxiliary *might* is very rare in academic prose (Biber et al 1999, 489).

Are all these people irrational agents, simply wanting to spend alot of money for things that can be acquired freely or for little cost? **I doubt** it. (Hu2B; 13.05.1999)

I don't know about Greek, but **I doubt** that it can do it. (Hu3A; 29.01.1990)

I wonder if the the philosophers are indeed ahead of the literary scholars in making use of e-texts. (Hu3A; 23.09.1992)

I don't know where you can get a copy, but the film was sponsored by the Council of Library and Information Resources in Washington, as a sequel to _Slow Fires_, on the problems caused by acid paper. (Hu3B; 18.01.2001)

Again **I wonder if** the model of the experimental sciences isn't a good one for us to use in fashioning our self-image. (MoB; 09.12.2000)

Examples of expressions of low probability with the modal *might*:

(26) **I might add**, regarding electronic publication, that it took us several years of hard arguing before we got our administration and faculty committees to accept _writing computer programs_ as tantamount to publication. (Hu4B; 15.10.2002)

Thus, **I might argue**, since sorting a list of words is a primitive, I don't need to be able to follow the code that does the sort. (MoB; 03.02.2001)

Examples of expressions of low probability with the adjectival expression *not sure*:

(27) For Hispanic studies in North America **I'm not sure that I would agree** with Willard. (Hu3A; 16.02.1990)

I wasn't aware that Willard said these were shortcomings, and **I'm not sure** I think so. (Hu4B; 17.01.2000)

Overall, the predominance of expressions of epistemic modality in my data gives evidence for the persuasive character of academic e-discourse. In addition, it reflects the character of the communicative situation in which the text is produced. Admittedly, participation in e-forum discussions involves carefully edited expression. However, the presence of expressions of epistemic modality proves the spontaneous and conversational character of academic e-discourse.

In the Hallidayan model of the interpersonal metaphor, deontic modality (modulation) subsumes the categories of obligation and inclination, and unlike epistemic modality, it refers to acts, not propositions.

According to Palmer, deontic modality "has much in common with the imperative. The speaker can give permission, lay an obligation or give an undertaking, in relation to possible future events" (1981, 153). Thus, deontic modality is concerned with the speaker's active relation to events[45]. The subjective expressions of deontic modality can be realised by means of the performative verb or modal auxiliary (for examples see Halliday 1985, 336). Modal auxiliaries, however, may be ambiguous as they each carry both deontic and epistemic meanings (Biber et al 1999, 485). Thus, in the present analysis, I have based my qualifications of deontic modality on the structural correlates of deontic modals indicated by Biber et al: (i) the subject is human, (ii) the main verb is dynamic, describing an activity that can be controlled.

To illustrate, the expressions of deontic modality realised by means of performative verbs are the uses of the suasive verbs *propose* and *urge* in (12) above (see Section 2.1.2). The examples of deontic modality with the use of modals are included in (28) below. In my data, the modals with the deontic meaning are *must* and *should*, used to mark respectively an obligation or a less absolute obligation. As the present analysis involves the study of the verbal group with the *I*-perspective, the addressee of the imposition is the subject himself. In general, the use of deontic modality, unless hedged by e.g. the adverbial *perhaps*, is decisive and authoritative, and thus enhances the author's decisive position.

I would also like to note that the use of the obligation/necessity modals *should* and *must* may point to the conversational character of academic e-discourse. It is because of the scholarly ethos that academics avoid the face-threatening force of directive expressions with an obligation meaning – hence, a lower frequency of obligation/necessity modals in academic prose (Biber et al 1999, 489). It appears again that the communicative context of the electronic medium proves to encourage indirectness and informality, as well as caution and tactfulness.

Examples of expressions of deontic modality:

> (28) **I should also add that** our facilitators consistently comment on how much _fun_ they have in the seminar, as it becomes a collaborative learning experience _for them_, with colleagues who share their considerable expertise and experience in thinking and talking about ideas which are both of interest "academically" and pertinent particularly to the art of teaching. (Hu1A; 14.12.1990)

---

[45] In his *Mood and Modality*, Palmer (2001) classifies deontic modality as a subcategory of "event modality".

In view of the crashing lack of response to my previous request for information or syllabi for a course on computational studies in Spanish, **perhaps I should amplify that** what I am primarily interested in is any material on humanities computing courses in general. (Hu3A; 19.06.1992)

though **I must note** one occasion upon which, when meeting face to face, the boy and girl didn't like each other after all. (Hu4A; 26.11.1989)

I should say that I was already a tenured full Professor when I began to learn to program, and that SSU has been hospitable to faculty who develop computer materials for teaching. (Hu4A; 03.10.1989)

But, **I must say**, I recall that in 1974, when I was touring the Western States with a program in Humanities for small towns under the aegis of the NEH, I was amused, together with my accompanying crew, to find a marquee above the entrance to Placerville Community College, in the Motherlode country of Placerville County of California, that announced, WELCOME, HUMANITARIANS! (Hu5A; 19.01.1991)

I also say the same thing, more or less. **I must** because I cannot afford to employ someone to do this work for me. (MoA; 12.09.1989)

I must object to the term "laborious", indeed to all the allegations that I am suffering under some intolerable burden. (MoA; 27.09.1989)

That certainly can be done, but **I must point out that** messages are not always received in the order they are sent from Toronto. (MoA; 30.09.1989)

By (this being England **I must mention**) NOT saying what might be said? (MoB; 15.11.2000)

I should also explain that the problem has been with us for a long time. (MoB; 10.04.2002)

5.6.2. Verbal group and the *we*-perspective: modality

Correspondingly to the analysis of the verbal group with the *I*-perspective, my objective was to examine the verbal group co-occurring with the pronoun *we* from the perspective of modality. I endeavoured to analyse the authors' qualifications of propositions in terms of certainty/ probability, and the authors' active stance towards events or situations.

With reference to epistemic modality, the orientation of the authors' choices with the pronoun *we* is intersubjective, to use a more precise term put forward by Nuyts (2000, 2001). Intersubjectivity of a qualification derives from its being shared or obtainable by a group of people, including the addressee, or from the fact of sharing or having common access to the evidence for the proposition. In my data, I also register the realisations of the three types of value enforced upon the participants' judgement - high, median and low – depending on the degree of certainty/probability and commitment.

The accomplishments of high probability in my material include the use of the modal *can*, adverbs of attitude such as *certainly* or *of course*, or adverbials *as we (all) know*, *as we say*. High probability is exemplified by sentences in (29) and (30) below:

(29) I suspect that the goals of the TEI are probably going to be achieved in much more limited and hard fought steps than Michael might think, but **we certainly agree that** >> quote << (Hu2B; 07.05.1999)

I find that fascinating -- **we know that** denial of responsibility is typical of our culture at its worst, but this is some sort of record-setting denial. (Hu3B; 13.10.2000)

A related point to be made is that although **we can spot** several determinisms at work in the development of a new technology, there seems to be considerable room for individual human desire to push that development one way or the other. (MoA; 17.05.1990)

We also, I think, know what a prescriptive manner of work is, and how demeaning and repugnant it is, and **we can all sense** the tendencies in modern life to impose prescriptive formulas if not technologies. (MoA; 03.08.1990)

Of course we all know that one can put old-fashioned essays online, indeed can compose prose arguments with HTML. (MoB; 17.02.2001)

Examples of high probability with adverbials:

(30) Most of what we have learned is quite forgettable, though it too often comes up out of the lower depths in hours of fever or delirium, **as we all know**. (Hu5A; 26.01.1990)

I am not myself altogether happy with the "challenge/response" generalization, since it seems to me, or to anyone who has ever worked with his or her own infant from the hour of birth, rather obvious for animal behavior, stimulus and response today being a notion that might well fit into the probabilistics of evolution, starting at the gross molecular organization...**as we know** now from the rapid variations in even such a primitive or rudimentary life as that of the HIV virus. (Hu5B; 21.10.2000)

As we all know, the giving of papers is only a part of what happens at conferences; (MoB; 29.05.1999)

As a result, engineering education today is, **as we say** in the humanities, contested terrain -- a site where different strategic goals collide. (MoB; 23.01.2003)

Just as with the pronoun *I*, the instances of median value are very frequent. The accomplishments of median value include the lexical verbs *suspect, hope, discover, think, find, view* and *anticipate*, the modal auxiliaries *may well* and *would,* and also *can* because it co-occurs with the tentative *suppose*, the adverbials *presumably* and *perhaps*, and the adverbial clause *as we've observed*. For examples of median probability (31) see below:

> (31) **Presumably we all know** the difficulties of the former method although without doubt good for strengthening the character, it keeps the student away from the language far too long. (MoA; 15.05.1991)
>
> **As we've observed** before, the electronic seminar is semiotically impoverished. (MoA; 07.09.1989)
>
> **We can reasonably suppose that** an oral storyteller, a Homer, might have looked on the newfangled written medium with disfavour and, from a not indefensible perspective, condemned it. (MoB; 23.09.1999)

Low probability is realised by the speculative linguistic items: the modal *might* and the verb *tend to*. Instances of low probability can be found among hedged opinions: they include examples with the tentative verb *tend to*, the modal *might* and the adverbial *perhaps*. For examples with *tend to* and *might* see (32) below:

> (32) **We might want to** "round up the usual suspects" -- you know who you are :-) -- and try again at ACH-ALLC at UVa. (Hu2B; 14.05.1999)
>
> I keep thinking that fundamentally we lack a clear understanding of how meaning arises from discourse, and with heads muddled about such a basic issue **we tend to misunderstand** how a phenomenon like Humanist really works. (MoA; 26.09.1989)
>
> If its end is articulation of stable formal methods, through algorithms and structures in metadata, then perhaps humanities computing is potentially akin to computer science at its theoretical end, offering us eventually what **we might call** a 'calculus for the arts and letters'. (MoB; 07.03.2000)
>
> **We tend**, I think, **to dismiss** such apparently trivial matters as sorting or reformatting, paying attention rather to complicated transformations of data, esp those involving substantial amounts of "computation". (MoB; 11.01.2001)

Overall, the analysis of the occurrences of epistemic modality shows, on the one hand, the authors' confidence and straightforwardness, which strengthen their scholarly authority (high value), and on the other, hesitancy and caution, resulting from their considerations of politeness and non-imposition (median and low value).

Unlike with the pronoun *I,* the occurrences of deontic modality completed by means of the pronoun *we* are very frequent. Their presence indicates the referents' shared and involved attitude towards situations and events. Such expressions of deontic modality contribute to discourse interactivity and persuasiveness: they are very stimulating, authoritative and direct, especially if the inclusive *we* is present. The instances of deontic modality in the data include those examples with the modal auxiliaries of obligation and necessity *must* and *should* – see (33) below:

(33) God forbid that **we should want to know** what Chaucer may have written or what he may have meant thereby...... (Hu4B; 13.10.2000)

Thank you Mr Bantz, for confirming what I have tried to point out, that stealing is stealing, and **we all should know** it, and do know it. (Hu5A; 14.12.1989)

Before we allow ourselves to be swept in the enthusiasm, the sense of the power of KNOWING, suggested by the being able to say 0, 01, and say everything, **we must realize that** we cannot say or say meaningful our own birth, our own death, o ur own next moment, even before it is known that the next thing I will type will be a [.] (Hu5A; 21.07.1990)

That there is cause for weeping and wiling and gnashing of teeth, we all agree, but we **must also look at** the case, which is not as you offer it, not at all. (Hu5A; 08.02.1991)

We simply must keep ourselves to our general topic, computing in the humanities, or like the creatures of fermentation, we will do ourselves in with our own most wonderful output. (MoA; 26.07.1989)

Now, however, **we must think** hard about what subset of things we want to deal with. (MoA; 31.10.1989)

To me this suggests that (a) our old wisdom about language and literature is called into play, and (b) **we must remember that** style and content, medium and message, are finally inseparable. (MoA; 27.02.1990)

So far the only answer I have been able to manage points to the fact that **we must objectify** our research methods before we can compute the artefacts we study, and in so doing we bring out into the open what has formerly been hidden from view. (MoB; 15.01.2000)

Perhaps rather than use the model of technological invention ("reinventing the wheel") **we should think** of one that happily allows for continuous repetition, such as making babies. (MoB; 24.10.2000)

Nor **should we call** it "multitasking", which is a degrading computational metaphor. (MoB; 22.03.2001)

5.7. Textual aspects of authorial presence

5.7.1 Global organisation of postings

According to Ivanič, discourse organisation[46] on the global level, just as well as on the local level, contributes towards how authors negotiate their identity relative to the aims and activities of their discourse community (Ivanič 1998, 274). In this way, discourse organisation becomes an aspect of the author's institutional voice.

In the analysis of the generic structure of the postings on the macro-level I focused on those elements which give direct information about the authors' identity, i.e. the header and signature (see Donath 1999). I also investigated the elements that concern the authors' relationship with their audience and other members of the e-seminar, i.e. the opening phrase (a salutation) and closing remark (a farewell). Additionally, a closing remark functions as a boundary marker, which separates the personalised message body from automatically generated material, and as an identity marker, which provides extended information about the sender: information typically not included in the header (Crystal 2001, 105). The investigation of the elements of the generic superstructure which I have singled out for my present purposes is an extension of the analysis of the employment of the *I/we* perspectives.

The investigated elements are to a large extent generated automatically, so usually follow fixed conventions imposed by the posting software. Yet, my data demonstrate some degree of variation in this respect, which suggests that the authors made conscious choices about how to present themselves in discourse. The presence or absence of the investigated elements may be explained in terms of the weight given to these elements by the author and the degree of accommodation to the preferred conventions.

As regards the header, its three standard lines (i.e. "Date", "From" and "Subject") were completed in every posting in the corpora from both periods of investigation, except for a few occasional cases, probably as a result of the errors of the archiving or posting software. "Date" and "From" lines are filled in automatically by the electronic mail software,

[46] Hoey's terminology to refer to the layout organisation of a text (see e.g. Hoey 1983, 1994, 2001).

but the sender has got a limited influence over what information will be included in the "From" line. Apart from the optional sender's name, the "From" line contains obligatorily the sender's account name (i.e. email address), which is an important identification signal (Donath 1999, 35–37). The domain in an e-mail address gives clues about the organisation that provides an account, and thus is a source of important contextual hints about the sender's affiliation and about the reliability of the header information. The *Humanists* under my study used sometimes a variety of e-mail accounts; however the majority of them were institutional, which was either indicated by .edu or included the abbreviated name of the institution. Commercial accounts were used by Hu1 in the earlier period of investigation, by Hu4 in the more recent period, and occasionally by Hu5 and Mo in the more recent period. The "From" line in my data nearly always contained the sender's full name. The exceptions are Hu5, who in the earlier period provided his surname only, and Hu3 whose "From" line in the more recent period contained just his e-mail address.

"Subject" line is one of the first elements that the recipient of the message receives, and thus is crucial for assigning priority to the message or rejecting it. In an e-seminar, the "Subject" line facilitates the categorisation of messages into topic threads and according to their relevance for the recipient's interests. The completion of the "Subject" line by the *Humanists* under study probably results from their wish to facilitate the screening procedures for other members and the archiving of the postings, and thus manifests the authors' adherence to the group's conventions.

The study of the opening phrases, closing remarks and signatures in the corpora demonstrates a considerable degree of variation and inconsistency, both within the postings by the same author and across the corpora (for figures see Tables 5–21 and 5–22). This may suggest that the expectations and constraints on what constitutes a prototypical discussion list posting were still evolving; or that adherence to the fixed structure of a posting was of minor importance; or that a conscious action was performed on the part of the author who appropriated the medium for his own purposes. Whether or not the elements in question are present in a posting, and the degree of how personalised they are, depends also on the frequency of contributions and the level of acquaintance among the interactants. In addition, it is expected that in an asynchronous CMC (such as an e-seminar), where the aim is to obtain information for the benefit of all, greetings, if present at all, will not be personalised, and messages will not generate personalised responses (Crystal 2001, 100).

In the initial period, over half of the postings (55,10%) were signed by the author's first name and surname, and the least frequent was the use of initials (0,42%). Also, a large proportion of signatures contained the author's surname and the name of the institution to which he was/is affiliated (27,55%). Almost one tenth of the postings was not signed at all. Lack of a signature creates an impression of directness, and shows the authors' demand for brevity rather than impoliteness or flouting of the *Humanist's* rules (from the beginning, the moderator discouraged anonymity within the *Humanist).*

Structural element	**Hu1A**	**Hu2A**	**Hu3A**	**Hu4A**	**Hu5A**	**MoA**	**Total for all members (715)**
Signature:							
Initial(s)	-	-	1 (0,74%)	-	2 (1,19%)	-	3 (0,42%)
First name + Surname	2 (3,92%)	9 (27,27%)	6 (4,41%)	10 (30,30%)	98 (58,33%)	269 (91,50%)	394 (55,10%)
First name + Surname + Name of college	27 (52,94%)	17 (51,51%)	86 (63,24%)	-	62 (36,90%)	5 (1,70%)	197 (27,55%)
Extended sig.	22 (43,14%)	2 (6,06%)	25 (18,38%)	-	-	1 (0,34%)	50 (6,99%)
No sig.	-	5[47] (15,15%)	18 (13,24%)	23 (69,70%)	6 (3,57%)	19 (6,46%)	71 (9,93%)
2 types of sig. in a posting	-	-	-	-	-	-	-
Opening phrase	-	-	-	-	41 (24,40%)	13 (4,42%)	54 (7,55%)
Closing remark	45 (88,23%)	5 (15,15%)	19 (13,97%)	-	26 (15,48%)	119 (40,48%)	214 (29,93%)

Table 5–21. The distribution of the selected elements of the postings' generic structure in the corpora from period A. The figures indicate the number of the investigated elements in the corpora. The percentages indicate the frequency of a given element relative to the total number of postings in a given corpus.

[47] Only in forwarded messages.

Structural element	Hu1B	Hu2B	Hu3B	Hu4B	Hu5B	MoB	Total for all members (505)
Signature:							
Initial(s)	-	1 (25,00%)	-	-	-	313 (84,59%)	314 (62,18%)
First name + Surname	2 (6,06%)	3 (75,00%)	-	-	2 (22,22%)	4 (1,08%)	11 (2,18%)
First name + Surname + Name of college	-	3 (75,00%)	-	-	-	-	3 (0,59%)
Extended sig.	25 (75,76%)	1 (25,00%)	37 (100,00%)	-	8 (88,89%)	290 (78,38%)	361 (71,49%)
No sig.	6 (18,18%)	-	-	52 (100,00%)	-	46[48] - (12,43%)	104 (20,59%)
2 types of sig. in a posting	-	4 (100,00%)	-	-	2 (22,22%)	282 (76,22%)	288 (57,03%)
Opening phrase	24 (72,73%)	-	1 (2,70%)	10 (19,23%)	-	4 (1,08%)	39 (7,72%)
Closing remark	28 (84,85%)	1 (25,00%)	2 (5,40%)	-	1 (11,11%)	301 (81,35%)	333 (65,94%)

Table 5–22. The distribution of the selected elements of the postings' generic structure in the corpora from period B. The figures indicate the number of the investigated elements in the corpora. The percentages indicate the frequency of a given element relative to the total number of postings in a given corpus.

The patterns of signing a posting vary so much in my data that it is difficult to talk of emergent general tendencies. Yet, some of the noted changes also reflect such general characteristics of contemporary discourse as pragmatism, conversalisation (see Fairclough 1995a) and abbreviation. Moreover, the changes suggest the authors' familiarisation with the medium and their readiness to exploit the possibilities it offers. Signatures may also show an author's creativity and individuality.

An interesting type of signature found in my data is an extended signature, a signature that resembles a business card and is typically characteristic for asynchronous types of CMC (e.g. Crystal 2001; Donath 1996). By extended signature I refer to the signature that includes a holder's full name, such real life academic credentials as title, position, department, college, etc., and also links to (personal) web pages, online

[48] Only in forwarded messages.

publications, and well-known sayings or quotations. Its contents are more or less regularly updated by the signature's holder. An extended signature is thus used "to anchor the virtual persona to the real world person", and informs the audience that its holder is "willing to publicly stand behind the statements" (Donath 1996, 40). In my data from the earlier period, 6,99% of the postings included an extended signature.

Interestingly, with time the number of postings with an extended signature increased markedly (to 71,49%), and the number of unsigned postings doubled. I also record a growth in the use of initials (62,18%), but in reality this was due to only one *Humanist*, the moderator. The least frequent were the signatures that include the author's first name and surname (2,18%), and the full name and the author's affiliation (0,59%). A novel element in the postings from the more recent period is the presence of two types of signature in one posting (57,03%), a feature non-existent in the earlier period. Again, the high proportion of a double signature in one posting was mainly due to the moderator (282 cases out of the total 288), Hu2 (4 cases) and Hu5 (2 cases). A double signature results from the authors' use of the option to have a signature inserted automatically by the email software, in addition to a customary signature. On the one hand, this proves the authors' growing acquaintance with the medium and taking advantage of the opportunities it offers. On the other, the members under study adhered to the "traditional" epistolary conventions of concluding a message with an autograph, though electronically.

With regard to the individual patterns of signing a posting, in the initial period, the members under study usually used a variety of types of a signature, but one type always prevailed. Furthermore, Hu1 was the only who always signed his post, and Hu4 had the greatest proportion of unsigned messages (69,70%). With time, individual preferences for one type of a signature more or less settled. An extended signature was used by all the members except for Hu4, whose messages were never signed. Thus, it appears that the *Humanists* under study "transferred" their offline identity to the electronic world, which proves the need for a stable and credible identity in a scholarly e-seminar. An extended signature appears also as an efficient way of promoting one's name and academic achievements.

Furthermore, some signatures found in my data demonstrate a creativity and an originality characteristic for e-discourse (see the creativity of Netspeak in e.g. Crystal 2001, 81–93), which opens up for academics new possibilities for constructing a unique voice. Such signatures are also the evidence of some degree of personalisation of academic discourse in an e-seminar. For examples of personalised signatures see (34) below.

(34) [Hu's Surname]@UCLA (Hu5A; 17.11.1989).

[Hu's Surname] here in LA. (Hu5A; 28.01.1990)

[Hu's Surname] cleaning up his email. (Hu5A; 23.05.1990)

Your friendly muser, and amuser, I hope, [Hu's Surname] here at UCLA, [Mo's First Name]. (Hu5A; 04.08.1990)

from [Hu's Surname], here in the desert of the LA Basin.... (Hu5A; 05.08.1990)

[Hu's Surname] here with an ice pack. (Hu5A; 08.08.1990)

[Hu's Surname] murmuring aloud. (Hu5A; 27.08.1990)

[Hu's Surname] out here on the Pacific Rim, a milli-second away from you all, us all, we all. (Hu5A; 20.02.1991)

[Hu's First Name and Surname] (lost in the Ozarks[49]), Drury College. (Hu1A; 20.12.1990)

Enthusiastic, but not ecstatic – [Hu's First Name and Surname], Drury College. (Hu1A; 30.11.1991)

In general, the inclusion of a welcoming address at the beginning of a posting is equally infrequent in the corpora from both periods of investigation (7,55% and 7,72%), which indicates the authors' need for brevity, their formality and lack of intimacy and the public character of the e-seminar, or, on the contrary, their direct stance towards their audience and the *Humanist* community. On the whole, a closing remark was present in 29,93% of the postings from the earlier period, and its proportion grew considerably to 65,94% in the more recent period. It appears then that a closing remark is a more popular indication of an author's commitment and polite attitude towards the audience.

As for the differences between particular *Humanists*, in the initial period only two members used an opening phrase, Hu5 and Mo. 24,40% of Hu5's postings and 4,42% of the moderator's postings included an opening phrase. Hu5 used an opening phrase only if directing his messages to one particular addressee, whereas the moderator used a general "Dear Colleagues". In the more recent period, although the overall increase in the proportion of opening phrases was insignificant, more *Humanists* included a salutation in their postings. Hu1 is the member who directly addressed

[49] The name of the region in Missouri, US.

his audience most often (72,73% of his messages included an opening phrase; e.g. "Colleagues", "Dear [Mo's First Name] and HUMANIST colleagues", "Dear Sister/Fellow Humanists", "[Mo's First Name] et al"). Opening phrases appeared in almost one fifth of Hu4's messages (19,23%). These were the messages directly addressed to the seminar's moderator by means of his first name, placed within the rest of the message body as in (35), not spaced away as it is usually the case.

(35) [Mo's First Name], I must admit to being less than enchanted by The Dialectizer. The Elmer Fudd and the Pig Latin work okay because they are simply rewrite rules (wewitc oolrays). But the others work at about the level of newspaper Sunday Supplements, which is to say, not hardly at all. Only as bad stereotyping of rich materials. Having lived in Redneck Territory for years and years, I find the presentation offensive, actually. (Hu4B; 04.02.2000; Subject: Re: 13.0371 linguistics: jobs, dialectical play)

Opening phrases were also found in one message from Hu3 and in four messages from Mo. Hu5 dropped using direct salutations, but as his participation in the *Humanist* in period B was shorter I do not have sufficient data to call it a general tendency.

As I have already stated, the presence of closing remarks was more frequent than of opening phrases and grew with time. In period A, the highest proportion of closing remarks is noted for Hu1 (88,23% of all his postings; for examples see (36) below) and for Mo (40,48%; for examples see (37) below).

(36) As always, thanks in advance. (Hu1A; 14.06.1989)

Proleptic thanks. (Hu1A; 21.06.1989)

With continued gratitude. (Hu1A; 06.10.1989)

Hope this helps. (Hu1A; 29.11.1989)

Advice and suggestions appreciated. (Hu1A; 16.08.1990)

In continual befuddlement. (Hu1A; 07.05.1992)

Any suggestions -- both experiential and philosophical -- would be appreciated. (Hu1A; 23.04.1990)

Thanks to one and all -- and peace. (Hu1A; 19.09.1990)

(37) Thanks very much. (MoA; 11.10.1990)

Many apologies. (MoA; 25.05.1989)

Comments? (MoA; 13.06.1989)

Suggestions? (MoA; 13.02.1991)

A heated argument, yes, please. (MoA; 13.05.1992)

The distribution at the level of ±15% is recorded for Hu2, Hu3 and Hu5. For examples of the closing remarks from their postings see (38), (39) and (40) below. Hu4 did not use any closing remarks in either of the investigated periods.

Examples from Hu2's postings:

(38) Thanks for the help. (Hu2A; 08.05.1989)

Thanks in advance. (Hu2A; 06.02.1990)

Any assistance would be greatly appreciated. (Hu2A; 02.03.1990)

Thank you very much for your interest. (Hu2A; 20.01.1993)

Examples from Hu3's postings:

(39) Any advice would also be most appreciated. (Hu3A; 11.10.1989)

Does anyone have a less drastic solution? (Hu3A; 22.11.1989)

Many thanks. (Hu3A; 29.01.1992)

I would be grateful for any help. (Hu3A; 06.01.1993)

Apologies for the duplication. (Hu3A; 13.01.1993)

HELP! (Hu3A; 14.04.1993)

Examples from Hu5's postings:

(40) Yours cordially. (Hu5A; 30.10.1989)

Yours at UCLA. (Hu5A; 21.11.1989)

Yours. (Hu5A; 16.02.1990)

Enjoy it, all! (Hu5A; 22.05.1990)

I take it back, just kidding. (Hu5A; 23.05.1990)

YOU MAY BE IN FOR A SURPRISE. (Hu5A; 22.05.1990)

Pazienza, all, please. (Hu5A; 31.05.1990)

Yrs. (Hu5A; 04.06.1990)

Yrs, this silly morning. (Hu5A; 21.08.1990)

Heigh Ho, and away we go. But let us be friends, all of us here on this list of alert folks. (Hu5A; 28.01.1993)

With time, the use of closing remarks dropped in the corpora of Hu1 (to 84,85%), Hu3 (two messages) and Hu5 (one message). Also, Hu2's one message contained a closing remark. A considerable increase is recorded for Mo (to 81,35%). It appears that the presence of closing remarks in my data not only demonstrates the authors' consideration of politeness and their growing commitment and familiarity with the *Humanist* community, but also their originality and resourcefulness. Frequently very personalised, opening phrases become a useful way of marking an author's distinctive voice. Examples of the closing remarks found in the later corpora are included in (41), (42), (43), (44) and (45).

Examples from Hu1's postings:

(41) Cheers (Hu1B; 02.11.1999)

Comments and suggestions welcome! Thanks in advance, and best wishes for the holidays and new year. (Hu1B; 22.12.1999)

Cheers and best wishes for the new year (as measured by the calendar prevailing in these parts...) (Hu1B; 30.12.2002)

Happy reading! (Hu1B; 09.09.2000)

Cheers and best wishes. (Hu1B; 09.09.2000)

Happy viewing! (Hu1B; 09.09.2000)

Hope that helps. (Hu1B; 07.02.2001)

Cheerfully (Hu1B; 05.03.2001)

With hopes for peace. (Hu1B; 03.11.2001)

Comments and suggestions also welcome! (Hu1B; 30.10.2002)

Hope this finds everyone well - cheers! (Hu1B; 10.02.2003)

An example from Hu2's postings:

(42) Let us all hack... ;-) (Hu2B; 07.05.1999)

An example from Hu3's postings:

(43) I'd love to have my cake and eat it, too. (Hu3B; 09.12.2002)

An example from Hu5's postings:

(44) Cordially. (Hu5B; 21.10.2000)

Mo's closing remarks mainly include "Yours", sometimes with the addition of one of the following:

(45) Ideas, comments? (MoB; 30.06.1999)

Save me (and my patient) from the sewer please. Many thanks. (MoB; 09.05.2001)

Yes, fascinating! (MoB; 18.11.1999)

Your reactions and comments, please. (MoB; 03.07.2000)

It appears that the presence of closing remarks not only demonstrates the authors' consideration of politeness and their growing commitment and familiarity with the *Humanist* community, but also their originality and resourcefulness. Frequently very personalised, opening phrases become a useful way of marking an author's distinctive voice.

As regards the types of signatures used by the moderator (see Tables 5–23 and 5–24), in the initial period his postings were mainly signed by his full name (in 91,50% of his post), whereas in the later period, his preferred convention was to use initials (found in 84,59% of his post). By contrast, in the postings of regular members from the initial period, the most frequent signatures included the member's full name and his academic affiliation (45,61%), or just full name (29,69%). For one thing, these preferences may be explained by the moderator's growing recognition within the group, his demand for brevity, or the fact of the presence of an additional, extended signature in one posting. For another, the regular *Humanists* may have found it more expedient to signal their real-life identity. Yet, the regular members were also more willing to remain anonymous (11,64% and 42,96% respectively for the two periods, to be contrasted with the moderator's 6,46% and 12,43%).

Further differences are revealed in the use of an extended signature. Initially, it is the regular *Humanists* who use an extended signature more extensively (the moderator's one case, to be contrasted with 49 cases in the postings of the regular members), whereas in the more recent period, an extended signature was present in 78,38% of the moderator's messages, and 52,59% of the regular *Humanists*' postings. As an extended signature is inserted automatically, its increased prominence is connected to the presence of two types of signature in one posting. As I have already stated, a double signature was mainly present in the moderator's postings from the later period (76,22% to be contrasted with 4,44% for regular members).

The moderator's well-recognised and respected position becomes evident in his patterns of opening, concluding and signing his post, especially if compared with the general patterns found in the postings of regular members. First of all, the moderator's use of opening phrases was much lower in comparison with the regular *Humanists* (4,42% vs. 9,74%), and decreased with time (to the level of 1,08%). This may indicate the moderator's direct attitude towards the *Humanist* community, resulting from his familiarity with the group, or his impersonal stance, deriving from compliance with the conventions of dropping a salutation in a public, open forum, whose audience is difficult to estimate.

Structural element	**MoA** **raw occ.(%)**	**Total for all regular *Humanists* (421)** **raw occ.(%)**
Signature: **Initial(s)**	-	3 (0,71%)
First name + Surname	269 (91,50%)	125 (29,69%)
First name + Surname + Name of college	5 (1,70%)	192 (45,61%)
Extended sig.	1 (0,34%)	49 (11,64%)
No sig.	19 (6,46%)	52 (12,35%)
2 types of sig. in a posting	-	-
Opening phrase	13 (4,42%)	41 (9,74%)
Closing remark	119 (40,48%)	95 (22,57%)

Table 5–23. The total distribution of the selected elements of the postings' generic structure for the regular members versus the moderator (period A).

Structural element	MoB raw occ.(%)	Total for all regular *Humanists* (135) raw occ.(%)
Signature:		
Initial(s)	313 (84,59%)	1 (0,74%)
First name + Surname	4 (1,08%)	7 (51,85%)
First name + Surname + Name of college	-	3 (2,22%)
Extended sig.	290 (78,38%)	71 (52,59%)
No sig.	46 [50](12,43%)	58 (42,96%)
2 types of sig. in a posting	282 (76,22%)	6 (4,44%)
Opening phrase	4 (1,08%)	35 (25,93%)
Closing remark	301 (81,35%)	32 (23,70%)

Table 5–24. The total distribution of the selected elements of the postings' generic structure for the regular members versus the moderator (period B).

5.7.2. Subgeneric repertoires

A person's identification with a particular community's values is manifested through the adoption of the community's discoursal practices and genres, and thus the study of the community's repertoire of (sub)genres provides further insights into how an individual's identity is negotiated in CMC discourse. In Swales' discourse community approach, the concept of a genre repertoire is crucial for regulating a community's integrity: "a discourse community utilizes and hence possesses one or more genres in the communicative furtherance of its aims" (Swales 1990, 26). Thus, genres owned by a discourse community have "a double generative capacity" (Swales 1990, 45): on the one hand, they settle a community's rhetorical goals, and on the other, they advance their accomplishment. In addition, Swales' conception allows us to grade membership to a discourse community (experts and novices), and thus members will differ in the degree of their discourse expertise, which may become evident in the repertoire of genres "owned" and employed by a given member. However advantageous, this view is also limiting as it neglects the relevance of such sociological factors as institutional ideologies and powers. Also, it does not fully account for individual variation which results from the need of members to accomplish their

[50] Only in forwarded messages.

particular communicative intentions, such as e.g. showing their originality and resourcefulness (see Bhatia 1993 and 2002).

Following Swales' conception of genre and discourse community, Ivanič points out that "genres are shaped by institutionally defined purposes, roles, and social relationships associated with them", and so they offer to individuals a range of possibilities within which to negotiate their identity (1998, 46). It must be stressed then that the factors responsible for genre formation and enactment additionally contribute to the complexity of mechanisms involved in the discoursal construction of individual identity. For one thing, repeated communicative situations decide about the stabilising effect of the emergent genres for a community's collective experience. For another, changeability is an inherent feature of genres: "genres are also in a state of constant evolution as members respond to professional and private exigencies in new and innovative ways" (Hyland 2000, 5). Moreover, there is always some tension involved between accommodation and resistance to the conventions, and thus a complex interweaving of factors implicates the negotiation of academic identity in discourse (see Ivanič 1998, 244).

With relation to e-discourse, I argued elsewhere (Sokół 2004) that the communicative situations of CMC reinforce the role of a genre repertoire owned by a community as a means of accomplishing such social purposes as the recruitment of new members, the maintenance of the community's cohesion, or the construction of individual identity. Yet, the electronic medium constitues a dynamic and unstable communicative environment. Its inherent capabilities such as flexibility, accessibility and speed, facilitate the processes of genre modification and emergence, accelerating the evolution of genres in general (see Erickson 1997, 1999). Moreover, Yates and Sumner (1997) point to the medium's destabilising effect on genre use and production. Digital texts are more mutable and dynamic, and consequently more indeterminate, which contributes to the loss of fixity and reliability of existing genres.

In addition, problems emerge if Swales' conception of genre and genre identification is applied to study of the genre of a discussion list posting (see Gruber 2000; Sokół 2005, 2006a, 2006b). My preliminary attempt to establish the generic status of the postings from the *Humanist* revealed that e-seminar postings were instances of the subgenres of a discussion list posting rather than instances of separate genres (Sokół 2005). Namely, in view of the criteria of genre classification in Bhatia's (1993) functional approach, I found that the communicative purposes of particular classes of postings were subordinated to the general purpose of the genre of a discussion list, i.e. debating and information exchange. Yet, following content analysis of all my data, which aimed at the identification of the communicative purpose of the postings, I extended the list of subgenres put forwarded in Sokół 2005. Thus, for the purposes of the present analysis I used the classification that included the following categories of subgenres of the genre of a discussion list posting:

- the categories related to the purpose of academic debate: "voice in a discussion", "initiation of a discussion";
- the categories related to the purpose of information exchange: "note", "report", "announcement", "request", "meta-message", "query", "book review", "obituary"[51].

As already stated, the above categories can be accommodated under the two dominant rhetorical purposes of the genre of a discussion list posting. However, they hold generic potential because of the social validity of these purposes and the emergent inner structuring that develops in response to distinctive social and technological aspects of the new communicative situation. The intrinsic differences between the emergent subgenres may be demonstrated through the analysis of the formal indicators of (sub)generic status. For instance, as I showed elsewhere (Sokół 2006a), the developed subgenres of announcement and note differed in the level of interactivity,[52] where interactivity was suggested as a vital factor in the maintenance and identification of electronic genres.

The focus on the communicative purpose provides relatively stable grounds for the generic analysis of the postings, as these emergent discourse structures are phenomena-in-progress and their form displays some degree of variation. However, such an analysis does not proceed without complications, and therefore must be supported by the analysis that takes into consideration formal indicators of genre development and identification. As for the problems, during my study I noted cases in which it was difficult to determine one dominant purpose of a posting, mainly because of the phenomenon of embedding. In addition, as the new medium facilitates the creation of novel electronic (sub)genres and innovative variants of "traditional" (sub)genres, I encountered problems in labelling the emergent structures.

As regards the purposes of my research, in this section my intention was to establish the repertoire of subgenres used by the *Humanists* under study. In this way I aimed to find out how these members position themselves through the discourse types they draw upon. In addition, I intended to test one of my initial hypotheses and discover whether the

[51] For the definitions and examples of the identified subgenres see Appendices A, B and C.

[52] As defined by Rafaeli (1988) and Rafaeli and Sudweeks (1997).

members' use of particular subgenres was dependent on the frequency of their contributions to the e-seminar.

The distribution of the subgenres identified in the corpora under investigation is presented in Tables 5–25 and 5–26.

Subgenre		Hu1A	Hu2A	Hu3A	Hu4A	Hu5A	MoA	Total for all members (715)
Voice in a discussion	**raw occ.**	6	9	47	17	120	63	262
	%	11,76	27,27	34,56	51,52	71,43	21,43	36,64
Initiation of a discussion	**raw occ.**	-	-	4	1	-	28	33
	%			2,94	3,03		9,52	4,62
Request	**raw occ.**	38	13	28	1	4	57	141
	%	74,51	39,39	20,59	3,03	2,38	19,39	19,72
Announcement	**raw occ.**	1	3	3	-	-	29	36
	%	1,96	9,09	2,21			9,86	5,03
Note	**raw occ.**	6	3	54	12	42	46	163
	%	11,76	9,09	39,71	36,36	25,00	15,65	22,80
"Meta-message"	**raw occ.**	-	-	-	1	-	50	51
	%				3,03		17,01	7,13
Query	**raw occ.**	-	-	-	1	2	2	5
	%				3,03	1,19	0,68	0,70
Book review	**raw occ.**	-	-	-	-	-	4	4
	%						1,36	0,56
Report	**raw occ.**	-	-	-	-	-	1	1
	%						0,34	0,14
Obituary	**raw occ.**	-	-	-	-	-	-	-
	%							
Forwarded message	**raw occ.**	-	5	-	-	-	14	19
	%		15,15				4,76	2,66

Table 5–25. The distribution of the subgenres identified in the corpora from period A. The figures indicate the number of raw occurrences of a given subgenre in the corpora. The percentages indicate the frequency of a given subgenre relative to the total number of postings in a given corpus.

Subgenre		Hu1B	Hu2B	Hu3B	Hu4B	Hu5B	MoB	Total for all members (505)
Voice in a discussion	raw occ.	11	4	15	34	5	93	162
	%	33,33	100	40,54	65,38	55,56	25,14	32,08
Initiation of a discussion	raw occ.	-	-	-	-	-	76	76
	%						20,54	15,05
Request	raw occ.	2	-	6	1	-	39	48
	%	6,06		16,22	1,92		10,54	9,50
Announcement	raw occ.	16	-	3	1	-	18	38
	%	48,48		8,11	1,92		4,86	7,52
Note	raw occ.	3	-	8	12	2	48	73
	%	9,09		21,62	23,08	22,22	12,97	14,46
"Meta-message"	raw occ.	-	-	2	1	2	37	42
	%			5,41	1,92	22,22	10,00	8,32
Query	raw occ.	-	-	1	1	-	4	6
	%			2,70	1,92		1,08	1,19
Book review	raw occ.	-	-	1	-	-	4	5
	%			2,70			1,08	0,99
Report	raw occ.	1	-	-	-	-	1	2
	%	3,03					0,27	0,40
Obituary	raw occ.	-	-	-	-	-	3	3
	%						0,81	0,59
Forwarded message	raw occ.	-	-	1	2	-	47	50
	%			2,70	3,85		12,70	9,90

Table 5–26. The distribution of the subgenres identified in the corpora from period B. The figures indicate the number of raw occurrences of a given subgenre in the corpora. The percentages indicate the frequency of a given subgenre relative to the total number of postings in a given corpus.

In general, the analysis of the generic identity of the postings revealed that the *Humanists* under study, through the range of subgenres used, position themselves as distinctive individuals who use the medium relative to their purposes, and/or status within the group (see the moderator's role). The growing experience with the medium brought the stabilisation of the members' expectations towards the use of the e-seminar, and the progressing diversification and specialisation of established discourse categories. The redistribution of subgenres in period B proves the evolution of the users' self-concept. At the same time, the results point to the consolidation of the emergent subgenres over time, providing evidence for some stability of these evolving discourse structures. The study also indicates the relevance of particular subgenres for users of a scholarly e-seminar, calling for the reconsideration of the status of these subgenres in the whole domain of the (sub)genres utilised by an academic community.

The percentage quotas for the identified subgenres demonstrate that the most essential subgenre in my data is "voice in a discussion", related to the purpose of academic debate. It is the most frequent subgenre in both periods of investigation, used by all the *Humanists* under study (the total proportional shares for the two periods are 36,64% and 32,08% respectively). Voice in a discussion is usually an extended argumentation and marks a member's turn in an ongoing debate, and thus his/her presence on the forum. Therefore, the frequency of a member's contributions to ongoing discussions decides about his/her strong position in the group, both as an active subscriber and knowledge generator. In fact, frequent or regular contributions to discussion are one of the necessary conditions associated with a successful scholarly e-seminar (Rojo 1995). An e-seminar belongs to collaborative mass media, which, in contrast to broadcasting mass media, are distinguished by the reciprocal interdependence among users. This means that individual users of collaborative media cannot achieve the potential benefits offered by the medium on their own, and that the very existence of the medium depends on users' participation. In addition, the number of voices in a discussion is also indicative of the longevity of topics relevant for the group's interests, and for particular members. The topic of a discussion is always specified in the "Subject" line of the header. For the ease of archiving and screening the postings, the same subject is repeated in a thread of postings, or at least includes the same key words or expressions.

The prominence of the voice in a discussion subgenre provides justification for the label "electronic seminar" (e-seminar), frequently assigned to academic electronic forums. As Allwood recounts, the academic seminar outside the electronic context is an institution whose "ideal purpose is often said to be the promotion of free and critical inquiry, in relation to a selected topic, in an academic scientific setting. Ideally, it should supplement the finding, teaching and learning of facts by providing teachers and students an opportunity to participate in a systematically critical discussion" (Allwood 1993, 1).

As regards the individual distribution of voices in a discussion, in the initial period the most active discussants were Hu5 (120 voices in a discussion out of a total of 262), Mo (63) and Hu3 (47). With time, the total number of voices in a discussion declined to 162, but the individual figures increased for Mo (to 93), Hu4 (34) and Hu1 (11). The rise may point to the growing involvement of these members, who probably continued to draw benefits from their participation in the *Humanist*. Hu3's contributions to ongoing debates declined to 15, as well as his general activity on the forum. Hu2 and Hu5 were still contributors of their voices (4 and 5 respectively), but as already stated, their participation in the forum during period B was considerably shorter than of the other members.

Two other crucial subgenres in may data, despite their declining distribution, are "note" and "request", which relate to the purpose of information exchange. These are the subgenres which also support the existence of an e-forum. Notes are brief, informal postings, whose major aim is to provide information, frequently including a personal comment. With their informational content relevant to members' personal interests, goals and needs, notes contribute to a pool of "public goods", from which all can profit. In addition, as my preliminary study indicates (Sokół 2006a), notes are largely interactive, probably because of their informality and personalised content. In contrast, requests direct the audience's attention to members' interests, goals and needs, and have the potential to initiate a response. Requests in my data differ in their level of formality and directness. Usually, they include inquiries for assistance or information related to various aspects of members' scholarly activity, e.g. an exchange of research materials or ideas, bibliographic searches, professional contacts, etc.

As concerns the distribution of notes in the corpora under study, their presence declined with time from 163 to 73 occurrences (the respective percentages are 22,8% and 14,46%). The decline may suggest that members of a scholarly e-seminar are less willing to engage in shorter, less formal forms of expression. They are rather inclined to produce more extended, and more carefully composed messages, which may be connected to their continued adherence to the general standards of academic public discourse. This observation, however, would have to be supported by a more extensive research, one that would include a socio-cognitive investigation of the medium's use by academics.

In period A, the *Humanists* whose use of notes was the highest were Hu3 (54 notes), Mo (46), Hu5 (42) and Hu4 (12). Over time, Hu4 an Mo's use of notes remained roughly at the same level, whereas it declined for the remaining *Humanists*. Still, the presence of notes strengthens the members' position as active and competent knowledge contributors.

An interesting change is presented in the distribution of requests, as their use decreased considerably with time for all members under investigation (from a total of 141 to 48 occurrences; the corresponding percentages are 19,72% and 9,50%). In the initial period of the medium's use, the *Humanists* were more eager to place requests, as their expectations about the potential gains might have been higher. In the more recent period, requests are rather infrequent in the corpora of regular *Humanists*: about 80% of requests were contributed by the moderator. The figures indicate the evolution of the members' beliefs about the usefulness of the medium: over time it may have turned out that the expected feedback from their audience was not satisfactory enough. Also, the members' self-perception evolved: once the *Humanists* got better acquainted with the group's needs, they were willing to provide knowledge and contribute to the ongoing debates rather than request information or put queries.

The *Humanists*' commitment to the group is also demonstrated by the considerable proportion of announcements (36 and 38 occurrences in the two periods; the respective percentages are 5,03% and 7,52%). Announcements are posting including a public, formal statement about a forthcoming event or enterprise, such as a conference, book or journal publication, scholarly project, etc. Their primary aim is to convey purely factual information. In the initial period, announcements were mainly sent by the moderator (29 cases). Hu1 contributed one announcement, and Hu2 and Hu3 three announcements each. In the more recent period, a large number of announcements came from the moderator (18 cases), and from Hu1, for whom I noted a substantial rise, from 1 to 16 occurrences. Three announcements were posted by Hu3 and one by Hu4. Announcements frequently give evidence about the member's established position as a competent researcher and scholar, as he is usually a(n) (co-)organiser or participant of an announced event or undertaking. Through the presentation of factual information that includes references to recognised academic institutions, announcements legitimise a member's institutional identity.

The group of the less numerous but important subgenres of a discussion list posting includes also "meta-messages" and "initiation of a discussion". By a meta-message I refer to a posting whose aim is to inform about or discuss matters related to the interaction in the e-seminar such as discussion topics, technical aspects of the functioning of the forum, organisational procedures, managing interpersonal relations that e.g. involve "flaming" situations, etc. The total distribution of meta-messages in the two periods is 51 and 42 occurrences (the corresponding percentages are 7,13% and 8,32%). In the initial period, virtually the only contributor of meta-messages is the moderator (50 occurrences), which can be explained by his role as the group's manager and administrator. One meta-message was posted by Hu4. In contrast, in the later period, more *Humanists* contributed meta-messages, which may be linked to their sense of group identity, their growing responsibility and involvement in the matters related to the e-seminar. In period B, the moderator was still the leading contributor of meta-messages (42 occurrences), Hu3 and Hu5 posted two meta-messages each and Hu4 one meta-message.

The study reveals interesting patterns in the distribution of the subgenre "initiation of discussion". Initiation of a discussion is a posting whose aim is to provoke a debate, by announcing a "niche" or "gap" in the Swalesean sense, so it is related to the seminar's general purpose of academic debate. Its existence is vital for the e-seminar's survival, provided the audience finds the suggested topics interesting enough to engage into debate. Members who introduce discussion topics show their engagement and sense of responsibility for the community. They probably themselves find their membership beneficial for their own scholarly discovery. The total distribution of initiations of a discussion for the two investigated periods is 33 and 76 (the respective percentages are 4,62% and 15,05%), so the rise is substantial. However, while in the initial period under study 3 *Humanists* contributed initiations of a discussion (the moderator 33 messages, Hu3 four messages and Hu4 one message), in the more recent period all initiations of a discussion came from the moderator. Again, such an activity of the moderator can be justified by his role as an activator and facilitator of discussion. The lack of eagerness to introduce discussion topics by the regular *Humanists* under study is probably related to the general decline of the activity on the forum.

The group of the least subgenres identified in the investigated corpora includes the following categories: query, book review, report and obituary. I classify them as the subgenres related to the general purpose of information exchange. The presence of these subgenres in my data is mainly thanks to the moderator's activity, resulting from performing his managerial duties. Only single examples of these categories were found in the corpora of the regular members.

Query is a brief posting that includes an inquiry to be answered or solved, or a rhetorical question. As they include direct or indirect questions, the value of queries lies in their interactive potential (see Rafaeli and Sudweeks 1987). Queries may have the power to activate action on the part of the audience. The distribution of queries in the two periods is 5 and 6 occurrences (the corresponding percentages are 0,7% and 1,19%). Hu5 and Mo contributed two queries each and Hu4 one query. In the more recent period, Mo posted four queries and Hu3 and Hu4 one query each. The presence of queries gives evidence about the author's direct attitude towards their audience, and his/her belief in its potential.

Book review is a posting that gives a critical evaluation of a book. It is an electronic variant of the "traditional" book review. In my data, book reviews include assessments of academic publications which might be of interest to the *Humanist* community. In the initial period, the only four book reviews were posted by the moderator. In the more recent period, also four reviews came from the moderator, but one from Hu3.

Report is also an electronic version of the "traditional" genre: it is a posting that includes a public, formal account of a past (academic) event or enterprise. In the initial period, the only report was sent by the moderator, while in the more recent period, the moderator and Hu1 contributed one report each. Finally, the only three postings that included a notice of someone's death (i.e. obituaries) were found in the moderator's corpus from period B.

One study that could be interesting would be to consider the status of forwarded messages in the repertoire of subgenres utilised by members of an e-seminar. For the purposes of the present research, however, I limited the analysis to the presentation of the occurrences of forwarded messages, as the *Humanists* under study were not the authors of their content. Still, forwarded messages mark the sender's presence on the forum, and their subject matter gives clues about the potential interests of both the sender and the group.

In the discussion of the subgeneres identified in my data, the moderator's role became apparent in the distinctive repertoire of subgenres he utilised. The comparison of the distribution of the subgenres for the moderator and for the regular members is presented in Tables 5–27 and 5–28. The power of the moderator lies in the greatest range of categories identified in his corpora, which is related to the moderator's multiple duties as the *Humanist's* leader, administrator, editor and promoter, whereas the power of the regular members lies mainly in how they contribute to ongoing debates (a high rate of voices in a discussion), and how they enlarge a pool of public goods through adding information relevant to the *Humanists'* interests (a high rate of notes and announcements).

Subgenre	**MoA** **raw occ.(%)**	**Total for all regular *Humanists* (421)** **raw occ.(%)**
Voice in a discussion	63 (14,81%)	199 (47,27%)
Initiation of a discussion	28 (3,67%)	5 (1,19%)
Request	57 (4,13%)	84 (19,95%)
Announcement	29 (3,10%)	7 (1,66%)
Note	46 (18,14%)	117 (27,79%)
"Meta-message"	50 (38,69%)	1 (0,24%)
Query	2 (6,77%)	3 (0,71%)
Book review	4 (2,87%)	-
Report	1 (4,36%)	-
Obituary	-	-
Forwarded message	14 (1,15%)	5 (1,19%)

Table 5–27. The total distribution of subgenres for the regular members versus the moderator (period A).

Subgenre	**MoB** **raw occ.(%)**	**Total for all regular *Humanists* (135)** **raw occ.(%)**
Voice in a discussion	93 (25,14%)	69 (51,11%)
Initiation of a discussion	76 (20,54%)	-
Request	39 (10,54%)	9(6,67%)
Announcement	18 (4,86 %)	20 (14,81%)
Note	48 (12,97%)	25 (18,52%)
"Meta-message"	37 (10,00%)	5 (3,70%)
Query	4 (1,08%)	2 (1,48%)
Book review	4 (1,08%)	1 (0,74%)
Report	1 (0,27%)	1 (0,74%)
Obituary	3 (0,81%)	-
Forwarded message	47 (12,70%)	3 (2,22%)

Table 5–28. The total distribution of subgenres for the regular members versus the moderator (period B).

The study of the repertoire of subgenres used by the *Humanists* involved also a statistical analysis whose aim was to find out whether there is any correlation between the use of particular subgenres and the number of members' contributions (i.e. the frequency of their contributions). To achieve this purpose, I used Chuprov's association coefficient. In the calculations I excluded the figures obtained for the moderator because of his special status within the group which determines his discursive practices. The values of the coefficient for the two periods respectively are T_{xy}=0,318 and T_{xy}=0,288[53]. The figures indicate that the correlation between the use of particular subgenres and the frequency of the members' contributions is not statistically significant. This led me to reject the hypothesis that there is a mutual dependency between the frequency of the *Humanists*' contributions to the forum and the subgenres employed by particular individuals. Thus, the members' repertoire of subgenres appears to depend on such external factors as the members' immediate purposes and needs, the community's norms and practices and on power relations.

To summarise this section, although the emergent subgenres are still phenomena-in-progress, their investigation gives insights into how academic identity is constructed in e-discourse. The study confirms that genre is a highly institutionalised textual event: the formation of new subgenres is largely based on the members' knowledge of previously encountered (sub)genres. More importantly though, the electronic context offers greater possibilities for making use of genre's natural "propensity for innovation and change" (Bhatia 2002: 24): the *Humanists* appropriate the medium to attain their individual communicative purposes, and thus actively contribute to the emergence of new electronic subgenres. It must be noted, however, that while in the offline world, the exploitation of the genre's full potential is reserved for the expert members of an academic community, in the electronic medium the manipulation with institutionalised generic forms is necessarily linked to the degree of an academic's e-competence. It seems then that the increased participation of academics in CMC in the last couple of decades has challenged the established, traditionally understood idea of scholarly authority and expertise.

[53] Appendix D includes the calculations of Chuprov's coefficient to test the hypothesis if there is a correlation between the use of particular subgenres and the frequency of the members' contributions.

CONCLUSIONS

The aim of the book was to discuss academic identity construction in CMC discourse, on the example of an e-seminar. An e-seminar is an asynchronous type of CMC, where private, public and institutional domains merge, and therefore it provides an interesting context for exploring academic communication phenomena in cyberspace. More specifically, my purpose was to search for the linguistic cues of academic identity on three levels of discourse organisation: the features of lexico-grammar, textual macrostructures and genres. In general, the analysis shows how these three levels of discourse organisation contribute towards how academics negotiate their identity relative to the aims and activities of their discourse community and relative to their individual goals. The discoursal construction of academic identity in electronic discourse depends also on such factors as the medium's defining properties and the lack of direct physical contact between interactants. An important finding is the confirmation of the individuating character of the medium: i.e. the authors' self-presentation in an e-seminar is characterised by their distinctive voice and increased self-disclosure. This allows me to put forward an argument that communication in this context enhances individuality, which bears important consequences for how academics negotiate their identity in electronic discourse, exploiting the possibilities offered by the new medium.

First of all, my investigation proves that the members under study maintain on the forum a stable and legitimate identity, which emerges as an extension and elaboration of their professional identity constructed in the offline world. This becomes evident on all three levels of discourse organisation that I have selected for my analysis. On the micro-level, the members' professional identity appears to be enhanced by means of such lexical and grammatical features as: the prominence of the pronoun *I* over *we*, the presence of the "*we*-the academic institution", the use of private and suasive verbs with the *I*-perspective, the manifestation of epistemic modality of high and median probability and of deontic modality. As regards the analysis on the macro-level, the members' authoritative and competent identity is built through the following: the presence of the members' personal data in the header of the posting, the inclusion of their real-life academic credentials in the signature, the use of the subgenres "voice in a discussion", "initiation of a discussion" and "announcement". Through these resources the *Humanists* mark their authorial presence as expert and recognised members of an academic community, active knowledge generators and legitimate owners of the property rights over their contributions.

The linguistic resources enumerated above point to the members' "institutional self". In other words, the presence of institutional aspects of self demonstrates how the *Humanists* validate their professional identity in cyberspace, and how they give it an institutional standing. This also shows how the collective identity of academic institutions becomes strengthened in the disembodied and unstable context of CMC. In addition, the findings prove that in cyberspace there is a strong influence of the norms and communicative practices associated with the "traditional", offline forms of scholarly exchange. The *Humanists* under study appear to adhere to the general standards of academic public discourse, which supports the results of the previous research, emphasising the role of offline experience in the perception of social interaction in cyberspace (see e.g. Wallace 1999; Żabicki 1999).

Self-promotion and the maintenance of a legitimate identity in an e-seminar arises from several reasons. Internationalisation and globalisation of scholarship, and the accompanying phenomena such as intensified competition and the commodification or marketisation of science (Duszak 2002; Fairclogh 1995), necessitate an increased drive for gaining and reconfirming scholarly authority and acclaim, also by recognised members of an academic community. The electronic medium has become a new forceful means of achieving this aim, mainly because of its communicative function. It turns out that the new medium has added to the "traditional" modes of scholarly exchange, extending for academics the repertoire of effective means of self-promotion. Active and reliable participation in e-discussions may enhance the members' career development and the propagation of their research and academic achievements.

Also, prominent authorial presence in electronic discourse may draw from the nature of interpersonal and group interaction in an e-seminar and the medium's defining properties. In particular, the lack of direct physical contact and reduced social context cues demand from the users controlled and personalised forms of self-presentation. This is linked to hybridity, one of the major constitutive properties of the electronic medium. In the Internet, being a mass medium, the blurred boundaries between the public and private domains of interpersonal communication result in the opposing characteristics of verbal expression: for instance, impersonal vs.

hyperpersonal communication; anonymity vs. highly controlled forms of self-presentation; disembodiment vs. re-embodiment (i.e. assuming new identities and roles); active participation vs. lurking (see Davis 1997).

In my research material, I have also noted a high presence of the private aspects of self ("private self"), which demonstrates that the interaction in an academic e-seminar is individuating. Namely, the members' self-presentation in this context is personalised, marked by their unique voice and increased self-disclosure. Therefore, on the one hand, in this potentially threatening communicative context, the users may show caution about their self-presentation, and hence their more "conservative" reliance on the established, institutionally sanctioned norms of an academic community. On the other hand, an informal character of the interaction in an e-seminar encourages indirectness, intimacy and spontaneity, resulting in the extended forms of self-presentation and revealing personal information. Such specificity of interaction also provides space for the users' greater autonomy and innovation. The members' resourcefulness is especially evident in the patterns of opening, closing and signing their postings to the *Humanist*. Thus, similarly to the results of other research on the linguistic behaviour in group CMCs (see e.g. Taylor 2000), my findings appear to contradict the de-individuation hypothesis, as advanced by Kiesler et al (1984).

The presence of the "private self", just as well as of the "institutional self", may be explained by the general changes in contemporary academic discourse, as discussed by Fairclough (1995). Following a social view of language use, Fairclough points to the interconnected developments in contemporary discursive practices of an academic community: next to the commodification or marketisation of public academic discourse, we also observe its conversalisation. Conversalisation is viewed as the infusion of private domain practices by the public domain, practices which are necessary for the complex processes of negotiating relationships and identities. Consequently, the related aspects of discourse are its personalisation and the realisation of promotional objectives. Overall, the commodification and conversalisation of public discourse provide evidence for a greater instrumentalisation of contemporary discursive practices, intensified by the development of the Internet and CMC.

In addition, an evolutionary perspective that I took in the present study allowed me to demonstrate how the patterns of scholars' authorial presence in electronic discourse evolve with the stabilisation of the medium's use. Generally, the observed changes reveal the evolution of the members' self-perception and their expectations towards the medium, the development of their sense of group identity, and their growing awareness of the audience. This transformation appears most evident on the micro-level of discourse organisation – in the members' pronoun choice, and on the textual level – in the global organisation of their postings and subgeneric repertoires. In the first place, the analysis of the data from the two periods of the *Humanists*' membership shows differences in how the scholars validate their professional identity in electronic discourse, and how they give it an institutional standing. It appears that in the initial period of their membership, the *Humanists* under study were introducing themselves to the group, simultaneously trying to estimate the potential gains from their participation on the forum. In order to reconfirm their scholarly authority, the *Humanists* were presenting themselves as affiliates to offline academic institutions, members of conference organising committees, book and journal editors, co-researchers taking part in various academic projects and undertakings, etc. This is exemplified by a high distribution of the "*we*-represented academic institution" and of the subgenre "announcement". At the same time, through the considerable number of requests, the *Humanists* were directing the audience's attention to their interests, goals and needs. With time, the *Humanists'* participation on the forum stabilised and their expectations shifted; hence, a falling distribution of the "*we*- represented academic institution" and of requests.

Instead, I found evidence for the members' growing familiarity and recognition within the *Humanist*, and their commitment and sense of group identity, which strengthened the group's cohesion. This conclusion is corroborated by the increased distribution of the "*we*-members of the e-seminar", the patterns of opening, closing and signing the postings, and the diversification and consolidation of the subgeneric repertoire of an e-seminar in the later period under study. An evolutionary perspective revealed also a considerable variation and inconsistency in the communicative practices of individual *Humanists*. This points to the fact that discursive practices in cyberspace are phenomena in progress. In addition, these findings may suggest the evolution of the members' expectations about what constitutes a prototypical contribution to an academic e-seminar.

Through the comparison of the discursive practices of the regular members of the *Humanist* to those of the group's moderator, I was able to show how identity is constructed relative to the individual's roles within the community. The analyses of the moderator's postings indicate his multiple duties as the *Humanist*'s leader, administrator, initiator of discussions, editor and promoter. This is exemplified by the fact that in both periods under study, the moderator generated the greatest number of subgeneric categories. By contrast, the power of the regular members lies mainly in how they contributed to ongoing debates (domination of the subgenre "voice in a discussion"), and how they enlarged a pool of public goods through adding information relevant to the *Humanists*' interests (a high rate of notes and announcements). The moderator's pronoun choice presents him as the *Humanist* with the biggest sense of group identity, and the lowest need to rely on his academic affiliation when creating his online persona. Finally, the moderator's well-recognised and respected position becomes evident in the patterns of the global organisation of his postings. He displays both his direct attitude towards the *Humanist* community, resulting from his familiarity with the group, and also his impersonal stance, deriving from compliance with the conventions of interaction in a public academic forum.

Overall, the analysis of authorial presence in academic electronic discourse demonstrates how particular linguistic choices of individuals relate to the socio-cultural context of the communicative situation. The *Humanists* under study negotiate their professional identity relative to the institutionally sanctioned norms and practices of an academic community. At the same time, they exploit the possibilities offered by the new medium and actively construct their unique voice of a competent member of academia. Although throughout the book, I have pointed to both individual and communal aspects of the discoursal construction of academic identity in cyberspace, the study proves the medium's potential for bringing about the revival of individuality. This I consider to be a great advantage of global and flexible CMC, which may contribute to enhancing the authority and uniqueness of the individual.

My study of the discoursal construction of academic identity in cyberspace opens up new perspectives for the future linguistic research. Admittedly, the increased participation of academics in CMC has challenged the established, traditionally understood idea of membership in an academic community, and of scholarly authority and expertise. It appears necessary, then, to specify what determines the universality of scholarship in cyberspace, and which discourse patterns distinguish an academic discourse community from other discourse communities. A useful approach for pursuing this thread of research may be Swales' conception of genre analysis, which allows us to focus on the community's shared communicative goals, norms and discursive practices as the factors that decide about the community's cohesion. The results of my present research show how the members of academia exploit the generic potential offered by the electronic medium in order to negotiate their individual and group identity. In this way they contribute to the modification of the existing (sub)genres, and cause the formation and enactment of novel, electronic ones. There is a need for a new, interdisciplinary theory of genre analysis, which would incorporate social and cognitive aspects of genre formation and enactment, and thus, it would be able to better account for the concept of genre as a script or frame (e.g. Grochowski 2004; Zaśko-Zielińska 2002). The investigation of the cognitive processes involved in the formation and maintenance of electronic genres can increase the generic awareness of language users, an awareness which remains a fundamental part of the communicative competence of language users.

APPENDIX A

DEFINITIONS OF SUBGENRES IDENTIFIED IN THE CORPORA

1. The subgenres related to the purpose of information exchange:

Announcement - a posting including a public, formal statement about a forthcoming event or enterprise, such as a conference, book or journal publication, scholarly project, etc.; the primary aim of an announcement is to convey purely factual information.

Note - a brief, informal posting, whose aim is to provide information, frequently including a personal comment.

Request - a posting including a formal or informal inquiry for information, appeal for assistance.

Meta-message - a posting whose aim is to inform about or discuss matters related to the interaction in the e-seminar, discussion topics, technical aspects of its functioning, organisational procedures, managing interpersonal relations that e.g. involve flaming situations, etc.

Report - a posting including a public, formal account of a past event or enterprise.

Query - a brief posting including an inquiry to be answered or solved, or a rhetorical question.

Book review - a posting that gives a critical evaluation of a book.

Obituary - a posting including a notice of someone's death; usually with a short biography.

2. The subgenres related to the purpose of academic debate:

Voice in a discussion - a posting which is a turn in an ongoing debate.

Initiation of a discussion - a posting whose aim is to provoke a debate, by announcing a "niche" or "gap" in the Swalesean sense.

APPENDIX B

EXAMPLES OF SUBGENRES IDENTIFIED IN THE CORPORA: THE SUBGENRES RELATED TO THE PURPOSE OF INFORMATION EXCHANGE

Announcement 1

Date: Fri, 14 Dec 90 13:53:52 CST
From: [Hu1's first name, surname and email address]
Subject: Facilitator sought

Drury College is seeking a facilitator for its Faculty Summer Seminar, to be held sometime during June, 1991.

The Seminar brings together Drury faculty for an intensive, two- week period of multi-disciplinary study and discussion, centered on topics of interest marked by both a general, "academic" perspective and by relevance to teaching in specific disciplines. (Recent topics have included "Classical Ethics, Carol Gilligan, and Teaching Ethics Across the Curriculum" [1988] and "The Canon" [1989], a study of how literary and other sorts of "canons" are formed, their rolc in culture and education, etc.)

Our topic this year is "Mind, Brain, and Creativity." The topic is occasioned by the observation that many of us, across a diversity of disciplines, have made regarding the impact of the computer: that the computer not only makes for a _quantitative_ difference in our work -- but also seems to offer an environment marked by _qualitative_ enhancements to our thinking and creativity. We are seeking a facilitator to guide our study first on a general level regarding theories of mind, brain, and creativity. We are open to a variety of approaches -- e.g., a fully philosophical approach reviewing both classical and contemporary theories (including the mind/brain discussion); a psychological approach with attention to contemporary views on creativity; the history of mathematics as an example of creative thinking and discussion of creativity in selected figures, etc.

The ideal facilitator will also have sufficient computer-based experience to present a series of examples of how the computer has served as a new kind of creative environment (e.g., through hypermedia, computer modeling in mathematics, etc.) -- though other sorts of examples (e.g. teaching students Japanese bookbinding and how to incorporate images as part of the writing process) would also be pertinent. _Critiques_ of the claim that the computer provides a new sort of creative environment are, of course, also welcome.

Typically, the facilitator will be asked to spend five days on campus to lead the seminar, as well as work with the Faculty Development Committee in planning the workshop schedule, reading list, and related activities. A modest honorarium for the facilitator's services, along with travel and per diem expenses, will be provided. I should also add that our facilitators consistently comment on how much _fun_ they have in the seminar, as it becomes a collaborative learning experience _for them_, with colleagues who share their considerable expertise and experience in thinking and talking about ideas which are both of interest "academically" and pertinent particularly to the art of teaching.

Interested persons should contact me directly, preferably by way of BITNET. A brief description of your background, and a proposed program of study should be included. Thanks to one and all.

Hu1's extended signature

Announcement 2

Date: Mon, 05 Aug 2002 09:25:03 +0100
From: [Hu3's email address]
Subject: Workshop on Transcription of Medieval MSS at Berkeley August 19

The Digital Scriptorium Project has prepared another revised version of the Document Type Definition (DTD) for the encoded transcription of medieval manuscripts using XML, documentation of that DTD, and a set of software tools to facilitate their use. These materials will be available after 8/19/02 to anyone, at UC Berkeley or elsewhere, at http://sunsite.berkeley.edu/Scriptorium/transcription.html

The Bancroft Library, U. of California, Berkeley, will sponsor a one-day hands-on workshop (9 a.m. - 4 p.m.) on Monday, August 19 (place TBA). The workshop will be led by Sharon Goetz and Charles Faulhaber and will cover all aspects of the use of the transcription guidelines and the software: downloading and installation, overview of text encoding principles for the preparation of machine-readable texts, and step-by-step instruction in the encoding and transcription of medieval manuscripts using the software.

Participants may use manuscripts available on the Digital Scriptorium website or provide their own. The workshop is open to anyone, whether affiliatied with UC Berkeley or not. Therre is no fee, but we can accomodate only 17 participants. If you are interested in attending the workshop, please contact Charles Faulhaber (cfaulhab@library.berkeley.edu).

The original DTD was prepared by Michael Sperberg-McQueen, former U.S. editor of the Text Encoding Initiative. An XML version was prepared by David Seaman (Electronic Text Center, U. of Virginia). This in turn has been extensively revised by Sharon Goetz (UC Berkeley). We are deeply indebted to all three for their work.

[Hu3's extended signature]

Note 1

Date: Wed, 7 Nov 90 15:09:27 EST
From: [Hu1's first name, surname and email address]
Forwarded by: Mo
Subject: Quotation Citation

"Education is the process, not the destination, the process of moving from cocksure ignorance to thoughtful uncertainty."

This is credited to T.H. Bell, U.S. Commissioner of Education -- unfortunately, with no further citation, in: L. M. Boyd _Boyd's Book of Odd Facts_New York: Signet, 1979 p. 147

Sorry not to have more details.

[Hu1's first name and surname]

Note 2

Date: Thu, 2 Nov 89 15:22:00 EST
From: [Hu5's surname and email address]
Subject: Re: 3.683 nuclear fiction? (34)

Recently read a fine novel called PRINCIPLES OF NUCLEAR CHEMISTORY, or PRINCIPLES OF AMERICAN NUCLEAR CHEMISTRY, An Irsh-named author, and from Atlantic Monthly about 20 years ago. Got it from UCLA library first edition last spring, recommended by e-mail from Toronto, in fact. First class novel.
[Hu5's first name initial and surname]

Request 1

Date: Thu, 08 Feb 90 15:27:50 CST
From: [Hu4's first name, surname and email address]
Subject: French periodical

I am trying to find Cahier 2 of _Mythes, Croyances et religions dans le monde Anglo-Saxon_ (specifically, an article on Chaucer's Prioress by Yvette Salviati, pp. 13-29 of that issue). Our Int. Library Loan, usually able to find most anything, drew a blank. I tried OCLC and found only 1 holding in all of the U.S.A., at Southern Illinois University at Carbondale----and they have only Cahier 4.

The Chaucer article looks very useful for a study I am just starting on the Prioress. If anyone knows of a library in Canada (or elsewhere on this side of the Atlantic) that has the journal, I would be most appreciative. (If I could get to Internet, I'd look myself, but while our MIS folks say it can be done, they have been in no hurry to make Internet available to faculty....)
[Hu4's first name, surname and email address]

Request 2

Date: Fri, 1 Sep 89 17:32:47 PDT

From: [Hu3's email address]
Subject: scanning and question data banks

We have a Mac II and an Apple scanner which we're going to use for a project to convert into machine-readable form the rather voluminous materials which generations of T.A.'s have developed for lower-division language instruction in Spanish.

My questions: Can anyone report on experience using Kurzweil's DataCopy or Caere's Omnipage software, especially with regard to foreign language usage?

Does anyone have suggestions for Mac software designed for setting up banks of questions for exercises and tests?

[Hu3's extended signature]

Meta-message 1

Date: Tue, 14 May 2002 06:14:38 +0100
From: [Hu3's email address]
Subject: Re: 16.001 Happy 15th Birthday!

Happy birthday, indeed! And I know that I speak for all of us in thanking Willard for his nurturing of Humanist from birth into its adolescent years.

This virtual, and real, community, could not exist without him.

[Hu3's extended signature]

Meta-message 2

Date: Sat, 29 May 1999 09:19:20 +0100
From: [Mo's first name, surname and email address]
Subject: hiatus

Dear Colleagues:

Humanist will be sporadically inactive over the next few weeks, from 31 May until approximately 14 June, while I am in transit, at

ACH/ALLC and otherwise preoccupied. Normally under such circumstances our able Assistant Editor, David Gants, would be standing in for me, but he is simultaneously in transit and at ACH/ALLC and so cannot. I will dart in from wherever I am when I can and do my job, but as I do not yet have a cellular phone and satellite uplink to the Internet -- AND DO NOT PLAN ON GETTING THUS HOOKED ANYTIME SOON -- there will be silences. Perhaps welcome silences! If wishes paid for tickets I'd have everyone at Charlottesville, since all signs are that this year's ACH/ALLC will be an event to remember with a glow, but wishes are a different sort of coin than the kind required.

The word "community" is mightily abused these days, often used to mean an aggregate of people many of whom neither know nor care about each other. (Have I said this before? Alas, it continues to be true.) Evidence from the gatherings of ACH/ALLC and others of computing humanists attests to a genuine intellectual and social community, however. As we all know, the giving of papers is only a part of what happens at conferences; it's a sine qua non, but I remember good ones for the boost they give to my sense of working together with others toward a common goal, however broadly that may be defined. Much more often than not, ACH/ALLC is exactly such an event, and even when I come away thinking it might have been better for this or that reason, I would not have missed the gathering of colleagues and friends for anything. Besides, the banquets and other peripheral activities are fabulous.

So, silences for a good reason. Still, apologies for them.

Yours,
[Mo's initials]

Report 1

Date: Fri, 19 Jan 2001 21:36:22 +0000
From: [Mo's first name, surname and email address]
Subject: new ACLS occasional report

Humanists will be interested in the latest ACLS Occasional Paper, No. 47, The Humanities and the Sciences, which includes papers by Jerome Friedman (theoretical physics, MIT), Peter Galison (History of Science and Physics, Harvard) and Susan Haack (Philosophy and Law, Miami). Billy E Frye (Chancellor, Emory) served as moderator. The volume is online at <http://www.acls.org/op47-1.htm>. (For those of you unfamiliar with the American Council of Learned Societies' series, allow me strongly to recommend it to you. Clifford Geertz's lecture, published a couple of years ago in the series, is a gem, for example; it is at <http://www.acls.org/op45geer.htm>.)

Friedman compares the qualities of the scientific and humanistic imaginations and the ideas of creativity and beauty in both. He finds some differences but stronger similarities. Those who have read scientists' writings on beauty and elegance in theoretical work (e.g. P.A.M. Dirac, G.H. Hardy) will be on familiar ground.

To my mind (and to that of James Gustafson, the theologian who starts off the concluding discussion) the central piece in this small collection is Peter Galison's. Galison is best known for his work on the history of experimental physics in the building of the atomic bomb. His book on the subject, Image and Logic, makes a major contribution to our understanding of the experimental sciences and to the way interdisciplinary collaborations work, as I have previously summarised on Humanist. His piece here, "Objectivity is Romantic", reports on research toward a book about the representations of objectivity in scientific publications from the end of the 18thC into the early 20th. He begins with an examination of collected photographs meant to train the young researcher or medic, e.g "atlases" of cloud-chamber photographs, anatomical drawings then photographs and so forth, and follows the changes in the conceptualisations of objectivity that they manifest, relating these changes to parallel developments in manufacture of goods and philosophical ideas, particularly in Germany and England, in Coleridge's thought. He finds that "the 'possibilities' in these various regimes of image-making are not purely conceptual.... we do not have a strategy of inquiry (an epistemology) followed by a morally-based reception (an ethics).... The machine is moralised from the get-go. Similarly, there is no accepted practice of neutral procedure of automatic image registration that later acquires a valuation.... For all these reasons, it might be more precise to speak about comportment (embracing the moral, technical, and epistemic), rather than concepts (capturing the ordered rules of combination imposed on statements)."

Haack, in “Science, Literature, and the Literature of Science”, seems mostly concerned to clear away what she regards as the nonsense about scientists making it all up so that she can approach the question of what a rhetoric of science might be like. The trouble I have with essays like this stems from the unitary conception of what science is, how it works -- as if there were one scientific method. (For arguments against this see Hacking, Feyerabend.) Galison’s historical awareness of contingent ideas is rare.

In the concluding discussion David Green (NINCH) asks a question put on Humanist some time ago, if memory serves -- why “we don’t have anything approaching a history [or philosophy] of the humanities” as we do of the sciences. Galison notes that the history of scholarship in the early modern and pre-modern periods have been studied for some time, e.g. by Anthony Grafton, but that the last two centuries have no such history. But why?

Inevitably in discussions on the topic of the sciences and the humanities someone mentions C.P. Snow’s “two cultures” argument. Galison responds that “Snow in the end wanted to make points [against Levis] about whether each side knew certain facts.... And I think that the knowledge of certain particular results is really not the issue. The issues that interest me in joining the humanities and the sciences... have to do with what counts as a demonstration or as an argument.” That, it seems to me, is *exactly* what we need to ask of ourselves for humanities computing.

Yours,
[Mo’s initials]

[Mo’s extended signature]

Report 2

Date: Sat, 03 Nov 2001 07:01:26 +0000
From: [Hu1’s first name, surname and email address]
Subject: preliminary report - internet research ethics

Colleagues:

I'm pleased to call to your attention the preliminary report of the ethics working committee of the association of internet researchers, as presented to the aoir 2.0 conference this past October in Minneapolis, MN. It can be found at aoir.org/reports/ethics.html

As the report notes, this is a very preliminary first effort at circumscribing the ways in which research into online behaviors is both similar to and, in specific circumstances, distinct from traditional human subjects research. Accordingly, the traditional guidelines for human subjects research (articulated in various national and disciplinary codes - some of which are collected as an addendum to our report) are ethically relevant to online research - but only up to a point. Beyond the point of strong analogies between traditional human subjects research and some contexts of online research - there further appear to be distinctive new contexts in online research that represent strong _dis-analogies with traditional human subjects research, thus calling for novel ethical reflection on what rights (e.g., to privacy, anonymity, confidentiality, informed consent) subjects may be reasonably expected to enjoy, and thereby what researchers may and may not do in the course of their studies.

There is general agreement - across a number of national borders (committee members represent cultures and traditions from around the world, as is required for a communications medium with a global reach) - regarding the basic values that should guide internet research, _and_ their application to specific cases - e.g., whether the communicative behavior of persons in chatrooms can be observed without consent. (The committee agrees that it can, given that peoples' behavior in public spaces, according to traditional guidelines, can be observed without consent - and given a strong analogy between a publicly-accessible chatroom and a public space in the embodied world.) Of course, there is also spirited disagreement as to the application of those values in other cases. We highlight one such case, as a way of illustrating that a) that distinctive details of a given research context can result in more than one ethical interpretation/application of the general guidelines, and b) that just as in our real-world efforts to ascertain generally binding values and apply them to specific cases (e.g., in law) - disagreement is common. This latter point is _not_ taken as an argument for ethical relativism. On the contrary, in keeping with ethics in other domains, there is consensus on a broad range of behaviors that are acceptable, as well as a broad range of behaviors that are not acceptable. Disagreement regarding the cases “in the grey” between those two ranges is to be expected and worked through. Another way of making this point: the application of ethical principles is _not_ to be taken as a mechanical - indeed, algorithmical! - process, in which general principles are somehow applied unproblematically to specific cases with specific rulings ‘yea’ or ‘nay’ somehow deductively cranked out. Rather, as ethicists from Aristotle through Simone de Beauvoir have noted, ambiguity, uncertainty, and disagreement are intrinsic to the process.

This further means, however, that despite the intriguing ways in which online research presents both strong analogies and important dis-analogies with traditional human subjects research - precisely the dis-analogies, and the correlative requirement that we struggle to extend our ethical judgment into new areas reiterate other ancient philosophical insights. What is needed, Aristotle noted, is _phronesis_, a kind of seasoned and informed ethical judgment that, partly through the lessons of experience and attempting to apply theory to _praxis_, gradually develops into a largely reliable ethical sensibility that can indeed cope with new contexts and situations. Confucius would not disagree.

As the report itself emphasizes, this document is but the first step in an on-going process. On behalf of the committee, I welcome any comments and feedback HUMANISTS may wish to provide.

With hopes for peace,

[Hu1’s extended signature including the following quotation:]
“...to be non-violent, we must not wish for anything on this earth which the meanest and lowest of human beings cannot have.” -- Gandhi

Query 1

Date: Sat, 09 Sep 2000 10:37:39 +0100
From: [Hu3’s email address]
Subject: Re: 14.0217 course buyout policies?

What is faculty course buyout? \

[Hu3’s extended signature]

Query 2

Date: Thu, 25 Mar 93 22:41:28 CST
From: [Hu4's first name, surname and email address]
Subject: Re: 6.0621 A4

The note about the length of A4 paper gives me a chance to ask something I have wondered about for years and years: why is it called A4 ? Are there other letters and numbers used for other sizes ? And what if anything is the rationale for such a system if it does indeed exist ?

[Hu4's first name, surname and email address]

Book review 1

Date: Sun, 18 Aug 2002 10:45:45 -0700
From: [Mo's first name, surname and email address]
Subject: digitization and work

Humanists interested in the broader effects of online communications will likely be glad for the following newly published book by a former Secretary of Labor in the U.S. government: Robert Reich, The Future of Success: Working and Living in the New Economy (Vintage, 2002; also published electronically). The book is reviewed by Paul Seabright, in the London Review of Books 24.16, 22 August 2002, pp. 24f.

The reviewer asks what is genuinely new? Among other things, he notes the standardization of procedures within organizations, "enabling knowledge of them to be transmitted from one individual to another without the apprenticeship of the craft tradition. This is not a new phenomenon – it's a pretty good description of what made the Roman army so much more powerful than its predecessors and rivals...." What is new, however, are two aspects of this communication of organizational method: (1) standardization to higher orders of flexibility; and, note well, (2) recording of standardization in digital form, hence ease and breadth of transmission.
"To learn the Roman Army's procedures you had to be a Roman soldier, whereas to copy a rival firm's accounting system you just have to buy (or pirate) its software."

By higher flexibility the reviewer means that whole processes of production can be standardized in such a way as to allow the individual steps to be modified. In scholarly work we are nowhere near that kind of thing -- for quite obvious reasons. But what is implied about computerization -- that its subject is the method by which things are done -- should be deeply familiar. Perhaps because Reich's concern is with the economics of industrial production , which is already mechanical and so more easily digitized than scholarship, he does not (apparently, from the review) talk about the discrepancy between human understanding and actual implementation as we must. The argument gives us, however, a way of talking about what we do to the public.

[Mo's initials]

[Mo's extended signature]

Book review 2

Date: Sat, 01 Sep 2001 06:26:24 +0100
From: [Mo's first name, surname and email address]
Subject: books of interest, with request for comments

Members of Humanist may be interested to know of the following, which are perhaps new only to me. Comments and further recommendations would be most welcome.

1. Caroline A Jones and Peter Galison, eds., Picturing Science, Producing Art (London: Routledge, 1998. I encountered this book because of Galison's fine essay, "Judgement Against Objectivity" (pp. 327-59), which is but one in a series of articles coming out of Galison's study of the historicity of the idea of objectivity; see also his paper in the ACLS Occasional Papers 47 volume, The Humanities and the Sciences, <http://www.acls.org/op47-1.htm>, which doubtless I have mentioned before. The editors of Picturing Science comment, "Analytic attempts to distinguish 'art' and 'science' often founder at the boundaries drawn between them" (p. 1). Indeed -- and much is in that past participle "drawn".

2. Charles Ess and Fay Sudweeks, eds., Culture, Technology, Communication: Towards an Intercultural Global Village (Albany NY:

State University of New York Press, 2001). This volume came out of a conference held in London in 1998, Cultural Attitudes Towards Technology and Communication, first in what has become a series. An intellectually exciting event (I was there but only made trouble on the sidelines) that has fortunately survived into print. The essays in the book work out consequences of the fact that, as Susan Herring says in her Foreward, "the world is getting smaller" in part through communication technologies. With our mobile phones, e-mail &c we tend to regard this as a good thing and think no more about it. What these essays do inter alia is to burn away the "good" as an unqualified qualifier. As a friend once said about another matter, "it isn't necessarily a good thing, but it is certainly a thing."

3. Mikael Hard and Andrew Jamison, eds., The Intellectual Appropriation of Technology: Discourses on Modernity, 1900-1939 (Cambridge MA: MIT Press, 1998). This book examines the social and intellectual responses to technology during the 1st four decades of the last century. It came out of a project at the Department of the Theory of Science at Gothenburg (Goteborg, Sweden) and so a most welcome majority of essays are from Scandinavian scholars. I have not read this book yet; comments from anyone who has would be welcome, of course.

4. Denis Donoghue, The Sovereign Ghost: Studies in Imagination (New York: Ecco Press, 1976). This is a literary-critical study of imagination in writers from Shakespeare to the modernists. I'm not sure what to say about it yet; I mention it here to solicit comments from anyone familiar with Donoghue, even more with the topic. I would be most greatful for pointers to studies from any discipline on this topic -- other than Northrop Frye's series of lectures, The Educated Imagination, which I have read.

[Mo's initials]

[Mo's extended signature]

Obituary 1

Date: Tue, 19 Oct 1999 21:36:34 +0100
From: [Mo's first name, surname and email address]

Subject: Don Fowler

Dear Colleagues:

I am deeply saddened and sorry to report to you that Don Fowler, an extraordinary human being, my friend and animi hortator, classicist and long-time computing humanist, died last Thursday of cancer. Don was one of the leading figures in literary criticism of the classics, one of those rare people whose scholarly imagination matched the kind of command of the languages and literatures in Greco-Roman studies that many only dream of. A real scholar, a real mensch.

The last time I saw Don was in his rooms at Jesus College Oxford; he had recently been given a Sun workstation, which he had tucked away in a little room to the side of his books-and-papers littered office, not exactly sure what he was going to do with it, but surely something interesting. We had a great time, as always. The first time I met Don was many years ago, I think Lou Burnard introduced us. Don set up a lecture for me at Jesus on my then newly begun research project on Ovid and managed somehow to get about 15-20 people there, quite a crowd for Oxford, including Richard Tarrant, *still* editor of the great edition of the Met we all want to see someday. I was terrified, but it all went well, and afterwards Don took me out to dinner with a group of students and, with the help of copious quantities of wine, we all sang "What a friend we have in Jesus", which was paying the bill, as I recall. On another occasion he arranged for me to have dinner with the fellows of the College; quite an experience, I can tell you, and no doubt he enjoyed watching as well as eating.

I will miss him.

Below is Michael Fraser's note, from which I learned of Don's death.

Yours,
[Mo's initials'

>--- Begin Forwarded Message ---
>Date: Mon, 18 Oct 1999 12:58:24 +0100 (BST)
>From: Michael Fraser <mike.fraser@computing-
>ervices.oxford.ac.uk>
>>

>I am very sorry to inform you that Don Fowler died last Thursday
>night at home. Don was a great friend of the CTI Centre. He was the
>longest-serving member of the Centre's management/advisory
>committees (a founding member of Oxford's CTI 'text searching'
>project in 1987). He inspired many of us in the Centre with his
>holistic view of the humanities, his real sense of play when it came to
>computers, and his humour to the end.
>
>I have been informed that Don's funeral service will be at Jesus
>College Chapel (and Hall) on Tuesday 26 October, at 10.30 a.m. The
>burial will be private. Rather than flowers, Don would like donations
>to be made to Imperial Cancer Research.
>
>Michael

- -

[Mo's extended signature]

Obituary 2

Date: Thu, 28 Oct 1999 11:15:26 +0100
From: [Mo's first name, surname and email address]
Subject: Leonard Boyle 1923-1999

Dear Colleagues:

It is my sad duty to tell you that Father Leonard Boyle, an extraordinary human being, one of the great palaeographers and a scholar keenly interested and involved in our field, has died at the age of 75. An obituary from the New York Times is included below.

Boyle was formerly Prefect of the Vatican Library. Before he went to Rome he was professor in the Pontifical Institute of Mediaeval Studies, Toronto, where he taught palaeography to generations of students in the Institute and in the Centre for Medieval Studies. I first encountered Boyle when I was a student of Old English, in a course taught by Angus Cameron (fons et origo of the Dictionary of Old English), at Toronto in 1976. For a final project I submitted to Angus a amateur's palaeographical study of some vernacular Anglo-Saxon hands (I had done palaeography on my own as a calligrapher years before). Much to my delight Angus thought well of the project. Without asking me he passed it on to Boyle, who then contacted me and asked me to see him. I went to the Institute expecting a stuffy academic scholar totally ignorant of the practical side of lettering.

Boyle, the speed of whose wit and clarity of mind recall many a story of samurai swordsmanship, quickly disabused me of such expectations; he knew all about the American Arts-and-Crafts Revival of calligraphy and had on his bookshelf most of the rather difficult-to-obtain books I was very proud of having in my collection. He knew of my mentor, Lloyd Reynolds, at Reed College. I was impressed! We became friends.

I saw him again from time to time in Toronto, always intending to take his palaeography course, but as a budding Miltonist never did, alas, alas. While working at the Records of Early English Drama project I became friends with a number of medievalists and as a result joined the long chain of beneficiaries of Boyle's insomnia. It seems that to while away the hours Boyle would read mystery novels, and at such a rate that a constant stream of them flowed from his study to the many others like myself needing some relief from our day jobs.

Boyle was then called to Rome. Some years later I found myself there for the first time, on a Sunday. I was approaching the Vatican when I spotted him walking briskly along in plain black. The only thing I remember about the conversation (other than the warmth of his greeting) was his telling me which of the nearby "bars" (Italian style) was the best place to get a sandwich. He explained that he could not go to the best one because the owner knew him and would refuse to take money from him. "I have a very dim view of a man not earning his living!" he exclaimed -- and walked on.

Some years after that I was giving a talk on computing at the Institute when Boyle turned up unexpectedly to introduce me. He commented that the sort of thing I was about to lecture on was precisely what he had had in mind when he established the lecture series 15 years previously. Computers were rather new to our academic world then, but Boyle was the kind of person who could recognise a good thing for scholarship when he saw it, however obscured by temporary crudities of form.

I referred above to samurai swordsmanship. The particular accomplishment I have in mind is the ability to slice a burning candle in half without disturbing the flame. But the metaphor doesn't do justice to his salt-of-the-earth wit, the sparkle of rebellious, conspiratorial delight in his eyes, the burning intelligence, the etymologically precise magnaminity, the passion for letterforms, for the life of the mind. A great loss to us all.

[Mo's initials]

>Date: Thu, 28 Oct 1999 09:53:51 +0100 (BST)
>To: [[Hu1's first name, surname and email address]
>>From: John Lavagnino <John.Lavagnino@kcl.ac.uk>
>Reply-to: John Lavagnino <John.Lavagnino@kcl.ac.uk>
>
>
> New York Times, October 28, 1999
>
>
> Leonard E. Boyle, Who
> Modernized Vatican Library,
> Dies at 75
>
> By WILLIAM H. HONAN
>
> The Rev. Leonard E. Boyle, the former keeper of
> manuscripts and chief librarian of the Vatican
> Library, who was dismissed from his post in 1997, died
> on Monday in Rome. He was 75.
>
> Boyle died of cancer, said Ambrogio Piazzoni, vice
> prefect of the Vatican Library.
>
> The library is one of the world's greatest storehouses of
> ancient books and manuscripts. Whether because of
> carelessness, shadowy ecclesiastical politics or plain
> bad luck, Boyle, a highly respected Oxford-trained
> paleographer, or student of manuscripts, became
> involved in several imbroglios toward the end of his
> 13-year tenure as keeper that tarnished an otherwise
> sterling reputation and led to his dismissal.

> Vatican officials refuse to discuss the circumstances
> surrounding Boyle's departure. Piazzoni would only
> say: "Everyone has to leave some time."
>
> Others outside the Vatican were more forthcoming.
> "What goes on inside the Vatican is anybody's guess,
> but Boyle's opening of access to materials in the library
> must have played a role in his departure," said James
> H. Marrow, an emeritus professor of art history at
> Princeton University who has worked at the Vatican
> Library. "He had a great impact on the place."
>
> Friends and supporters praise Boyle for having
> computerized the library's ancient catalogs, wired the
> main reading room for laptops, hired women for the
> first time and liberalized the strict dress code. Others
> suggest that the liberalization measures and Boyle's
> trustfulness were the seeds of his downfall.
>
> In May 1995 Anthony Melnikas, a professor of art at
> Ohio State University, was found to have stolen from
> the Vatican Library two leaves from a medieval
> manuscript once owned by Petrarch, the 14th-century
> Italian poet. Melnikas was sentenced to 14 months in
> prison.
>
> Boyle was stunned by the theft by a man he considered
> a friend; he was criticized as an unwitting accomplice
> for having granted Melnikas many special privileges in
> the library, including allowing him the free run of the
> institution in August, when it is closed to the general
> public.
>
> In 1996, a year after the Melnikas affair, the Vatican
> was obliged to pay $8.8 million plus $1.3 million in
> attorneys' fees to settle a lawsuit stemming from
> Boyle's sale to a California entrepreneur of exclusive
> world rights to reproduce the images in the Library.
>
> His object, he insisted, had been to raise money to pay
> for a modernization program, but the Holy See accused

> him of acting without authority -- a charge he
> contested. Boyle's offer to take early retirement in
> order to discourage gossip was not accepted; he was
> dismissed three weeks before the 13th anniversary of
> his arrival.
>
> Leonard Eugene Boyle was born on Nov. 13, 1923, in
> Ballintra, County Donegal, Ireland. He was educated in
> Gaelic and entered the Dominican order at Cork in
> 1943. He then went to Oxford University, where he
> discovered his passion for medieval manuscripts. He
> was ordained a priest in 1949 and soon became a widely
> published and prize-winning scholar.
>
> Moving to Toronto, he taught at the Pontifical Institute
> of Mediaeval Studies, and in 1961 also taught at the
> neighboring Center for Medieval Studies at the
> University of Toronto. He was employed by the Vatican
> Library in 1984.
>
> A playfully witty man, Boyle disparaged suggestions
> that he might be positioning himself to become a
> cardinal. "I'm not interested in some second-rate job,"
> he said. "The papacy or nothing!"
>

[Mo's extended signature]

APPENDIX C

EXAMPLES OF SUBGENRES IDENTIFIED IN THE CORPORA: THE SUBGENRES RELATED TO THE PURPOSE OF ACADEMIC DEBATE

Voice in a discussion 1

Date: Thu, 3 Aug 89 13:48:59 EDT
From: [Hu1's first name, surname and email address]
Subject: Re: 3.317 MIPSy workstations; multitasking (153)

The current debate over whether a 12.5 MIPs Sun workstation is a good choice for humanist computing hits nicely on a central problem – hot hardware that is lightyears ahead of available software.

The comments by Scott Myers make this conflict clear. He rightly praises the high screen resolution of the Sun, and its relative speed vis-a-vis the Macintosh -- and strikes a chord with one of my major complaints with the Macintosh: the screen is just too small to exploit the possibilities of hypermedia display. For that, he points out, while the software for all this is not available, it *could* be developed.

Certainly it could. It only took some five years and a few million dollars to develop Intermedia for the Macintosh. And now that Intermedia has entered its commercial release phase, anyone who can afford the (admittedly expensive) hardware can make use of an extraordinary hypertext authoring system that is far more powerful than, say, Hypercard -- and its ease of use makes scripting in Hypertalk look like writing dissertations in UNIX (possible, but probably not the route most of us would take). And all this for $125.00...

Perhaps in a few years, some brave soul will have developed equivalent software for the SUN -- i.e., powerful, user-friendly, and relatively affordable -- which will thus open up the SUN to humanities faculty who can (a) afford the equipment, and (b) do not care to become power users to exploit its 12.5 MIPS. Until that time, despite my aggravation with the current size limitations on the Macintosh display, -- if a choice must be made between available software and powerful hardware, I would prefer to have the software in hand and get to work, rather than become embroiled with the dubious joys of trying to create my own programs.

Note: I do not hold stock in either IRIS (the source of Intermedia) or Apple Computer, Inc. I _am_ interested in software applications which bend technology to the traditional goals and functions of humanities scholarship and teaching.

Finally, speed is, as has been commented on several times, highly relative. Compared to the Sun, yes the Mac is slow. Compared to my beloved PC -- which is perfectly adequate for most of my tasks -- the Mac is astonishingly fast. I suggest that the term "slow" belongs to the family of terms which includes "obsolete." In the face of the rapidly changing technology of computers, the term "obsolete" is obsolete: it has, at best, a highly relative meaning, and in general conveys something of the sense of a given user's aesthetic habits and preferences. While this may be useful information, it is hardly a term of damnation from a more general standpoint.

Hope all this is taken in the spirit it is sent -- i.e., just a friendly comment from from a humanities professor at a small college.

[Hu1's first name, surname and name of college]

Voice in a discussion 2

Date: Wed, 31 May 89 12:41:43 EDT
From: [Hu3's first name, surname and email address]
Subject: Re: 3.76 scholarly microcomputing (110)

We are on the very edge of the massive use of computers in humanities scholarship. For people interested primarily in texts the big stumbling block right now is the lack of primary materials in machine-readable form. Where such materials have become available, they have caused a revolution in the way scholars work in the discipline. The primary example is the TLG. Having these materials available does not change the sorts of things scholars want to do. It will not convert everyone into stylometricians (stylomeretricians?), but it will allow them to explore hunches, to follow up leads that would have been literally impossible before.

Take Willard's question about ivory and marble in classical Latin poetry. If we had a machine-readable corpus of Latin texts that question could be solved in an hour. Without such a corpus it becomes an enormously tedious and time-consuming exercise with, ultimately, less than satisfactory results.

Besides the texts we also need suitable tools for text analysis. These include not only the standard sorts of searching tools (boolean and contextual) but also thesauri. To take up Willard's problem again, one would like to be able to search on a semantic field which includes the concepts of ivory and marble, regardless of the specific words used to convey those concepts. That is why the text-encoding initiative is so important, so that search software can be standardized in terms of the SGML tags.

In this sense I disagree with Bob Kraft. I don't think that the humanities scholar should have to become a computing specialist to do this kind of work, any more than he has had one in order to use a computer for word processing.

[Hu1's first name and surname]

Initiation of a discussion 1

Date: Wed, 30 Jun 1999 10:15:10 -0400
From: [Mo's first name, surname and email address]
Subject: ways of teaching humanities computing

Dear colleagues,

As our subject becomes more popular, numbers of students will increase -- as they already have begun to do where I ply my trade. At some point, it becomes difficult to accommodate all those who want to take a practically orientated humanities computing course in a single lab. What does one do then -- without simply hiring another full-time lecturer?

There are other pressures too. As single intro courses develop into programmes, interested departments may want more choices. Unlike most if not all departments we serve, humanities computing necessarily has a prominent service component. Requests from other departments must be welcomed and dealt with. (This does not mean that h.c. is necessarily in a passive role or must be content with a lesser status, only that *collegial* service is a very important part of what it does.)

Thus the need for alternative models for teaching the subject, even at institutions where courses or programmes are in place and working successfully. Where should we look for those models?

Because teaching our subject involves equipment (except perhaps under rather special circumstances), it seems to me that we should look to the laboratory sciences, e.g. chemistry, physics, biology. The model I know from having taken courses in those fields specifies the large lecture section followed by practical tutorials with relatively small numbers of students per tutorial/lab. In other words, the explicitly conceptual part of the subject is separated from the explicitly practical. Because our field is interdisciplinary, this might allow us to have tutorials/labs with different emphases, though managing such a scenario might be impossibly difficult.

What do the sciences do, I wonder, with the need to process the “poets” -- i.e. students in the humanities who need to take a science course, or those who simply (and laudably!) want to know what a particular science is like? In particular, how do the sciences handle a student who has taken an “X for poets” course then wants to switch into the mainstream of that subject? Is the time spent in the poets’ course necessarily wasted?

Because our field is a neophyte, we can hardly afford to take the robust approach, as one might call it -- do it our way or get lost.

Ideas, comments?

[Mo’s initials]

[Mo's extended signature]

Initiation of a discussion 2

Date: Tue, 13 Feb 90 10:45:21 PST
From: [Hu3's first name, surname and email address]
Subject: electronic critical editions

For an introduction to a special issue on textual criticism for <emp>Romance Philology</emp> I am writing an introduction on the critical edition of the 21st century, which, as I see it, will be essentially some sort of hypertext system.

I am currently struggling to figure out the relationship between hypertext and SGML, not so much as SGML descriptions of hypertext systems (the subject of one query not so long ago), but rather the relative merits of coding a particular feature via SGML or linking a region of text to another node in the system.

Let us suppose, for example, that one is interested in marking all examples of religious imagery in a particular text. Under SGML one would tag each of those samples with something like <rel.img></rel.img>. In a hypertext system one would mark off the region of text, and link it to a node called "Religious imagery," which might or might not have a short description of some kind with it. The link in turn would be coded with one or more attributes, such as TYPE = imagery.

The user, presumably, would be able to use a filter in both systems to locate all of the examples of religious imagery and then work with that set for whatever purposes he or she might conceive.

One of my problems is that I have little experience with an SGML system and no experience with hypertext. In terms of text preparation, however, coding for imagery in both systems would take roughly the same amount of time (a lot), since all of the coding and linking would have to be done manually.

In some other examples, such as indication of sources and parallels, it seems to me that hypertext is clearly superior because of the fact that it allows for linkages between two separate texts. But for text-internal references I'm not so sure.

In any case, I would greatly appreciate hearing from anyone who has either knowledge or strongly held opinions.

[Hu3's extended signature]

APPENDIX D

THE CALCULATIONS OF THE STATISTICAL PARAMETERS

I. The calculation of the correlation between the frequency of members' contributions and the total number of words.

1. The formulae for Pearson's Correlation Coefficient used in the calculations:

$$r_{xy} = \frac{c(x, y)}{S(x) \cdot S(y)}$$

$$c(x\,y) = \overline{x \cdot y} - \overline{x} \cdot \overline{y}$$

$$c(x\,y) = \frac{\sum_{i=1}^{n} (x_i - \overline{x}) \cdot (y_i - \overline{y})}{n}$$

$$\overline{x \cdot y} = \frac{\sum_{i=1}^{n} x_i y_i}{n}$$

2. The raw data used in the calculations for the two periods respectively:

x → np (number of postings)

y → nw (number of words)

np	nw
51	10570
33	5274
136	16702
33	6368
168	33488

Table D–1. The number of postings and the number of words contributed by the regular *Humanists* in period A.

$r_{xy} = 0{,}932271$

np	nw
51	10570
33	5274
136	16702
33	6368
168	33488

Table D–2. The number of postings and the number of words contributed by the regular *Humanists* in period B.

$r_{xy} = 0{,}47449$

II. The calculation of the correlation between the use of particular subgenres and the number of members' contributions:

1. The formulae for Chuprov's Coefficient (T_{xy}) used in the calculations:

$$T_{xy} = \sqrt{\frac{x^2}{n\sqrt{(k-1)(l-1)}}}$$

$$x^2 = \sum_{i=1}^{k}\sum_{j=1}^{l}\frac{(n_{ij} - \hat{n}_{ij})^2}{\hat{n}_{ij}}$$

$$\hat{n}_{ij} = \frac{n_i \cdot n_j}{n}$$

n_{ij} – partial frequencies in the independence table
n_i – edge frequencies for factor 1
n_j – edge frequencies for factor 2
n – total number of occurrences
$i = 1,2, \ldots, k$ – row number in the independence table
$j = 1,2,\ldots, l$ – column number in the independence table

2. The raw data used in the calculations for the two periods respectively:

	Number of postings					Total
	Hu2	Hu1	Hu3	Hu4	Hu5	
Voice in a discussion	9	6	47	17	120	199
Initiation of a discussion	0	0	4	1	0	5
Request	13	38	28	1	4	84
Announcement	3	1	3	0	0	7
Note	3	6	54	12	42	117
Meta-message	0	0	0	1	0	1
Query	0	0	0	1	2	3
Book review	0	0	0	0	0	0
Report	0	0	0	0	0	0
Obituary	0	0	0	0	0	0
Forwarded message	5	0	0	0	0	5
Total	33	51	136	33	168	421

Table D–3. The independence table for period A includes the numbers of particular subgenres contributed by the regular *Humanists* in the earlier period.

$T_{xy} = 0{,}318$

	Number of postings					
	Hu2	Hu1	Hu3	Hu4	Hu5	Total
Voice in a discussion	11	4	15	34	5	69
Initiation of a discussion	0	0	0	0	0	0
Request	2	0	6	1	0	9
Announcement	16	0	3	1	0	20
Note	3	0	8	12	2	25
Meta-message	0	0	2	1	2	5
Query	0	0	1	1	0	2
Book review	0	0	1	0	0	1
Report	1	0	0	0	0	1
Obituary	0	0	0	0	0	0
Forwarded message	0	0	1	2	0	3
Total	33	4	37	52	9	135

Table D–4. The independence table for period B includes numbers of particular subgenres contributed by the regular *Humanists* in the more recent period.

$T_{xy} = 0{,}288$

BIBLIOGRAPHY

Allwood, Jens. *The Academic Seminar as an Arena of Conflict and Conflict Resolution*. Gothenburg: University of Gothenburg, 1993.

Anderson, Benedict. *Wspólnoty wyobrażone*. Translated by Stefan Amsterdamski. Kraków: Znak, 1997.

Argyle, Michael and Adam Kendon. "The experimental analysis of social performance." Reprinted in *Communication in Face to Face Interaction,* edited by John Laver and Sandy Hutcheson, 19–63, London: Penguin Books, 1972/1967.

Argyle, Michael. *Psychologia stosunków międzyludzkich* (Third edition). Translated by Waldemar Domachowski. Warszawa: Wydawnictwo Naukowe PWN, 2002.

Aycock, Alan. "'Technologies of the self': Foucault and Internet discourse." *Journal of Computer Mediated Communication* 1 no 2 (1995) (accessed January 21, 2002).

Bardini, Thierry. "Bridging the gulfs: From hypertext to cyberspace." *Journal of Computer-Mediated Communication* 3 no 2 (1997) (accessed April 13, 2003).

Barnes, Susan B. *Computer-Mediated Communication. Human-to-Human Communication Across the Internet*. New York: Pearson Education, 2003.

Baron, Naomi. *Alphabet to Email. How Written English Evolved and Where It's Heading*. London: Routledge, 2000.

Bartmiński, Jerzy, ed. *Współczesny język polski*. Wrocław: Wiedza o Kulturze, 1993.

Bartmiński, Jerzy. "Opozycja ustności i literackości." Reprinted in *Antropologia słowa. Zagadnienia i wybór tekstów,* edited by Grzegorz Godlewski, Andrzej Mencwel and Roch Sulima, 430–434. Warszawa: Wydawnictwa Uniwersytetu Warszawskiego, 2003/1989.

Bartmiński, Jerzy and Stanisława Niebrzegowska-Bartmińska, eds. *Tekstologia Part 2*. Lublin: Wydawnictwo UMSC, 2004.

Bauman, Richard and Joel Sherzer, eds. *Explorations in the Ethnography of Speaking*. Cambridge: Cambridge University Press, 1974.

Baym, Nancy K. "The emergence of on-line community." In *Virtual Culture: Identity and Communication in Cybersociety,* edited by

Steven G. Jones, 35–68. Thousands Oaks, London, New Delhi: Sage Publications, 1998.

Beaugrande, Robert-Alain de and Wolfgang Ulrich Dressler. *Introduction to Text Linguistics*. London: Longman, 1981.

Beniger, James R. "Personalization of mass media and the growth of pseudo-community." *Communication Research* 14 no 3 (1987): 352–371.

Benschop, Albert. "Virtual communities. Networks of the future." 1997. (http://www.sociosite.org/network.php) (accessed January 25, 2002).

Benwell, Bethan and Elizabeth Stokoe. *Discourse and Identity*. Edinburgh: Edinburgh University Press, 2006.

Berge, Zane L. and Maureen Collins. "The founding and managing of IPCT -L: A listowners' perspective." *Interpersonal Computing and Technology: An Electronic Journal for the 21st Century* 1 no 2 (1993) (accessed January 25, 2002).

Bergs, Alexander. "Analyzing online communication from a social network point of view: questions, problems, perspectives." *language@internet* 1 (2006) (accessed September 26, 2006).

Bernard, Jessse. *The Sociology of Community*. Glenview, IL: Scott Foresman, 1973.

Berquist, Magnus and Jan Ljungberg. "Genres in action: Negotiating genres in practice." In *Proceedings of the 32nd Hawaii International Conference on System Sciences* 2 (2009) (http://csdl2.computer.org/comp/proceedings/hicss/1999/0001/02/0001 2009.PDF) (accessed March 02, 2002).

Bhatia, Vijay K. *Analysing Genre: Language Use in Professional Settings*. New York: Longman, 1993.

—. "A generic view of academic discourse." In *Academic Discourse*, edited by John Flowerdew , 21–39. London: Pearson Education, 2002.

Biber, Douglas. *Variation Across Speech and Writing*. Cambridge: Cambridge University Press, 1988.

Biber, Douglas, Susan Conrad and Randi Reppen. *Corpus Linguistics: Investigating Language, Structure and Use*. Cambridge: Cambridge University Press, 1998.

Biber, Douglas, Geoffrey Leech and Susan Conrad. *Longman Grammar of Spoken and Written English*. Harlow: Longman, 1999.

Biniewicz, Jerzy and Anna Starzec. "Styl naukowy." In *Przewodnik po stylistyce polskiej*, edited by Stanisław Gajda, 397–430. Opole: Uniwersytet Opolski, 1995.

Bizell, Patricia. "Cognition, convention and certainty: What we need to know about writing." *PRE/TEXT* 3 (1982): 213–143.

Blom, Jan-Petter and John J Gumperz. "Social meaning in linguistic structures: Code-switching in Norway." In *Directions in Sociolinguistics: The Ethnography of Communication*, edited by John J. Gumperz and Dell Hymes, 407–34. New York: Holt, Rinehart and Winston, 1972.

Bolter, Jay David. *Writing Space. The Computer, Hypertext, and the History of Writing*. New Yersey: Lawrence Erlbaum Associates, 1991.

Borg, Erik. "Discourse community." *ELT Journal* 57 no 4 (2003): 398–400.

Bralczyk, Jerzy and Katarzyna Mosiołek-Kłosińska, eds. *Język w mediach masowych*. Warszawa: Upowszechnianie Nauki – Oświata „UN-O", 2000.

Breivega, Kjersti Rongen, Trine Dahl and Kjersti Fløttum. "Traces of self and others in research articles. A comparative pilot study of English, French and Norwegian research articles in medicine, economics and linguistics." *International Journal of Applied Linguistics* 12 no 2 (2002): 218–239.

Brown, Penelope and Stephen C Levinson. *Politeness. Some Universals in Language Usage*. Cambridge: Cambridge University Press, 2000/1987.

Bucholtz, Mary. "<Why be normal?>: Language and identity practices in a community of nerd girls." *Language in Society 28* (1999): 203–223.

Bucholtz, Mary and Kira Hall. "Identity and interaction: A sociocultural linguistic approach." *Discourse Studies* 7 no 4–5 (2005): 585–614.

Bunz, Ulla and Scott W Campbell. "Accommodating politeness indicators in personal electronic mail messages." A paper presented at the Association of Internet Researcher's 3rd Annual Conference, Maastricht, The Netherlands, October 13–16, 2002. (http://www.scils.rutgers.edu/~bunz/AoIR2002politeness.pdf.) (accessed July 14, 2004).

Burszta, Wojciech J. „Język hiperrzeczywistości – hiperrzeczywistośc języka. Rozważania bardzo wstępne." 2002. (http://www.cyberforum.edu.pl) (accessed July 14, 2004).

Candlin, Christopher N. and Maurizio Gotti, eds. *Intercultural Aspects of Specialized Communication*. Bern: Peter Lang, 2004.

Carretero, Marta. "The influence of genre and register on epistemic modality in spoken English: a preliminary study", *Estudios Ingleses de la Universidad Complutense* 10 (2002): 11–41.

Castells, Manuel. *The Information Age: Economy, Society and Culture: Power of Identity.* Oxford & Cambridge, MA: Blackwell, 1997.

Chafe, Wallace L. and Johanna Nichols, eds. *Evidentiality : The Linguistic Coding of Epistemology*. Norwood, N.J.: Ablex Publishing, 1986.

Chambers, Jack, Peter Trudgill and Natalie Schilling-Estes, eds. *Handbook of Language Variation and Change*. Oxford: Blackwell, 2002.

Chomsky, Noam. *Aspects of the Theory of Syntax.* Cambridge, Mass.: MIT Press, 1965.

Chyła, Wojciech. "Kruszenie słowa przez maszyny tekstualne." *Principia* XXVI (2000).

Clark, Herbert H. "Communities, commonalities, and communication." In *Rethinking Linguistic Relativity*, John J. Gumperz and Stephen C. Levinson, 324–355. Cambridge: Cambridge University Press, 1996.

Clyne, Michael "Culture and discourse structure." *Journal of Pragmatics* 11 (1987): 211–247.

—. *Inter-Cultural Communication at Work. Cultural Values in Discourse*. Cambridge: Cambridge University Press, 1994.

Collot, Milena and Nancy Belmore. "Electronic language: A new variety of English." In *Computer-Mediated Communication: Linguistic, Social and Cross-Cultural Perspectives,* edited by Susan Herring, 13–28. Amsterdam: Benjamins, 1996.

Condon, Sherri L. and Claude G Čech. "Functional comparisons of face-to-face and computer-mediated decision making interactions." In *Computer-Mediated Communication: Linguistic, Social and Cross-Cultural Perspectives,* edited by Susan Herring, 65–80. Amsterdam: Benjamins, 1996.

Connor, Ulla. *Contrastive Rhetoric.* Cambridge: Cambridge University Press, 1996.

Conoscenti, Michelangelo. "Virtual diplomacy: A case study of conversational practices in an intercultural setting." In *Intercultural Aspects of Specialized Communication,* edited by Christopher N. Candlin and Maurizio Gotti, 343–360. Bern: Peter Lang, 2004.

Cortese, Giuseppina and Philip Riley, eds. *Domain-specific English. Textual Practices Across Communities and Classrooms*. Bern: Peter Lang, 2002.

Cortese, Giuseppina and Anna Duszak eds. *Identity, Community, Discourse: English in Intercultural Settings*. Bern: Peter Lang, 2005.

Coulmas, Florian, ed. *The Handbook of Sociolinguistics.* Oxford & Cambridge, MA: Blackwell, 1998.

Coulthard, Malcolm, ed. *Advances in Written Text Analysis*. London: Routledge, 1994.

Crismore, Avon, Raija Markkanen and Margaret S Steffensen. "Metadiscourse in persuasive writing: a study of texts written by American and Finnish university students." *Written Communication* 10 no 1 (1993): 39–71.

Crystal, David. *The Cambridge Encyclopedia of Language* (Second edition.) Cambridge: Cambridge University Press, 1998.

—. *Language and the Internet.* Cambridge: Cambridge University Press, 2001.

Cutler, Richard H. "Distributed presence and community in cyberspace." *Interpersonal Computing and Technology: An Electronic Journal for the 21st Century* 3 no 2 (1995): 12–32 (accessed July 14, 2004).

Dahl, Trine. "Textual metadiscourse in research articles: a marker of national culture or of academic discipline?" *Journal of Pragmatics* 36 (2004): 1807–1825.

Davis, Mike. "Fragmented by technologies: A community in cyberspace." *Interpersonal Computing and Technology: An Electronic Journal for the 21st Century* 5 no 1–2 (1997): 7–18 (accessed July 14, 2004).

Davis, Boyd H. and Jeuttone P. Brewer. *Electronic Discourse. Linguistic Individuals in Virtual Space.* Albany: State University of New York Press, 1997.

Dąbrowska, Marta. "Język e-maila jako hybryda mowy i pisma." In *Język a komunikacja 1. Język trzeciego tysiąclecia I,* edited by Grzegorz Szpila, 95–111. Kraków: Tertium, 2000.

December, John. "Characteristics of oral culture in discourse on the net." A paper presented at the 12th Annual Penn State Conference on Rhetoric and Composition, University, Park, Pennsylvania, July 8, 1993. (http://www.december.com/john/papers/pscrc93.txt) (accessed January 10, 2002).

De Fina, Anna, Deborah Schiffrin and Michael Bamberg, eds. *Discourse and Identity.* Cambridge: Cambridge University Press.

Del Lungo Camiciotti, Gabriella and Elena Tognini Bonelli, eds. *Academic Discourse – New Insights into Evaluation.* Bern: Peter Lang, 2004.

Dendale, Patrick and Liliane Tasmowski. "Introduction: Evidentiality and related notions." *Journal of Pragmatics* 33 (2001): 339–348.

Derrida, Jacques. *O gramatologii.* Translated by Bogdan Banasiak. Warszawa: KR, 1999.

Dijk, Teun van and Walter Kintsch. *Strategies of Discourse Comprehension.* New York: Academic Press, 1983.

Dil, Anwar S., ed. *Language in Social Groups.* Essays by John J. Gumperz, selected and introduced by Anwar S. Dil. Stanford: Stanford University Press, 1971.

Donath, Judith S. *Inhabiting the Virtual City: The Design of Social Environments for Electronic Communication.* A PhD thesis, Massachusetts Institute of Technology 1996.

(http://smg.media.mit.edu/people/Judith/Thesis.html) (accessed July 14, 2004).
—. "Identity and deception in the virtual community." In *Communities in Cyberspace,* edited by Marc A. Smith and Peter Kollock, 29–59. London: Routledge, 1999.
Durant, Alan. "Orality and literacy." *The Johns Hopkins Guide to Literary Theory and Criticism,* 1997. (http://www.press.jhu.edu/books/hopkins_guide_to_literary_theory/orality_and_literacy.html) (accessed July 14, 2004).
Duszak, Anna. "Academic discourse and intellectual styles." *Journal of Pragmatics* 21 (1994): 291–313.
—. "Cross-cultural academic communication: A discourse community view." In *Culture and Styles of Academic Discourse,* edited by Anna Duszak, 11–39. Berlin: Mouton de Gruyter, 1997a.
—. "Analyzing digressiveness in Polish academic texts." In *Culture and Styles of Academic Discourse,* edited by Anna Duszak, 323–341. Berlin: Mouton de Gruyter, 1997b.
—. *Tekst, dyskurs, komunikacja międzykulturowa.* Warszawa: Wydawnictwo Naukowe PWN, 1998a.
—. "Academic writing in English and Polish: comparing and subverting genres." *International Journal of Applied Linguistics* 8 no 2 (1998b): 191–213.
—. "Języki, kultury, wspólnoty." In *Język rodzimy a język obcy: komunikacja, przekład, dydaktyka,* edited by Andrzej Kopczyński and Urszula Zaliwska-Okrutna, 7–22. Warszawa: Wydawnictwa Uniwersytetu Warszawskiego, 2001.
—. "Us and Others: An introduction." In *Us And Others: Social Identities Across Languages, Discourses and Cultures,* edited by Anna Duszak, 1–28. Amsterdam/Philadelphia: John Benjamins Publishing Company, 2002a.
—. "Retoryczny charakter dyskursów naukowych: o wartościowaniu w świecie nauki." In *Konteksty kulturowe w dyskursie edukacyjnym*, edited by Jan Ożdżyński and Teodozja Rittel, 49–63. Kraków: Oficyna Wydawnicza "Edukacja", 2002b.
Duszak, Anna ed.
—. *Culture and Styles of Academic Discourse*. Berlin: Mouton de Gruyter, 1997.
—. *Us And Others: Social Identities Across Languages, Discourses and Cultures.* Amsterdam/Philadelphia: John Benjamins Publishing Company, 2002.

Duszak, Anna and Urszula Okulska, eds. *Speaking from the Margin: Global English from a European Perspective*. Frankfurt am Main-New York: Peter Lang, 2004.

—. *Bridges and Barriers in Metalinguistic Discourse*. Frankfurt am Main-New York: Peter Lang, 2006.

DuVal Smith, Anna. "Problems of conflict management in virtual communities." In *Communities in Cyberspace*, edited by Marc A. Smith and Peter Kollock, 134–163. London: Routledge, 1999.

Eckert, Penelope and Sally McConnel-Ginet. "Think practically and look locally: Language and gender as community-based practice." *Annual Review of Anthropology* 21 (1992): 461–490.

—. "New generalizations and explanations in language and gender research." *Language in Society* 28 (1999): 185–201.

Edwards, John. *Language, Society and Identity*. Oxford & Cambridge, MA: Basil Blackwell, 1985.

Eelen, Gino. *A Critique of Politeness Theories*. Manchester, UK & Northampton MA: St. Jerome Publishing, 2001.

Ekeblad, Eva. "Contact, community and multilogue: Electronic communication in the practice of scholarship." A paper presented at The 4th Congress of the International Society for Cultural Research and Activity Theory (ISCRAT), Aarhus University, Denmark, June, 1998. (http://hem.fyristorg.com/evaek/writings/iscrat98/cocomu.html) (accessed August 09, 2002).

—. "The emergence and decay of multilogue on a scholarly mailing list." A paper presented at 8th European Conference for Research on Learning and Instruction, August, 1999, Göteborg, Sweden. (http://hyperion.math.upatras.gr/commorg/ekeblad/multdyn.html) (accessed August 09, 2002).

Erickson, Thomas. "Social interaction on the net: Virtual community as participatory genre." In *Proceedings of the 30th Hawaii International Conference on System Sciences (HICSS 30)* 6 (1997): 13–21. (http://www.pliant.org/personal/Tom_Erickson/VC_as_Genre.html) (accessed August 09, 2002).

—. "Making sense of computer-mediated communication (CMC): Conversations as genres, CMC systems as genre ecologies." (http://www.pliant.org/personal/Tom_Erickson/genreEcologies.html) (accessed August 09, 2002).

Fairclough, Norman. *Critical Discourse Analysis: The Critical Study of Language*. London and New York: Longman, 1995a.

—. *Media Discourse*. London: Arnold, 1995b.

—. *Analysing Discourse. Textual Analysis for Social Research.* London and New York: Routledge, 2003.

Fasold, Ralph. *The Sociolinguistics of Society.* Oxford & Cambridge, MA: Basil Blackwell, 1984.

Fernback, Jan and Brad Thompson. "Virtual Communities: Abort, Retry, Failure?" A version of the paper "Computer-Mediated Communication and the American Collectivity: The Dimensions of Community Within Cyberspace" presented at the annual convention of the International Communication Association, Albuquerque, New Mexico, May 1995. (http://www.well.com/user/hlr/texts/VCcivil.html) (accessed August 07, 2002).

Fernback, Jan. "The individual within the collective: Virtual ideology and the realisation of collective principles." In *Virtual Culture: Identity and Communication in Cybersociety,* edited by Steven G. Jones, 36–54. Thousands Oaks, London, New Delhi: Sage Publications, 1997.

Firth, John R. "On sociological linguistics." In *Language in Culture and Society. A Reader in Linguistics and Anthropology,* edited by Dell Hymes, 66–70. New York, Evanston and London: Harper & Row, 1964.

Fish, Stanley. *Is There a Text in This Class?: The Authority of Interpretive Communities.* MA and London: Harvard University Press, 1980.

Fishman, Joshua A. "The sociology of language." In *Readings in the Sociology of Language,* edited by Joshua A. Fishman, 3–13. The Hague, Paris: Mouton, 1968.

Fishman, Joshua A., ed. *Readings in the Sociology of Language.* The Hague, Paris: Mouton, 1968.

Fitneva, Stanka A. "Epistemic marking and reliability judgements: Evidence from Bulgarian." *Journal of Pragmatics* 33 (2001): 401–420.

Fløttum Kjersti, Trine Gedde-Dahl and Torodd Kinn. *Academic Voices.* Amsterdam, Philadelphia: John Benjamins, 2006.

Flowerdew, John ed. *Academic Discourse.* London : Pearson Education, 2002.

Foley, William A. *Anthropological Linguistics. An Introduction.* Blackwell, 1997.

Fortanet-Gómez, Inmaculada. "The use of *we* in university lectures: reference and function", *English for Specific Purposes* 23 (2004a): 45–66.

—. "Verbal stance in spoken academic discourse." In *Academic Discourse – New Insights into Evaluation,* Gabriella Del Lungo Camiciotti and ElenaTognini Bonelli, 99–119. Bern: Peter Lang, 2004.

—. "Interaction in academic spoken English: The use of *I* and *you* in the MICASE." In *Information Technology in Language for Specific Purposes. Issues and Prospects,* edited by Elisabet Arnó Macià, Antonia Soler Cervera and Carmen Rueda Ramos, 35–51. New York: Springer, 2006.

Foucault, Michel. *The Archaeology of Knowledge and Discourse on Language*. New York, NY: Harper and Row, 1972.

—. "Truth, power, self: An interview with Michel Foucault." In *Technologies of the Self: A Seminar with Michel Foucault,* edited by Luther H. Martin, Gutmanand Patrick H. Hutton, 9–15. London: Tavistock, 1988.

Frawley, William ed. *The Expression of Modality*. Berlin, New York: Mouton de Gruyter, 2006.

Fuertes Olivera, Pedro A. ed. *Lengua y Sociedad: Investigaciones recientes en lingüística aplicada. Lingüística y Filología no 61.* Valladolid: Universidad de Valladolid, 2005.

Gabrielatos, Costas and Tony McEnery. "Epistemic modality in MA dissertations." In *Lengua y Sociedad: Investigaciones recientes en lingüística aplicada. Lingüística y Filología no 61,* edited by Pedro A. Fuertes Olivera, 311–331. Valladolid: Universidad de Valladolid, 2005.

Gajda, Stanisław. *Podstawy badań stylistycznych nad językiem naukowym.* Warszawa: PWN, 1982.

—. *Współczesna polszczyzna naukowa. Język czy żargon?* Opole: Instytut Śląski w Opolu, 1990.

—. "Styl naukowy." In *Współczesny język polski,* edited by Jan Bartmiński, 173–189. Wrocław: Wiedza o Kulturze, 1993.

—. "Styl osobniczy uczonych." In *Styl a tekst,* edited by Stanisław Gajda and Mieczysław Balowski, 251–261. Opole: Uniwersytet Opolski, 1996.

—. "Media – stylowy tygiel współczesnej polszczyzny." In *Język w mediach masowych,* edited by Jerzy Bralczyk and Katarzyna Mosiołek-Kłosińska, 19–27. Warszawa: Upowszechnianie Nauki – Oświata „UN-O," 2000.

—. "Współczesny polski dyskurs humanistyczny." In *W kręgu wiernej mowy,* edited by Maria Wojtak and Małgorzata Rzeszutko, 49–58. Lublin: Wydawnictwo Uniwersytetu Marii Curie-Skłodowskiej, 2004.

Gajda, Stanisław ed. *Przewodnik po stylistyce polskiej.* Opole: Uniwersytet Opolski, 1995.

—. *Dyskurs naukowy – tradycja i zmiana.* Opole: Uniwersytet Opolski, 1999.

Gajda, Stanisław and Mieczysław Balowski, eds. *Styl a tekst*. Opole: Uniwersytet Opolski, 1996.

Gergen, Kenneth J. "Social understanding and the inscription of self." In *Cultural Psychology: Essays on Comparative Human Development*, edited by James W. Stigler, Richard A. Shweder and Gilbert S. Herdt, 569–606. Cambridge: Cambridge University Press, 1990.

—. "Technology and the self. From the essential to the sublime." In *Constructing the Self in a Mediated World,* edited by Debra Grodin – Thomas R. Lindlof, 127–140. London: Sage, 1996.

Giddens, Anthony. *The Constitution of Society*. Berkeley: University of California Press, 1984.

—. *Nowoczesność i tożsamość. „Ja" i społeczeństwo w epoce późnej nowoczesności.* Warszawa: Wydawnictwo Naukowe PWN, 2001.

Giles, Howard. "Sociolinguistics and social psychology: An introductory essay." In *Language and Social Psychology,* edited by Howard Giles and Robert N. Stlair, 1–20. Oxford: Basil Blackwell, 1979.

Giles, Howard and Robert N. Stlair, eds. *Language and Social Psychology*. Oxford: Basil Blackwell, 1979.

Gilson, Etienne. "Słowo mówione i słowo pisane." Reprinted in *Antropologia słowa. Zagadnienia i wybór tekstów,* edited by Grzegorz Godlewski, Andrzej Mencwel and Roch Sulima, 416–422. Warszawa: Wydawnictwa Uniwersytetu Warszawskiego, 2003/1969.

Goban-Klas, Tomasz. *Media i komunikowanie masowe*. Warszawa: PWN, 1999.

Godlewski, Grzegorz, Andrzej Mencwel and Sulima, Roch, eds. *Antropologia słowa. Zagadnienia i wybór tekstów*. Warszawa: Wydawnictwa Uniwersytetu Warszawskiego, 2003.

Godzic, Wiesław. "Czy nowe media potrzebują nowej estetyki? Humanista w Internecie." In *Piękno w sieci: estetyka a nowe media,* edited by Krystyna Wilkoszewska, 257–272. Kraków: Universitas, 1999.

—. "Język w Internecie: czy piszemy to, co myślimy?" In *Język w mediach masowych*, edited by Jerzy Bralczyk and Katarzyna Mosiołek-Kłosińska, 176–185. Warszawa: Upowszechnianie Nauki – Oświata „UN-O," 2000.

—. "Tożsamość analogowa w obrazie cyfrowym." In *Blaustein. Koncepcja odbioru mediów,* by Zofia Rosińska, 142–150. Warszawa: Prószyński i S-ka, 2001.

Godzic, Wiesław, ed. *Humanista w cyberprzestrzeni*. Kraków: Rabid, 1999.

Goffman, Erving. "On face-work: An analysis of ritual elements in social interaction." *Psychiatry* 18 (1955): 213–231. Reprinted in *Communication in Face to Face Interaction*, edited by John Laver and Sandy Hutcheson, 319–346. London: Penguin Books, 1972.

Gotti, Maurizio. *Specialized Discourse: Linguistic Features and Changing Conventions*. Bern: Peter Lang, 2003.

Graddol, David. "In search of identity." *British Studies Now* 8 (1997): 8–9.

Gresham, John L. Jr. "From invisible college to cyberspace college: Computer conferencing and the transformation of informal scholarly communication networks." *Interpersonal Computing and Technology: An Electronic Journal for the 21st Century* 2 no 4 (1994): 37–52. (accessed January 25, 2002).

Griffin, Em. *Podstawy komunikacji społecznej*. Translated by Olga Kubińska, Wojciech Kubiński, Magdalena Kacmajor. Gdańsk: Gdańskie Wydawnictwo Psychologiczne, 2002.

Grochowski, Grzegorz. "Czy istnieje tekst poza gatunkiem?" In *Gatunki mowy i ich ewolucja 2. Tekst a gatunek,* edted by Danuta Ostaszewska, 20–28. Katowice: Wydawnictwo Uniwersytetu Śląskiego, 2004.

Grodin, Debra and Thomas R Lindlof, eds. *Constructing the Self in a Mediated World.* London: Sage, 1996.

Gruber, Helmut. "Scholarly email discussion list postings: A single new genre of academic communication?" In *Words on the Web: Computer Mediated Communication*, edited by Lyn Pemberton and Simon Shurville, 36–43. Exeter/Portland, OR: Intellect Books, 2000.

Grzelak, Janusz Ł. and Maria Jarymowicz. "Tożsamość i współzależność." In *Psychologia. Podręcznik Akademicki Tom 3*, edited by J. Strelau, 107–145. Gdańsk: Gdańskie Wydawnictwo Psychologiczne, 2000.

Gumperz, John J. "Types of linguistic communities." *Anthropological Linguistics* 4 (1962): 28–40. Reprinted in *Language in Social Groups*. Essays by John J. Gumperz, selected and introduced by Anwar S. Dil, 97–113, Stanford: Stanford University Press, 1971a.

—. "The speech community." In *Language in Social Groups*. Essays by John J. Gumperz, selected and introduced by Anwar S. Dil, 114–128. Stanford: Stanford University Press, 1971b.

—. "The relation of linguistic to social categories." In *Language in Social Groups*. Essays by John J. Gumperz, selected and introduced by Anwar S. Dil, 220–229. Stanford: Stanford University Press, 1971c.

—. "The sociolinguistics of interpersonal communication." *Working Papers and prepublications* 33 (1974).

—. *Discourse Strategies*. Cambridge: Cambridge University Press, 1982.

—. "Introduction to Part IV." In *Rethinking Linguistic Relativity,* edited by John J. Gumperz and Stephen C. Levinson, 359-373. Cambridge: Cambridge University Press, 1996.

Gumperz, John J., ed. *Language and Social Identity.* Cambridge: Cambridge University Press, 1982.

Gumperz, John J. and Jenny Cook-Gumperz. "Introduction: language and the communication of social identity." In *Language and Social Identity,* edited by John J. Gumperz, 1–21. Cambridge: Cambridge University Press, 1982.

Gumperz, John J. and Dell Hymes, eds. *Directions in Sociolinguistics: The ethnography of Communication.* New York: Holt, Rinehart and Winston, 1972.

Gumperz, John J. and Stephen C. Levinson. "Introduction: linguistic relativity re-examined." In *Rethinking Linguistic Relativity,* edited by John J. Gumperz and Stephen C. Levinson, 1–18. Cambridge: Cambridge University Press, 1996.

Gumperz, John J. and Stephen C. Levinson, eds. *Rethinking Linguistic Relativity*. Cambridge: Cambridge University Press, 1996.

Gunnarsson, Britt Louise. "On the sociohistorical construction of scientific discourse." In *Text and Talk in Professional Contexts,* edited by Britt Louise Gunnarsson, Per Linnel and Bengt Nordberg, 99–126. Uppsala: ASLA, 1994.

Gunnarsson, Britt Louise, Per Linnel and Bengt Nordberg, eds. *Text and Talk in Professional Contexts*. Uppsala: ASLA, 1994.

Halliday, Michael A. K. *Language as Social Semiotic. The Social Interpretation of Language and Meaning*. London: Arnold, 1978.

—. *An Introduction to Functional Grammar* (Second edition). London: Arnold, 1994.

Haan de, Ferdinand. "Typological approaches to modality." In *The Expression of Modality,* edited by William Frawley, 27–69. Berlin, New York: Mouton de Gruyter, 2006.

Hanks, William H. "Language form and communicative practices." In *Rethinking Linguistic Relativity,* edited by John J. Gumperz and Stephen C. Levinson, 232–270. Cambridge: Cambridge University Press, 1996.

Harwood, Nigel. "*Nowhere has anyone attempted ... In this article I aim to do just that*' A corpus-based study of self-promotional *I* and *we* in academic writing across four disciplines." *Journal of Pragmatics* 37 (2005): 1207–1231.

Heller, Monica. "Globalization, the new economy, and the commodification of language and identity." *Journal of Sociolinguistics* 7 no 4 (2003): 473–492.

Helmbrecht, Johannes. "Grammar and function of *we*." In *Us And Others: Social Identities Across Languages, Discourses and Cultures,* edited by Anna Duszak, 31–49. Amsterdam/Philadelphia: John Benjamins Publishing Company, 2002.

Herring, Susan, ed. *Computer-Mediated Communication: Linguistic, Social and Cross-Cultural Perspectives.* Amsterdam: Benjamins, 1996.

Hill, Jane H. "Styling locally, styling globally: What does it mean?" *Journal of Sociolinguistics* 4 no 3 (1999): 542–556.

Hoey, Michael. *On the Surface of Discourse*. London: George Allen & Unwin, 1983.

—. "Signalling in discourse: A functional analysis of a common discourse pattern in written and spoken English." In *Advances in Written Text Analysis*, edited by Malcolm Coulthard, 26–45. London: Routledge, 1994.

—. *Textual Interaction: An Introduction to Written Discourse Analysis.* London, New York: Routledge, 2001.

Holliday, Adrian. "Small cultures." *Applied Linguistics* 20 no 2 (1999): 237–264.

Holmes, Janet and Miriam Meyerhoff. "The Community of Practice: Theories and methodologies in language and gender research." *Language in Society* 28 (1999): 173–183.

Hongladarom, Krisadawan and Soraj Hongladarom. "Politeness ideology in Thai Computer-mediated Communication." A paper presented at the International Symposium on Linguistic Politeness: Theoretical Approaches and Intercultural Perspectives (ISLP 99), 7–9 December 1999, Chulalongkorn University, Bangkok, Thailand. (http://pioneer.netserv.chula.ac.th/~hsoraj/web/Politeness.pdf) (accessed August 10, 2004).

Hudzik, Jan P. and Jadwiga Mizińska, eds. *Pamięć, miejsce, obecność. Współczesne refleksje nad kulturą i ich implikacje pedagogiczne*. Lublin: Wydawnictwo UMSC, 1997.

Hunston, Susan. "Organisation and evaluation in a sample of written academic discourse." In *Advances in Written Text Analysis,* edited by Malcolm Coulthard, 191–218. London: Routledge, 1994.

Hyland, Ken. *Disciplinary Discourses: Social Interactions in Academic Writing*. Harlow: Pearson Education, 2000.

—. "Activity and evaluation: Reporting practices in academic writing." In *Academic Discourse*, edited by John Flowerdew, 115–130, London : Pearson Education, 2002a.

—. "Authority and invisibility: authorial identity in academic writing." *Journal of Pragmatics* 34 (2002b): 1091–112.

—. *Metadiscourse: Exploring Interaction in Writing*. New York: Continuum International Publishing Group, 2005.

Hymes, Dell. *Language in Culture and Society. A Reader in Linguistics and Anthropology*. New York, Evanston and London: Harper & Row, 1964a.

—. "Introduction to Part VII. Social structure and speech community." In *Language in Culture and Society. A Reader in Linguistics and Anthropology,* by Dell Hymes, 385–390, New York, Evanston and London: Harper & Row, 1964b.

—. "The ethnography of speaking." In *Readings in the Sociology of Language*, edited by Joshua A. Fishman, 99–137, The Hague, Paris: Mouton, 1968.

—. *Foundations in Sociolinguistics: An Ethnographic Approach.* Philadelphia: University of Pennsylvania Press, 1974.

Ivanič, Roz. *Writing and Identity. The Discoursal Construction of Identity in Academic Writing.* Amsterdam/Philadelphia: John Benjamins Publishing Company, 1998.

Jacher, Władysław. *Więź społeczna w teorii i praktyce*. Katowice: Wydawnictwo Uniwersytetu Śląskiego, 1987.

Jackson, Michelle H. "Assessing the structure of communication on the World Wide Web." *Journal of Computer-Mediated Communication* 3 no 1 (1997) (accessed August 09, 2002).

Johns, Ann M. *Text, Role and Context. Developing Academic Literacies.* Cambridge: Cambridge University Press, 1997.

Johnstone, Barbara. *The Linguistic Individual. Self-Expression in Language and Linguistics*. New York & Oxford: Oxford University Press, 1996.

Jones, Quentin. "Virtual communities, virtual settlements and cyber-archaeology: A theoretical outline." *Journal of Computer-Mediated Communication* 3 no 3 (1997) (accessed August 09, 2002).

Jones, Steven G. "The Internet and its social landscape." In *Virtual Culture: Identity and Communication in Cybersociety,* edited by Steven G. Jones, 7–35. Thousands Oaks, London, New Delhi: Sage Publications, 1997.

—. "Information, Internet, and community: Notes Toward an understanding of community in the Information Age." In *Cybersociety*

2.0. Revisiting Computer-Mediated Communication and Community, editedby Steven G. Jones, 1–34. Thousands Oaks, London, New Delhi: Sage Publications, 1998.

Jones, Steven G., ed. *Virtual Culture: Identity and Communication in Cybersociety*. Thousands Oaks, London, New Delhi: Sage Publications, 1997.

—. *Cybersociety 2.0. Revisiting Computer-Mediated Communication and Community*. Thousands Oaks, London, New Delhi: Sage Publications, 1998.

Joseph, John E. *Language and Identity: National, Ethnic, Religious*. Houndmills: Palgrave Macmillan, 2004a.

—. "Linguistic identity and the limits of global English." In *Speaking from the Margin: Global English from a European Perspective*, edited by Anna Duszak and Urszula Okulska, 17–33. Frankfurt am Main-New York: Peter Lang, 2004b.

Kerckhove de, Derrick. *Inteligencja otwarta. Narodziny społeczeństwa sieciowego*. Translated by Andrzej Hildebrandt and Ryszard Glegoła. Warszawa: Mikom, 2001a.

—. *Powłoka kultury. Odkrywanie nowej elektronicznej rzeczywistości*. Translated by Witold Sikorski and Piotr Nowakowski. Warszawa: Mikom, 2001b.

Kerrick, Douglas T., Steven L. Neuberg and Robert B. Cialdini. *Psychologia społeczna. Rozwiązane tajemnice*. Gdańsk: Gdańskie Wydawnictwo Psychologiczne, 2002.

Kiesler, Sara, ed. *Culture of the Internet*. Hillsdale, NY: Lawrence Erblaum, 1997.

Kiesler, Sara, Jane Siegal and Timothy W. McGuire. "Social psychological aspects of CMC." *American Psychologist* 39 no 10 (1984): 1123–1134.

Koku, Emmanuel, Nancy Nazer and Barry Wellman. "Netting scholars: Online and offline." *American Behavioral Scientist* 44 no 10 (2001): 1752–1774.

Kolko, Beth and Elizabeth Reid. "Dissolution and fragmentation: Problems in on-line communities." In *Virtual Culture: Identity and Communication in Cybersociety*, edited by Steven G. Jones, 211–229. Thousands Oaks, London, New Delhi: Sage Publications, 1998.

Kolko, Beth, Lisa Nakamura and Gilbert Rodman, eds. *Race in Cyberspace*. New York: Routledge, 2000.

Kollock, Peter and Marc A. Smith. "Communities in cyberspace." In *Communities in Cyberspace*, edited by Marc A. Smith and Peter Kollock, 3–25. London: Routledge, 1999.

Kopczyński, Andrzej, Urszula Zaliwska-Okrutna, eds. *Język rodzimy a język obcy: komunikacja, przekład, dydaktyka*. Warszawa: Wydawnictwa Uniwersytetu Warszawskiego, 2001.

Kopytko, Roman. "Linguistics pragmatics and the concept of 'face'." *Vienna English Working Papers* 2 no 2 (1993): 90–102.

—. *The Mental Aspects of Pragmatic Theory: An Integrative View*. Poznań: Motivex, 2002.

—. "The idea of 'self' and modern pragmatics." *Scripta Neofilologica Posnaniensia* 5 (2003): 85–105.

Kosiński, Stanisław. *Socjologia ogólna. Zagadnienia podstawowe*. Warszawa: PWN, 1987.

Koutsantoni, Dimitra. "Certainty across cultures: A comparison of the degree of certainty expressed by Greek and English speaking scientific authors." *Journal of Pragmatics* 2 no 2 (2005): 121–149.

Kress, Gunther and Theo Van Leeuwen. *Multimodal Discourse*. London: Arnold, 2001.

Kubacka-Jasiecka, Dorota, ed. *Człowiek wobec zmiany. Rozważania psychologiczne*. Kraków: Wydawnictwo Uniwersytetu Jagiellońskiego, 2002.

Labocha, Janina. "Operatory tekstu." In *Gramatyka polska. Składnia, (Podstawy analizy wypowiedzi)* by Janina Labocha. Kraków: Księgarnia Akademicka, 1996. Reprinted in *Tekstologia Part 2*, edited by Jerzy Bartmiński and Stanisława Niebrzegowska-Bartmińska, 145–150. Lublin: Wydawnictwo UMSC, 2004.

Labov, William. *Principles of Linguistic Change. Volume 2: Social Factors*. Oxford & Cambridge, MA: Blackwell, 2001.

Lakoff, Robin Tolmach. "Some of my favorite writers are literate: The mingling of oral and literate strategies in written communication." In *Spoken and Written Language: Exploring Orality and Literacy,* edited by Deborah Tannen. Norwood, NJ: Ablex, 1982.

Lanham, Richard A. *The Electronic Word: Democracy, Technology, and the Arts*. Chicago: University of Chicago Press, 1993.

Lave, Jean and Etienne Wenger. *Situated Learning: Legitimate Peripheral Participation*. Cambridge and New York: Cambridge University Press, 1991.

Laver, John and Sandy Hutcheson, eds. *Communication in Face to Face Interaction*. London: Penguin Books, 1972.

Le Page, Robert B. and Andrée Tabouret-Keller. *Acts of Identity: Creole-based Approaches to Language and Ethnicity*. Cambridge: Cambridge University Press, 1985.

Leech, Geoffrey. *Principles of Pragmatics*. London and New York: Longman, 1983.

Liu, Geoffrey Z. "Virtual community presence in Internet relay chatting." *Journal of Computer-Mediated Communication* 5 no 1 (1999). (accessed August 15, 2002).

Loska, Krzysztof. *Dziedzictwo McLuhana – między nowoczesnością a ponowoczesnością*. Kraków: Rabid, 2001.

Lubański, Adam and Lucy Matthew. 1998."Socio-economic impact of the Internet in the academic research environment." A paper presented at IRISS (Internet Research and Information for Social Scientists) International Conference, March 1998, Bristol, UK, (http://www.sosig.ac.uk/iriss/papers/paper18.html) (accessed August 15, 2002).

Macià, Elisabet Arnó, Antonia Soler Cervera and Carmen Rueda Ramos, eds. *Information Technology in Language for Specific Purposes. Issues and Prospects*. New York: Springer, 2006.

Martin, James R. and Peter R. R. White. *The Language of Evaluation. Appraisal in English*. London: Palgrave Macmillan, 2005.

Martin, Luther H., Huck Gutman and Patrick H. Hutton, eds. *Technologies of the Self: A Seminar with Michel Foucault*. London: Tavistock, 1988.

Mauranen, Anna. *Cultural Differences in Academic Rhetoric*. Frankfurt am Main: Peter Lang, 1993.

—. " 'A Good Question': Expressing Evaluation in Academic Speech." In *Domain-specific English. Textual Practices across Communities and Classrooms*, edited by Giuseppina Cortese and Philip Riley, 115–140. Bern: Peter Lang, 2002.

Matzat, Uwe. *Social Networks and Cooperation in Electronic Communities. A Theoretical-empirical Analysis of Academic Communication and Internet Discussion Groups*. Amsterdam: Thela Publisher, 2001. (http://www.ub.rug.nl/eldoc/dis/ppsw/u.matzat/) (accessed September 02, 2004).

—. "Academic communication and Internet discussion groups: Transfer of information or creation of social contacts?" *Social Networks* 26 no 3 (2004): 221–255.

Mazur, Jan and Małgorzata Rzeszutko-Iwan, eds. *Teksty kultury. Oblicza komunikacji XXI wieku Tom 1*. Lublin: Wydawnictwo UMSC, 2006.

McCarty, Willard. "*Humanist*: Lessons from a global electronic seminar." *Computers and the Humanities* 26 (1992): 205–22.

McEnery, Tony and Nazareth Amselom Kifle. "Epistemic modality in argumentative essays of second-language writers." In *Academic*

Discourse, edited by John Flowerdew, 182–195. London : Pearson Education, 2002.

McLuhan, Marshall. *Understanding Media: The Extensions of Man.* New York: McGraw-Hill, 1964.

—. *Wybór tekstów*. Poznań: Wydawnictwo Zysk i S-ka, 2001.

Mead, George Herbert. *Umysł, osobowość i społeczeństwo.* Translated by Zofia Wolińska. Warszawa: PWN, 1975.

Meyerhoff, Miriam. "Community of practice." In *Handbook of Language Variation and Change*, edited by Jack Chambers, Peter Trudgill and Natalie Schilling-Estes, 526–548. Oxford: Blackwell, 2002.

Meyrowitz, Joshua. *No Sense of Place: The Impact of Electronic Media on Social Behavior*. New York: Oxford University Press, 1985.

Mika, Stanisław. *Psychologia społeczna*. 3rd edition. Warszawa: PWN, 1981.

Mikołajczak, Stanisław. *Składnia tekstów naukowych: dyscypliny humanistyczne*. Poznań: Wydawnictwo Naukowe UAM, 1990.

Milroy, Lesley. *Language and Social Networks*. Oxford: Blackwell, 1980.

—. "Social networks." In *Handbook of Language Variation and Change,* edited by Jack Chambers, Peter Trudgill and Natalie Schilling-Estes, 549–572. Oxford: Blackwell, 2002.

Milroy, Lesley and Matthew Gordon. *Sociolinguistics: Method and Interpretation.* Oxford: Blackwell, 2003.

Mitra, Ananda. "Virtual commonality: Looking for India on the Internet." In *Virtual Culture: Identity and Communication in Cybersociety,* edited by Steven G. Jones, 55–79. Thousands Oaks, London, New Delhi: Sage Publications, 1997.

—. "Characteristics of the WWW text: Tracing discursive strategies." *Journal of Computer-Mediated Communication* 5 no 1 (1999) (accessed February 03, 2002).

Mizrach, Steven. "From orality to teleliteracy." 1998. (http://www.fiu.edu/~mizrachs/orality.htm) (accessed February 05, 2002).

Montgomery, Martin. *An Introduction to Language and Society*. London and New York: Routledge, 1986.

Morand, David A. and Rosalie J. Ocker. "Politeness Theory and Computer-Mediated Communication: A sociolinguistic approach to analyzing relational messages." *Proceedings of the 36th Hawaii International Conference on System Sciences (HICSS'03),* 2002. (http://csdl.computer.org/comp/proceedings/hicss/2003/1874/01/18741 0017b.pdf) (accessed July 03, 2004).

Morris, Merrill and Christine Ogan. "The Internet as Mass Medium." *Journal of Computer-Mediated Communication* 1 no 4 (1996) (accessed September 20, 2005).

Mudyń, Krzysztof. „Technoświadomość. O zmieniającym się poczuciu realności i własnej tożsamości u użykowników cyberprzestrzeni." In *Człowiek wobec zmiany. Rozważania psychologiczne*, edited by Dorota Kubacka-Jasiecka, 145–156. Kraków: Wydawnictwo Uniwersytetu Jagiellońskiego, 2002.

Nawojczyk, Maria. *Przewodnik po statystyce dla socjologów*. Kraków: SPSS Polska, 2002.

Negroponte, Nicholas. *Being Digital*. London: Hodder & Stoughton, 1995.

Nickols, Fred. "Communities of Practice. Definition, indicators, & identifying characteristics." 2000. (http://home.att.net/~discon/KM/CoPCharacteristics.htm) (accessed July 15, 2003).

Nuyts, Jan. *Epistemic Modality, Language and Conceptualization. A Cognitive-Pragmatic Perspective*. Amsterdam/Philadelphia: John Benjamins, 2000.

—. "Subjectivity as an evidential dimension in epistemic modal expressions." *Journal of Pragmatics* 33 (2001): 383–400.

—. "Modality: Overview and linguistic issues." In *The Expression of Modality,* edited by William Frawley, 1–26. Berlin, New York: Mouton de Gruyter, 2006.

O'Driscoll, Jim. "A face model of language choice." *Multilingua* 20 no 1 (2001): 245–268.

O'Halloran, Kay L., ed. *Multimodal Discourse Analysis. Systemic Functional Perspectives*. London: Continuum, 2004.

Olsson, David and Nancy Torrance, eds. *Literacy and Orality*. Cambridge: Cambridge University Press, 1991.

Ong, Walter J. *Orality and Literacy: The Technologizing of the Word*. London: Blackwell, 2002/1982.

Orlikowski, Wanda J. and JoAnne Yates. "Genre repertoire: The structuring of communicative practices in organizations." *Administrative Science Quarterly* 39 no 4 (1994): 542–574.

Ostaszewska, Danuta, ed. *Gatunki mowy i ich ewolucja 2. Tekst a gatunek*. Katowice: Wydawnictwo Uniwersytetu Śląskiego, 2004.

Ożdżyński, Jan and Teodozja Rittel, eds. *Konteksty kulturowe w dyskursie edukacyjnym*. Kraków: Oficyna Wydawnicza "Edukacja", 2002.

Ożóg, Kazimierz. "Operatory metatekstowe w polszczyźnie potocznej." In *Z polszczyzny historycznej i współczesne,j* edited by Teresa Ampel. Rzeszów: Wydawnictwo Wyższej Szkoły Pedagogicznej, 1997.

Reprinted in *Tekstologia Part 2*, edited by Jerzy Bartmiński and Stanisława Niebrzegowska-Bartmińska, 134–144. Lublin: Wydawnictwo UMSC, 2004.

Paccagnella, Luciano. "Getting the seats of your pants dirty: Strategies for ethnographic research on virtual communities." *Journal of Computer-Mediated Communication* 3 no 1 (1997). (accessed February 15, 2002).

Palmer, Frank Robert. *Semantics*. Second edition. Cambridge: Cambridge University Press, 1981.

—. *Mood and Modality*. Second edition. New York: Cambridge University Press, 2001.

Paolillo, John. "The virtual speech community: Social network and language variation on IRC." *Journal of Computer-Mediated Communication* 4 no 4 (1999). (accessed February 15, 2002).

Patrick, Peter L. "The Speech Community." In *Handbook of Language Variation and Change*, edited by Jack Chambers, Peter Trudgill and Natalie Schilling-Estes, 573–597. Oxford: Blackwell, 2002.

Pemberton, Lyn and Simon Shurville. *Words on the Web: Computer Mediated Communication*. Exeter/Portland, OR: Intellect Books, 2000.

Pękala, Teresa. "Wirtualne światy słowa i obrazu." In *Pamięć, miejsce, obecność. Współczesne refleksje nad kulturą i ich implikacje pedagogiczne*, edited by Jan P. Hudzik and Jadwiga Mizińska, 95–104. Lublin: Wydawnictwo UMSC, 1997.

Pisarkowa, Krystyna. "O spójności tekstu mówionego." In *Tekst i język. Problemy semantyczne,* edited by Maria Renata Mayenowa. Wrocław, Warszawa, Kraków, Gdańsk: Wydawnictwo ZNiO, 1974. Reprinted in *Tekstologia Part 2*, edited by Jerzy Bartmiński and Stanisława Niebrzegowska-Bartmińska, 121–133. Lublin: Wydawnictwo UMSC, 2004.

Plungian, Vladimir. "The place of evidentiality within the universal grammatical space." *Journal of Pragmatics* 33 (2001): 349–357.

Pluskota, Jolanta. "Metatekst w tekstach felietonów Stefana Kisielewskiego." *Poznańskie Studia Polonistyczne. Seria Językoznawcza* V (XXV) (1998). Reprinted in *Tekstologia Part 2,* edited by Jerzy Bartmiński and Stanisława Niebrzegowska-Bartmińska, 162–174. Lublin: Wydawnictwo UMSC, 2004.

Postman, Neil. *Technopoly: The Surrender of Culture to Technology*. New York: Vintage Books, 1993.

Preece, Jenny and Diane Maloney-Krichmar. "Online communities: Theory, design, and practice." *Journal of Computer-Mediated Communication* 10 no 4 (2005). (accessed September 14, 2006).

Rafaeli, Sheizaf. "Interactivity: From new media to communication." *Sage Annual Review of Communication Research: Advancing Communication Science* 16 (1988): 110–134.

Rafaeli, Sheizaf and Fay Sudweeks. "Networked interactivity." *Journal of Computer-Mediated Communication* 2 no 4 (1997). (accessed July 03, 2003).

Rampton, Ben. *Crossing: Language and Ethnicity Among Adolescents.* London: Longman, 1995.

—. "Styling the Other: Introduction." *Journal of Sociolinguistics* 4 no 3 (1999): 421–427.

Reid, Elizabeth M. *Electropolis: Communication and Community On Internet Relay Chat.* An unpublished Honours Thesis, 1991. (http://www.ee.mu.oz.au/papers/emr/index.html) (accessed February 14, 2002).

—. *Cultural Formations in Text-Based Virtual Realities.* An unpublished Master of Arts Thesis, 1994. (http://www.ee.mu.oz.au/papers/emr/index.html) (accessed February 14, 2002).

—. "Hierarchy and power. Social control in cyberspace." In *Communities in Cyberspace*, edited by Marc A. Smith and Peter Kollock, 107–133. London: Routledge, 1999.

Rheingold, Howard. *The Virtual Community. Homesteading on the Electronic Frontier.* Reading, MA: Addison-Wesley, 2000/1993.

Ricoeur, Paul. "Mowa i pismo", 1976. Reprinted in *Antropologia słowa. Zagadnienia i wybór tekstów,* edited by Grzegorz Godlewski, Andrzej Mencwel and Roch Sulima, 423–429. Warszawa: Wydawnictwa Uniwersytetu Warszawskiego, 2003.

Riley, Philip. "Epistemic communities: The social knowledge system, discourse and identity." In *Domain-specific English. Textual Practices Across Communities and Classrooms,* edited by Giuseppina Cortese and Philip Riley, 41–64. Bern: Peter Lang, 2002.

Rojo, Alejandra. *Participation in Scholarly Electronic Forums.* A University of Toronto Ph.D. thesis, 1995. (http://web.archive.org/web/19990224193318/www.oise.on.ca/~arojo/tabcont.html) (accessed February 09, 2002).

Romaine, Suzanne. *Language in Society: An Introduction to Sociolinguistics.* 2nd edition. Oxford: Oxford University Press, 2000/1994.

Rosińska, Zofia. *Blaustein. Koncepcja odbioru mediów.* Warszawa: Prószyński i S-ka, 2001.

Rowley-Jolivet, Elizabeth and Shirley Carter-Thomas. "Scientific conference Englishes: Epistemic and language community variations." In *Identity, Community, Discourse: English in Intercultural Settings,* edited by Giuseppina Cortese and Anna Duszak, 295–320. Bern: Peter Lang, 2005.

Röska-Hardy. "*I* and the first person perspective." A paper given at the Twentieth World Congress of Philosophy, Boston, Massachusettes, USA, August 1998. (http://www.bu.edu/wcp/Papers/Lang/LangRosk.htm) (accessed February 15, 2004).

Saeed, John I. *Semantics*. Oxford: Blackwell, 1997.

Sánchez-Macarro, Antonia and Ronald Carter, eds. *Linguistic Choice Across Genres. Variation in Spoken and Written English.* Amsterdam/Philadelphia: John Benjamins Publishing Company, 1998.

Saville-Troike, Muriel. *The Ethnography of Communication. An Introduction*. 2nd edition. Oxford: Blackwell, 1989.

Schenk, David. *Data smog – Surviving the Information Glut*. New York: Harper Colins, 1997.

Scheunemann, Dietrich, ed. *Orality, Literacy, and Modern Media*. Columbia: Camden House, 1996.

Schiffrin, Deborah. *Approaches to Discourse*. Oxford UK & Cambridge USA: Blackwell, 1994.

Schulze, Rainer, ed. *Making Meaningful Choices in English. On Dimensions, Perspectives, Methodology and Evidence.* Gunter Narr Verlag Tűbingen, 1998.

Scollon, Ronald and Susanne W. Scollon. *Intercultural Communication: A Discourse Approach*. Oxford: Basil Blackwell, 1995.

Shepherd, Michael and Carolyn Watters. "The functionality attribute of cybergenres", *Proceedings of the 32nd Hawaii International Conference on System Sciences (HICSS 32),* 1999. (http://www.computer.org/proceedings/hicss/0001/00012/00012007.PDF) (accessed February 04, 2002).

Smith, Greg. "Virtual community in real reality...." An abridged version of a paper given to the Communities Online conference in October 1995, Sheffiled, UK. (http://www.partnerships.org.uk/itf/virtreal.html) (accessed February 06, 2002).

Smith, Marc A. and Peter Kollock, Peter. eds. *Communities in Cyberspace*. London: Routledge, 1999.

Snow, David. "Collective identity and expressive forms." *Centre for the Study of Democracy* Paper 01–07, 2001. (http://repositories.cdlib.org/csd/01-07) (accessed February 04, 2002).

Sobczyk, Mieczysław. *Statystyka* (Fourth edition). Warszawa: PWN, 2005.

Sokół, Małgorzata. "Towards an identity of an academic virtual community. A discourse community approach." In *Speaking from the Margin: Global English from a European Perspective*, edited by Anna Duszak and Urszula Okulska, 91–103. Frankfurt am Main-New York: Peter Lang, 2004.

—. "Academic identity construction in e-discussion lists: A case study." In *Identity, Community, Discourse: English in Intercultural Settings*, edited by Gusepinna Cortese and Anna Duszak, 321–344. Bern: Peter Lang, 2005.

—. "Genre analysis and digital communication: New approaches to genre theory." In *Bridges and Barriers in Metalinguistic Discourse,* edited by Anna Duszak and Urszula Okulska, 167–180. Frankfurt am Main-New York: Peter Lang, 2006a.

—. "Komunikacja elektroniczna a ewolucja gatunków mowy: repertuar gatunków mowy emaila." In *Teksty kultury. Oblicza komunikacji XXI wieku Tom 1,* edited by Jan Mazur and Małgorzata Rzeszutko-Iwan, 175–186. Lublin: Wydawnictwo UMSC, 2006b.

Starzec, Anna."Wartościowanie w tekstach popularnonaukowych." In *Styl a tekst*, edited by Stanisław Gajda and Mieczysław Balowski, 271–283. Opole: Uniwersytet Opolski, 1996.

Stigler, James W., Richard A. Shweder and Gilbert S. Herdt, eds. *Cultural Psychology: Essays on Comparative Human Development*. Cambridge: Cambridge University Press, 1990.

Strelau, Jan, ed. *Psychologia. Podręcznik Akademicki Tom 3*. Gdańsk: Gdańskie Wydawnictwo Psychologiczne, 2000.

Stryker, Sheldon. *Symbolic Interactionism: A Social Structural Version.* Menlo Park, Calif.: Benjamin/Cummings, 1980.

Stryker, Sheldon and Peter J. Burke. "The past, present, and future of an identity theory." *Social Psychology Quarterly* 63 (2000): 284–297.

Swales, John G. *Genre Analysis: English in Academic and Research Settings.* Cambridge: Cambridge University Press, 1990.

—. "Genre and Engagement." *Revue Belge de Philologie et d'Histoire* 71 (1993): 687–698.

—. *Other Floors, Other Voices: A Textography of a Small University Building*. Mahwah NJ: Lawrence Erblaum Associates, 1998.

Szczepański, Jan. *Elementarne pojęcia socjologii*. Warszawa: PWN, 1963.

Szpila, Grzegorz, ed. *Język a komunikacja 1. Język trzeciego tysiąclecia I.* Kraków: Tertium, 2000.

Sztompka, Piotr. *Socjologia. Analiza społeczeństwa*. Kraków: Wydawnictwo Znak, 2002.

Tabouret-Keller, Andrée. "Language and identity." In *The Handbook of Sociolinguistics,* edited by Florian Coulmas, 315–326. Oxford & Cambridge, MA: Blackwell, 1998.

Tannen, Deborah "Agonism in academic discourse." *Journal of Pragmatics* 34 (2002): 1651–1669.

Tannen, Deborah, ed. *Spoken and Written Language: Exploring Orality and Literacy*. Norwood, NJ: Ablex, 1982.

Tanno, Dolores and Alberto Gonzáles. "Introduction: Sites of identity in communication and culture." In *Communication and Identity Across Cultures,* edited by Dolores Tanno and Alberto Gonzáles, 3–7. Thousand Oaks; London; New Delhi: Sage, 1998.

Tanno, Dolores and Alberto Gonzáles, eds. *Communication and Identity Across Cultures*. Thousand Oaks; London; New Delhi: Sage, 1998.

Taylor, Jacqueline. "Electronic mail, communication and social identity: A social psychological analysis of computer-mediated group interaction." In *Words on the Web: Computer Mediated Communication,* edited by Lyn Pemberton and Simon Shurville, 96–105. Exeter/Portland, OR: Intellect Books, 2000.

Teufel, Simone and Marc Moens. "What's yours and what's mine: Determining intellectual attribution in scientific text." In *Proceedings of the 2000 Joint SIGDAT Conference on Empirical Methods in Natural Language Processing and Very Large Corpora*. Hong Kong, October 2000. (http://acl.ldc.upenn.edu/W/W00/W00-1302.pdf) (accessed September 16, 2004).

Thompson, Neil. *Communication and Language. A Handbook of Theory and Practice*. Houndmills, New York: Palgrave Macmillan, 2003.

Thoms, Lesley and Mike Thelwell. "Academic home pages: Reconstruction of the self." *First Monday* 10 no 12 (2005) (accessed September 16, 2006).

Turkle, Sherry. *Life on the Screen. Identity in the Age of the Internet.* New York: Touchstone Books, 1995.

—. "Who Am We?" *Wired Archive* 4.01 (1996) (accessed Februaty 10, 2002).

—. "Tożsamość w epoce Internetu." In *Blaustein. Koncepcja odbioru mediów,* by Zofia Rosińska, 133–141. Warszawa: Prószyński i S-ka, 2001.

Valle, Ellen. "A scientific community and its texts: a historical discourse study." In *Text and Talk in Professional Contexts*, edited by Britt

Louise Gunnarsson, Per Linnel and Bengt Nordberg, 76–97. Uppsala: ASLA, 1994.

Van Leeuwen, Theo. *Introducing Social Semiotics*. London: Routledge, 2005.

Vande Kopple, William J. "Some exploratory discourse on metadiscourse." *College Composition and Communication* 36 (1985): 89–93.

Vassileva, Irena. *Who Is the Author? A Contrastive Analysis of Authorial Presence in English, German, French, Russian and Bulgarian academic discourse*. Sankt Augustin: Asgard, 2000.

Ventola, Eija. "Modalization: Probability – an exploration into its role in academic writing." In *Culture and Styles of Academic Discourse,* edited by Anna Duszak, 157–179. Berlin: Mouton de Gruyter, 1997.

—. "Meaningful choices in academic communities." In *Making Meaningful Choices in English. On Dimensions, Perspectives, Methodology and Evidence,* edited by Rainer Schulze, 277–294. Gunter Narr Verlag Tűbingen, 1998a.

—. "Interpersonal choices in academic work." In *Linguistic Choice Across Genres. Variation in Spoken and Written English,* edited by Antonia Sánchez-Macarro and Ronald Carter, 117–136. Amsterdam/ Philadelphia: John Benjamins Publishing Company, 1998b.

Verstraete, Jean-Christophe. "Subjective and objective modality: Interpersonal and ideational functions in the English modal auxiliary system." *Journal of Pragmatics* 33 (2001): 1505–1528.

Wallace, Patricia. *Psychologia Internetu*. Translated by Tomasz Hornowski. Poznań: Dom Wydawniczy Rebis, 2001.

Watson, Nessim. "Why we argue about virtual community: A case study of the Phish.Net fan community." In *Virtual Culture: Identity and Communication in Cybersociety,* edited by Steven G. Jones, 102–132. Thousands Oaks, London, New Delhi: Sage Publications, 1997.

Weinreich, Frank. "Establishing a point of view toward virtual communities," *CMC Magazine* 2 (1997) (accessed July 14, 2003).

Welch, Kathleen E. *Electric Rhetoric. Classical Rhetoric, Oralism, and a New Literacy*. Cambridge, MA, London: The MIT Press, 1999.

Wellman, Barry. "An Electronic Networking is Virtually a Social Network." In *Culture of the Internet*, edited by Sara Kiesler, 179–205. Hillsdale, NY: Lawrence Erblaum, 1997.

Wellman, Barry, Milena Gulia. "Virtual communities as communities: Net surfers don't ride alone." In *Communities in Cyberspace*, edited by Marc A. Smith and Peter Kollock, 167–194. London: Routledge, 1999.

Wenger, Etienne. *Communities of Practice: Learning, Meaning and Identity*. Cambridge and New York: Cambridge University Press,1998.

Werry, Christopher C. "Linguistic and interactional features of Internet Relay Chat." In *Computer-Mediated Communication: Linguistic, Social and Cross-Cultural Perspectives,* edited by Susan Herring, 47–64. Amsterdam: Benjamins,1996.

Wierzbicka, Anna. "Metatekst w tekście." In *O spójności tekstu,* Maria Renata Mayenowa. Wrocław, Warszawa, Kraków, Gdańsk: Wydawnictwo ZNiO, 2001. Reprinted in *Tekstologia Part 2,* edited by Jerzy Bartmiński and Stanisława Niebrzegowska-Bartmińska, 109–120. Lublin: Wydawnictwo UMSC, 2004.

Wilk, Eugeniusz. *Nawigacje słowa. Strategie werbalne w przekazach audiowizualnych.* Kraków: Rabid, 2000.

Wilkoń, Aleksander. "Ponadgatunkowe typy wypowiedzi." In *Gatunki mowy i ich ewolucja 2. Tekst a gatunek,* edited by Danuta Ostaszewska, 15–19. Katowice: Wydawnictwo Uniwersytetu Śląskiego, 2004.

Wilkoszewska, Krystyna, ed. *Piękno w sieci: estetyka a nowe media.* Kraków: Universitas, 1999.

Winiarska, Justyna. "Operatory podkreślające aktualne rozczłonkowanie zdania – *jeśli chodzi o, co, to.*" In *Operatory metatekstowe w dialogu telewizyjnym,* by Justyna Winiarska, Kraków: Universitas, 2001. Reprinted in *Tekstologia Part 2,* edited by Jerzy Bartmiński and Stanisława Niebrzegowska-Bartmińska, 151–161. Lublin: Wydawnictwo UMSC, 2004.

Wojtak, Maria and Małgorzata Rzeszutko, eds. *W kręgu wiernej mowy.* Lublin: Wydawnictwo Uniwersytetu Marii Curie-Skłodowskiej, 2004.

Wray, Alison, Kate Trott and Aileen Bloomer. *Projects in Linguistics. A Practical Guide to Researching Language.* London: Arnold, 1998.

Yates, Simeon J. "Oral and written aspects of computer conferencing: A corpus based study." In *Computer-Mediated Communication: Linguistic, Social and Cross-Cultural Perspectives,* edited by Susan Herring, 19–46. Amsterdam: Benjamins, 1996.

Yates, Simeon J. and Tamara R.Sumner. "Digital genres and the new burden of fixity." *Proceedings of the 30th Hawaii International Conference on System Sciences (HICSS 30)* 6 (1997): 3–12. (http://www.cs.colorado.edu/~sumner/articles/trs97-HICSS.pdf) (Accessed February 05, 2002).

Zaśko-Zielińska, Monika. *Przez okno świadomości. Gatunki mowy w świadomości użytkowników języka.* Wrocław: Wydawnictwo Uniwersytetu Wrocławskiego, 2002.

Zwiefka-Chwałek, Agnieszka. „Słowo Internetu: Współczesne hieroglify", 2002 (http://www.cyberforum.edu.pl) (accessed July 14, 2003).

Żabicki, Piotr. „Internet – (r)ewolucja w komunikacji międzyludzkiej. Semiotyczno-socjologiczne spojrzenie na listę dyskusyjną." In *Humanista w cyberprzestrzeni*, edited by Wiesław Godzic, 65–76. Kraków: Rabid, 1999.